OFFICIAL SAST PAPERS WITH ANSWERS

ADVANCED HIGHER

ENGLISH
2006-2009

2006 EXAM – page 3
2007 EXAM – page 51
2008 SQP – page 101
2008 EXAM – page 135
2009 EXAM – page 177

© Scottish Qualifications Authority
All rights reserved. Copying prohibited. No part of this publication may be reproduced, stored in a retrieval system, or transmitted in any form or by any means, electronic, mechanical, photocopying, recording or otherwise.

First exam published in 2006.
Published by Bright Red Publishing Ltd, 6 Stafford Street, Edinburgh EH3 7AU
tel: 0131 220 5804 fax: 0131 220 6710 info@brightredpublishing.co.uk www.brightredpublishing.co.uk

ISBN 978-1-84948-074-1

A CIP Catalogue record for this book is available from the British Library.

Bright Red Publishing is grateful to the copyright holders, as credited on the final page of the book, for permission to use their material. Every effort has been made to trace the copyright holders and to obtain their permission for the use of copyright material. Bright Red Publishing will be happy to receive information allowing us to rectify any error or omission in future editions.

ADVANCED HIGHER
2006

X115/701

| NATIONAL QUALIFICATIONS 2006 | FRIDAY, 12 MAY 1.00 PM – 4.00 PM | ENGLISH ADVANCED HIGHER |

There are four sections in this paper.

- Section 1—Literary Study   pages   2 – 13
- Section 2—Language Study   pages   14 – 24
- Section 3—Textual Analysis   pages   25 – 39
- Section 4—Reading the Media   pages   40 – 44 (plus colour inserts)

Depending on the options you have chosen, you must answer **one** or **two** questions.

If you have submitted a Creative Writing folio, you must answer only **one** question.

Otherwise, you must answer **two** questions.

If you are required to answer only **one question**

- it must be taken from **Section 1—Literary Study**
- you must leave the examination room **after 1 hour 30 minutes**.

If you are required to answer **two questions**

- your first must be taken from **Section 1—Literary Study**
- your second must be taken from **a different section**
- each answer must be written in **a separate answer booklet**
- the maximum time allowed for any question is **1 hour 30 minutes**.

You must identify each question you attempt by indicating clearly

- **the title of the section** from which the question has been taken
- **the number of the question** within that section.

You must also write inside the front cover of your Literary Study answer booklet

- **the topic** of your Specialist Study (Dissertation)
- **the texts** used in your Specialist Study (Dissertation).

Section 1—Literary Study

This section is **mandatory** for all candidates.

You must answer **one question only** in this section.

DRAMA

1. **Bridie**

   How far do you agree that the key to the success of Bridie's plays is his careful shaping of dramatic structure?

   You should support your answer with evidence from **each** of the specified plays.

2. **Byrne**

   "*For all its riotous comedy, **The Slab Boys Trilogy** articulates a passionately serious political vision.*"

   Discuss.

3. **Chekhov**

   "*Central to the dramatic effectiveness of a Chekhov play is not so much action or incident but the changing perceptions and feelings of characters.*"

   How far do you agree?

   You may base your answer on *The Cherry Orchard* **or** on *Uncle Vanya* **or** on both plays.

4. **Glover**

   Discuss Glover's dramatic treatment of human loneliness in *The Straw Chair* **and** in *Bondagers*.

5. **Lindsay**

   "*Lindsay's shift in focus—from the allegorical figures which dominate Part One to the social types that come to the fore in Part Two—is vital to the successful promotion of his central argument.*"

   Analyse the structure of *Ane Satyre of the Thrie Estaitis* in the light of this assertion.

6. **Lochhead**

   Analyse and evaluate the various ways in which Lochhead uses humour in *Mary Queen of Scots Got Her Head Chopped Off* **and** in *Dracula*.

7. **McLellan**

   Drawing evidence from *Jamie the Saxt* **and** *The Flouers o Edinburgh*, describe and evaluate some of the distinctive features of McLellan's dialogue.

8. **Pinter**

   Discuss the extent to which variations of tone and mood contribute to the dramatic effectiveness of **each** of the specified plays.

9. **Shakespeare**

   (a) Make a detailed examination of Shakespeare's dramatic treatment of kingship in *Hamlet* **or** in *King Lear*.

   OR

   (b) Compare and contrast the principal features of Shakespeare's dramatic treatment of kingship in *Hamlet* with the principal features of his dramatic treatment of kingship in *King Lear*.

10. **Shaw**

    "***Major Barbara*** and ***St Joan*** *present us with heroines who are models of what Shaw has called 'creative evolution'—ideals of human aspiration and innovation.*"

    How far do you agree?

11. **Stoppard**

    "*Dramatic tension in Stoppard's plays arises from the presentation of protagonists confronted by destructive and unpredictable forces.*"

    Discuss with reference to *Rosencrantz and Guildenstern are Dead* **and** *Arcadia*.

12. **Williams**

    Discuss Williams's dramatic exploration of the relationship between the "old South" and the "new South" in *The Glass Menagerie* **and** in *A Streetcar Named Desire*.

    [Turn over

POETRY

13. Chaucer

"*The interest is not simply in the Tale itself but in the Tale as characteristic of the teller.*"

Discuss with reference to *The Pardoner's Prologue and Tale* and to any **one** other Tale.

14. Coleridge

"*In the poetry of Coleridge, Nature is seen not only as a source of wonder but also as a moral guide and teacher.*"

Discuss.

15. Donne and the metaphysical poets

"*The most notable characteristic of metaphysical poetry is its preoccupation with individual experience, its unabashed concentration upon the self.*"

How far do you agree?

You should support your answer with evidence drawn from the language, imagery and tone of **three** or **four** metaphysical poems.

16. Duffy

"*Duffy's character studies—the affectionate, the gently ironic, the bitingly satirical—always impress with the firmness of the poet's control of tone.*"

Discuss with reference to **three** or **four** poems.

17. Dunbar

Examine Dunbar's poetic treatment of particular aspects of the social life of his day in **two** or **three** poems.

18. Dunn

"*One of the distinguishing features of Dunn's poetry is the sensitivity with which it portrays ordinary people—with all their human weaknesses.*"

Analyse **three** or **four** poems in the light of this assertion.

19. Fergusson

With reference to **two** or **three** poems, analyse some of the principal techniques employed by Fergusson to satirise human folly and corruption.

20. **Heaney**

*The following poem, **Sunlight**, is the first of two poems dedicated to Mossbawn, Heaney's childhood home, and written for Mary Heaney.*

Read the poem carefully and then answer the questions that follow it.

Mossbawn: Two Poems in Dedication
For Mary Heaney

1 Sunlight

There was a sunlit absence.
The helmeted pump in the yard
heated its iron,
water honeyed

5   in the slung bucket
and the sun stood
like a griddle cooling
against the wall

of each long afternoon.
10 So, her hands scuffled
over the bakeboard,
the reddening stove

sent its plaque of heat
against her where she stood
15 in a floury apron
by the window.

Now she dusts the board
with a goose's wing,
now sits, broad-lapped,
20 with whitened nails

and measling shins:
here is a space
again, the scone rising
to the tick of two clocks.

25 And here is love
like a tinsmith's scoop
sunk past its gleam
in the meal-bin.

(a) "And here is love" (line 25). Analyse the means by which Heaney explores aspects of love in this poem.

(b) Go on to discuss the means by which he explores aspects of love in **two** or **three** other poems.

[Turn over

21. Hopkins

What do you consider to be the most distinctive features of Hopkins's use of imagery?

Support your answer with evidence drawn from a range of poems.

22. Morgan

The following poem refers to a painting of a Glasgow scene by the Scottish artist, Joan Eardley, which Morgan owned.

Read the poem carefully and then answer the questions that follow it.

TO JOAN EARDLEY

    Pale yellow letters
    humbly straggling across
    the once brilliant red
    of a broken shop-face
5 CONFECTIO
    and a blur of children
    at their games, passing,
    gazing as they pass
    at the blur of sweets
10 in the dingy, cosy
    Rottenrow window—
    an Eardley on my wall.
    Such rags and streaks
    that master us!—
15 that fix what the pick
    and bulldozer have crumbled
    to a dingier dust,
    the living blur
    fiercely guarding
20 energy that has vanished,
    cries filling still
    the unechoing close!
    I wandered by the rubble
    and the houses left standing
25 kept a chill, dying life
    in their islands of stone.
    No window opened
    as the coal cart rolled
    and the coalman's call
30 fell coldly to the ground.
    But the shrill children
    jump on my wall.

(*a*) Analyse the means by which Morgan explores aspects of Glasgow in this poem.

(*b*) Go on to discuss the means by which he explores aspects of Glasgow in **two** or **three** other poems.

23. **Plath**

   Read the following poem carefully and then answer the questions that follow it.

   Morning Song

   Love set you going like a fat gold watch.
   The midwife slapped your footsoles, and your bald cry
   Took its place among the elements.

   Our voices echo, magnifying your arrival. New statue.
   5   In a drafty museum, your nakedness
   Shadows our safety. We stand round blankly as walls.

   I'm no more your mother
   Than the cloud that distills a mirror to reflect its own slow
   Effacement at the wind's hand.

   10 All night your moth-breath
   Flickers among the flat pink roses. I wake to listen:
   A far sea moves in my ear.

   One cry, and I stumble from bed, cow-heavy and floral
   In my Victorian nightgown.
   15 Your mouth opens clean as a cat's. The window square

   Whitens and swallows its dull stars. And now you try
   Your handful of notes;
   The clear vowels rise like balloons.

   (a) Make a detailed analysis of Plath's poetic treatment of the relationship between mother and child in this poem.

   (b) Go on to discuss distinctive aspects of her poetic treatment of the relationship between mother and child in **two** or **three** other poems.

24. **The Scottish Ballads**

   Make a comparative study of some of the ways in which death is given significance in **three** or **four** Scottish ballads.

   [Turn over

PROSE FICTION

25. Achebe

Discuss the significance within Achebe's fiction of his use of proverbs, popular adages, folktales and any other characteristics of Ibo language and culture that you think are important.

26. Austen

"*Emma* is a good-humoured, benevolent social comedy that never falters in its tone; *Persuasion* is an altogether darker novel, almost tragic in its implications and much more acerbic in its criticism of society."

How far do you agree?

27. Dickens

Examine Dickens's treatment of wealth and its effects upon the individual in *Great Expectations* **or** in *Bleak House* **or** in both novels.

28. Forster

Compare and contrast the role of Mrs Wilcox in *Howards End* with that of Mrs Moore in *A Passage to India*.

29. Galloway

Analyse and evaluate the means by which Galloway engages the reader with the inner lives of her main protagonists in *The Trick is to Keep Breathing* **and** in *Foreign Parts*.

30. Gray

Discuss the use of different narrative voices within *Lanark* **and** within *Poor Things*.

31. Gunn

*The following extract is taken from **Highland River**.*

Read the extract carefully and then answer the questions that follow it.

An hour later, he left the white shore and encountered two or three tiny lochs, called dubh lochs. The inland moors were full of them. He had heard stories of their treacherous depths. The one in front of him was barely six feet across, its water hardly a foot deep. When his stick touched bottom in the middle it went sinking into the soft,
5 dark ooze under its own weight. With his finger tip and the slightest of pressures, he sank it its full five feet. He had only to take one step forward and not all his struggles or clawings at the bank would save him from being sucked to death.

He was aware of an irrational pleasure, arising out of an absolute absence of fear. He had once thought of Radzyn's mind as a remote place with chasms.

10 As he looked back at Loch Braighe na h'Aibhne, his lips moved in their characteristic humour, but in his eyes was a deep, secret tenderness.

The intimacy was very close now. In the last few moments before he had risen he had seen himself walking towards the mountain, much as, in the last year or two, he had seen the little figure of the boy Kenn adventuring into the strath. What older
15 mind, in this curious regress, was now the observer might be difficult to say, for its apprehension seemed profounder than individual thought. Pict, and Viking too, and Gael; the folk, through immense eras of time; sea and river, moor and loch; the abiding land: of which the departing figure was a silent emanation, more inevitable than any figure in any vision.

20 From the high summit, the solitary figure would watch the dawn come up behind the Orkneys; would see on the mountain ranges of Sutherland the grey planetary light that reveals the earth as a ball turning slowly in the immense chasm of space; would turn again to the plain of Caithness, that land of exquisite lights, and be held by a myriad lochs and dubh lochs glimmering blood-red. He could then bow his head and see what
25 lay in his heart and in his mind.

Kenn withdrew his eyes from the source of his river and, turning, saw about him here and there on the moor the golden spikes of the bog asphodel. He picked one and found it had a scent. He searched for the name of the scent and remembered the taste of a golden candy Sans used to sell out of a glass bottle. At that, little Kenn's face
30 vanished goblin-like across his mind. He could not all at once throw the flower from him nor could he put it in his buttonhole, so he forgot it in his hand as he went over the watershed and down into the valley that lay between him and the base of the mountain.

(*a*) Analyse in detail the means by which Gunn explores the relationship between Kenn and the natural world in this extract.

(*b*) Go on to discuss some of the ways in which Gunn gives significance to the natural world elsewhere in *Highland River* **or** in *The Silver Darlings*.

[Turn over

32. Hardy

"*In Henchard and Tess Hardy presents us with characters who are responsible for their own suffering.*"

How far do you agree?

33. Hogg

Analyse the narrative structure of *The Private Memoirs and Confessions of a Justified Sinner* and comment on its effectiveness.

34. Joyce

Discuss the portrayal of young love in *A Portrait of the Artist as a Young Man* **and** in any **two** of the short stories from *Dubliners*.

35. Spark

The following extract is taken from the opening chapter of **The Girls of Slender Means**.

Read the extract carefully and then answer the questions that follow it (*Page twelve*).

Long ago in 1945 all the nice people in England were poor, allowing for exceptions. The streets of the cities were lined with buildings in bad repair or in no repair at all, bomb-sites piled with stony rubble, houses like giant teeth in which decay had been drilled out, leaving only the cavity. Some bomb-ripped buildings looked like the ruins
5   of ancient castles until, at a closer view, the wallpapers of various quite normal rooms would be visible, room above room, exposed, as on a stage, with one wall missing; sometimes a lavatory chain would dangle over nothing from a fourth- or fifth-floor ceiling; most of all the staircases survived, like a new art-form, leading up and up to an unspecified destination that made unusual demands on the mind's eye. All the nice
10 people were poor; at least, that was a general axiom, the best of the rich being poor in spirit.

There was absolutely no point in feeling depressed about the scene, it would have been like feeling depressed about the Grand Canyon or some event of the earth outside everybody's scope. People continued to exchange assurances of depressed feelings
15 about the weather or the news, or the Albert Memorial which had not been hit, not even shaken, by any bomb from first to last.

The May of Teck Club stood obliquely opposite the site of the Memorial, in one of a row of tall houses which had endured, but barely; some bombs had dropped nearby, and in a few back gardens, leaving the buildings cracked on the outside and shakily
20 hinged within, but habitable for the time being. The shattered windows had been replaced with new glass rattling in loose frames. More recently, the bituminous black-out paint had been removed from landing and bathroom windows. Windows were important in that year of final reckoning; they told at a glance whether a house was inhabited or not; and in the course of the past years they had accumulated much
25 meaning, having been the main danger-zone between domestic life and the war going on outside: everyone had said, when the sirens sounded, "Mind the windows. Keep away from the windows. Watch out for the glass."

The May of Teck Club had been three times window-shattered since 1940, but never directly hit. There the windows of the upper bedrooms overlooked the dip and
30 rise of treetops in Kensington Gardens across the street, with the Albert Memorial to

be seen by means of a slight craning and twist of the neck. These upper bedrooms looked down on the opposite pavement on the park side of the street, and on the tiny people who moved along in neat-looking singles and couples, pushing little prams loaded with pin-head babies and provisions, or carrying little dots of shopping bags. Everyone carried a shopping bag in case they should be lucky enough to pass a shop that had a sudden stock of something off the rations.

From the lower-floor dormitories the people in the street looked larger, and the paths of the park were visible. All the nice people were poor, and few were nicer, as nice people come, than these girls at Kensington who glanced out of the windows in the early mornings to see what the day looked like, or gazed out on the green summer evenings, as if reflecting on the months ahead, on love and the relations of love. Their eyes gave out an eager-spirited light that resembled near-genius, but was youth merely. The first of the Rules of Constitution, drawn up at some remote and innocent Edwardian date, still applied more or less to them:

The May of Teck Club exists for the Pecuniary Convenience and Social Protection of Ladies of Slender Means below the age of Thirty Years, who are obliged to reside apart from their Families in order to follow an Occupation in London.

As they realized themselves in varying degrees, few people alive at the time were more delightful, more ingenious, more movingly lovely, and, as it might happen, more savage, than the girls of slender means.

*

"I've got something to tell you," said Jane Wright, the woman columnist.

At the other end of the telephone, the voice of Dorothy Markham, owner of the flourishing model agency, said, "Darling, where have you been?" She spoke, by habit since her débutante days, with the utmost enthusiasm of tone.

"I've got something to tell you. Do you remember Nicholas Farringdon? Remember he used to come to the old May of Teck just after the war, he was an anarchist and poet sort of thing. A tall man with—"

"The one that got on to the roof to sleep out with Selina?"

"Yes, Nicholas Farringdon."

"Oh rather. Has he turned up?"

"No, he's been martyred."

"What-ed?"

"Martyred in Haiti. Killed. Remember he became a Brother—"

"But I've just been to Tahiti, it's marvellous, everyone's marvellous. Where did you hear it?"

"Haiti. There's a news paragraph just come over Reuters. I'm sure it's the same Nicholas Farringdon because it says a missionary, former poet. I nearly died. I knew him well, you know, in those days. I expect they'll hush it all up, about those days, if they want to make a martyr story."

"How did it happen, is it gruesome?"

"Oh, I don't know, there's only a paragraph."

"You'll have to find out more through your grapevine. I'm shattered. I've got heaps to tell you."

*

The Committee of Management wishes to express surprise at the Members' protest regarding the wallpaper chosen for the drawing room. The Committee wishes to point out that Members' residential fees do not meet the running expenses of the Club. The Committee regrets that the spirit of the May of Teck foundation has apparently so far deteriorated that such a protest has been made. The Committee refers Members to the terms of the Club's Foundation.

Joanna Childe was a daughter of a country rector. She had a good intelligence and strong obscure emotions. She was training to be a teacher of elocution and, while attending a school of drama, already had pupils of her own. Joanna Childe had been drawn to this profession by her good voice and love of poetry which she loved rather as it might be assumed a cat loves birds; poetry, especially the declamatory sort, excited and possessed her; she would pounce on the stuff, play with it quivering in her mind, and when she had got it by heart, she spoke it forth with devouring relish. Mostly, she indulged the habit while giving elocution lessons at the club where she was highly thought of for it. The vibrations of Joanna's elocution voice from her room or from the recreation room where she frequently rehearsed, were felt to add tone and style to the establishment when boy-friends called. Her taste in poetry became the accepted taste of the club. She had a deep feeling for certain passages in the authorized version of the Bible, besides the Book of Common Prayer, Shakespeare and Gerard Manley Hopkins, and had newly discovered Dylan Thomas. She was not moved by the poetry of Eliot and Auden, except for the latter's lyric:

> Lay your sleeping head, my love,
> Human on my faithless arm;

Joanna Childe was large, with light shiny hair, blue eyes and deep-pink cheeks. When she read the notice signed by Lady Julia Markham, chairwoman of the committee, she stood with the other young women round the green baize board and was given to murmur:

"He rageth, and again he rageth, because he knows his time is short."

It was not known to many that this was a reference to the Devil, but it caused amusement. She had not intended it so. It was not usual for Joanna to quote anything for its aptitude, and at conversational pitch.

(*a*) Identify the distinctive aspects of Spark's narrative method evident in this extract.

(*b*) How far are such aspects as you have identified characteristic of her narrative method elsewhere in this novel **and** in *The Prime of Miss Jean Brodie*?

36. Stevenson

How important is Stevenson's evocation of mood and atmosphere to the success of *The Strange Case of Dr Jekyll and Mr Hyde* **and** of *Weir of Hermiston*?

PROSE NON-FICTION

37. Autobiography

In what ways have any **two** of the specified autobiographies contributed to your interest in and understanding of the times in which the writers lived?

38. Autobiography

How effectively does the writer reveal or create or explore his or her identity in any **one** of the specified autobiographies?

39. Travel Writing

"*Representations of place often tell us more about the culture of the writer than about the culture of the place or places visited.*"

Discuss with reference to **one** or **more than one** of the specified texts.

40. Travel Writing

"*In many ways, the best travel writers work like novelists: they select; they cast light on this object or shadow on that; they shape character; they imagine.*"

Discuss the work of **one** or **more than one** of the travel writers you have studied in the light of this assertion.

41. Writing about Scotland

"*Writing about Scotland from the last hundred years is marked by a bleakness of vision, by anger and dismay at what the writer observes.*"

Discuss with detailed reference to any **two** of the specified texts.

42. Writing about Scotland

"*There is no such thing as a Scottish national identity; what there is is a multiplicity of small local identities.*"

To what extent is this view reflected in **one** or **more than one** of the specified texts?

[Turn over

Section 2—Language Study

You must answer **one question only** in this section.

Topic A—The use of English in a particular geographical area

1. Describe the distinctive linguistic features of a particular regional variety of English and go on to discuss **one** or **more than one** of the following: who speaks it, its history, its relationship to other regional varieties, its relationship to Standard English, the contexts in which it is used.

2. Describe in detail the vocabulary, grammar and pronunciation of a particular overseas variety of English.

Topic B—Variations in the use of English related to social class

3. *"People's perception of linguistic differences across social classes has more to do with their prejudices than with any substantial variations in language use."*

   How far do you agree?

   You should support your answer with detailed reference to vocabulary, grammar and pronunciation.

4. If you were to investigate the relationship between language and social class, how would you collect your data and how would you analyse it?

Topic C—Variations in the use of English related to gender

5. Some researchers have claimed that in male-female conversations men's talk is more competitive and less co-operative than that of women.

   What evidence can be drawn upon to support or challenge such a claim?

6. From your own experience and from your reading and research, compare and contrast the typical features of conversation in male-only groups with the typical features of conversation in female-only groups.

Topic D—The linguistic characteristics of informal conversation

For both questions on this topic (see *Page sixteen*), you are provided with a transcript of a conversational exchange between Addie and Brianne, two young American women.

NB The examples used to illustrate the transcription key that precedes the transcript are **not** taken from the transcript itself.

Each line of the transcript contains a single intonation unit, and the conventions of transcription are as follows:

Transcription Key

She's out.	— *A full stop shows falling tone in the preceding element.*
Oh yeah?	— *A question mark shows rising tone in the preceding element.*
Well, okay	— *A comma indicates a continuing intonation, drawing out the preceding element.*
Damn	— *Italics show heavy stress.*
bu–but?	— *A single dash indicates a cut-off with a glottal stop.*
says "Oh"	— *Double quotes mark speech that is set off by a shift in the speaker's voice.*
[and so-] [Why] her?	— *Square brackets on successive lines mark the beginning and end of overlapping talk.*
{sigh}	— *Curly brackets enclose editorial comments.*

Transcript

1	Addie:	you know my mom and I went to Monroe today.
2	Brianne:	uh-huh
3	Addie:	and anyway, so –
4		Keith swore that it was Sheila in the car.
5		now Sheila heard all this through Alison.
6		because Alison, I guess, worked today.
7		and, um, sh–
8		he swore that it was her riding in the car. {laughs}
9	Brianne:	{laughing} no way.
10	Addie:	and I guess he said to Alison,
11		cause Alison, um,
12		he asked her, Alison,
13		if she could stay a little later
14		and she said "No,
15		because I have to go to Monroe to get some things,
16		y'know I have to run some errands."
17		and he thought that it was a scam
18		that Sheila was going with them.
19	Brianne:	oh, no.
20	Addie:	and that's why Sheila didn't come in to work.
21	Brianne:	oh, no.

[Turn over

22	Addie:	and so he said, y'know,
23		"I–If I find out that–
24		that you and Sheila were in Monroe
25		you *both* are going to be fired" {laughs}
26	Brianne:	"yeah, sure,
27		go ahead and fire them, y'know,
28		then you could just work that much more, Keith,
29		y'know, you want to work forty hours a day,
30		don't you?"
31	Addie:	{laughing} and so I guess, Sheila,
32		[Sheila was so mad]
33	Brianne:	[oh, man.]
34		not to trust your employees at all.
35	Addie:	yeah.

[Source: Neal R. Norrick (2000) *Conversational Narrative: Storytelling in Everyday Talk* Amsterdam/Philadelphia: John Benjamins, pp 210–11 ISBN 90–272–3710–7]

7. How typical do you find this extract as an example of storytelling in informal conversation?

   In answering this question, you should discuss matters such as narrative structures, interactions between speakers and the purposes of storytelling in informal conversations.

8. What choices are involved in transcribing speech? Base your answer on the transcript given above and on your study of other transcripts of informal conversation.

Topic E—The linguistic characteristics of political communication

9. Describe and give examples of the kinds of linguistic strategies used by politicians to:

   - present their own party's image
   - comment on rival parties' statements and actions
   - represent particular events.

10. In this question you are provided with an excerpt from the *Official Report* of the Scottish Parliament (8th September 2004). This excerpt is an edited transcript (in which for ease of reference each paragraph is numbered) of a debate following the First Minister's Question Time of the previous day. On that day, the First Minister, Jack McConnell, had outlined his government's economic strategy.

    How effective do you find this excerpt as an example of political communication?

    In answering this question, you should examine as many of the following as you consider appropriate:

    - the conventions of debates such as this
    - the degree of formality
    - the choice of vocabulary
    - the degree of grammatical complexity
    - the description of rival parties
    - the use of humour.

[1] **Mr Ted Brocklebank (Mid Scotland and Fife) (Con):** I want to explore in further detail some of the things that the First Minister said yesterday and, perhaps more important, some of the things that he did not say.

[2] A couple of years ago, Jack McConnell said that his Executive was going to "do less, better". If that were an alternative to doing a lot of things badly, few could question the logic. However, it turned out that, while the coalition was, indeed, doing fewer things, it was not necessarily doing them better. So, as we discovered in yesterday's statement, it is time to raise the goalposts again. The softly-softly approach has been abandoned, and no fewer than 12 major pieces of legislation will be introduced this year. However, as we say in my part of Fife, it is a poor cadger that shouts "stinking fish".

[3] I had to pinch myself to realise that the litany of supposed achievements and aspirations that the First Minister was talking up yesterday had happened in the same small country that I live in. Like Jack McConnell, I believe that Scotland is one of the best small countries in the world. However, I believe that despite, rather than because of, the efforts of the coalition. The coalition had nothing to do with the creation of our wonderful scenery—although its policies, in particular those on wind farms, might go a long way towards destroying it. The coalition has done nothing to improve the quality of Scottish education, which was once recognised as of international class but which is now too often regarded as second rate. The coalition has turned the thrifty, entrepreneurial country that Scotland once was into a land in which one in every four employees works in a public sector that accounts for an extraordinary 52 per cent of the country's gross domestic product.

[4] However, this week, Jack McConnell seems to have seen the light. His latest big media message is that the balance between the public and private sectors has swung too far in favour of the state and must be redressed, but—wait for it—that will be done not by reducing the public sector in places such as Fife, where council employment has increased by another 5 per cent, or 600 employees, this year, but by increasing the private sector. Apparently, we can do one but we cannot do the other. Does the First Minister intend to follow Gordon Brown's example and make public service job cuts? If he does not, was his latest soundbite an example of how he intends to raise the game in Parliamentary debates?

[5] **Christine May (Central Fife) (Lab):** Will the member give way?

[6] **Mr Brocklebank:** A little later, perhaps.

[7] I am reminded of my days in the Salvation Army and the old hymn:
"Tell me the old, old story, for I forget so soon . . .
Tell me the story simply, as to a little child
For I am weak and weary and helpless and defiled."
I expect that that strikes a chord with many Scots as we enter this Executive's sixth year.

[8] **Christine May:** Mr Brocklebank talked about the increases in public sector employment. Given that most of those employees are teachers, social workers and workers in the health service, will he tell us how many doctors, nurses and social workers the Tories would get rid of?

[9] **Mr Brocklebank**: In Christine May's part of Fife—the part that we both come from—by far the largest employer is the public sector. Indeed, that is true for the whole of Fife. I will not guess at how many teachers, doctors and others there are, but is Christine May happy with that statistic? I do not believe so.

[10] Jack McConnell told members that his job is not to create jobs, but to create the climate in which enterprise, innovation and risk taking can grow. That sounded great until he sat down after more than an hour without having once mentioned the Scottish industry that led the world in risk taking, innovation and sheer hard work. Of course, I am talking about the Scottish fishing industry.

[11] **Jeremy Purvis (Tweeddale, Ettrick and Lauderdale) (LD)**: Will the member give way?

[12] **Mr Brocklebank**: A little later, perhaps.

[End]

[Source:http://www.scottish.parliament.uk/business/officalReports/meetingsParliament/archive/or-04/sor0908-02.htm#Col10024]

Topic F—The linguistic characteristics of tabloid journalism

11. For this question, you are provided with an extract from *The Sun* newspaper of Friday, September 3, 2004.

    Make a detailed analysis of the page provided in which you identify and discuss those aspects of style and language which a reader would expect of tabloid journalism.

WE BEAT BARMY PARLY BAN

Crunch talks... Tory MSP Bill Aitken enjoys our toast outside the parliament yesterday and thanks Sun man Kenny for bringing him breakfast

THE SCOTTISH Sun IS THE TOAST OF HOLYROOD

MSPs line up for our breakfast

By KENNY McALPINE

HUNGRY Holyrood MSPs found out which side their bread is buttered on—after we served them up some tasty TOAST.

We revealed yesterday how crusty parly bosses banned the breakfast dish in case it sets off smoke alarms.

But we were the toast of Holyrood when we set up our own brekkie stall outside their offices.

Equipped with dozens of loaves and a toaster, we gave away free buttered toast to hundreds of MSPs and parly workers. Tory MSP Bill Aitken said: "Had it not been for the Scottish Sun we would not have been able to get our toast today.

"It is ridiculous that we can spend £430 million on a parliament building but we cannot make or eat toast in it."

The Executive banned the making of toast after smoke from the kitchens' toasters caused a spate of false fire alerts.

Hot topic... our story

Burnt offering... toaster pops up

Buttering 'em up... Kenny feeds grateful workers

12. With reference to content and style, mode of address and typical stance, discuss how any **one** tabloid newspaper presents its view of the world.

If you choose to discuss *The Sun* newspaper in your answer to this question, you may include reference to the text provided for question 11.

Topic G—The use of Scots in a particular geographical area

13. What have you observed about the use of the Scots language in the 21st century?

In your answer you must refer in detail to your own research and you may refer to **one** or **more than one** geographical area.

14. What are the main influences that have shaped Scots vocabulary in **one** or **more than one** geographical area?

Topic H—The linguistic characteristics of Scots as used in informal conversation

15. From your own systematic study, identify and describe some of the ways you or other people you know or have observed use Scots in informal conversation.

16. Discuss the ways in which Scots is used in the following transcript.

The transcript is part of a conversation involving Annie and Joe, who live beside a railway, and Neil, their neighbour. Annie tells the story of her daughter Jean's poodle, Cherie. The text is lightly transcribed as follows.

```
<NA>XXXX<NA>      signifies inaudible speech
<NA>laughs</NV>   signifies non-verbal behaviour
<-->              signifies pause
```

    Annie: Many a cat we lost on that railway.

    Joe: Ken what we used tae like on the railway? See when they –

    Annie: They used tae go past. The puffies, the puffies used tae go past and they flung aw the coal off in the garden, Neil, and ye went oot and there was huge coal . . . Oh!

    Joe: Aye, the old steam-tails went past, Neil. And they cairted the coal. And they <NA>XXXX<NA> there <NA>XXXX<NA> there the boy that <NA>XXXX<NA> the coal. Big lumps is rollin oot the door, rollin oot the door, rolling oot the door.

10   **Neil:** <NV>laughs</NV>

    Joe: . . . an eh we'd tae get along wae the barrie, Neil eh? . . . And we used tae go through wi' the barrie and get the coal and all them . . . Aye, we used tae walk that line and that.

    Annie: And then they used tae throw it in the garden. As <--> Ken the bit at the
15   back? They used tae full it fu' for us and hoot their horn . . . And then, on a Sunday we'd to hurry and get the coal, and then, on a Sunday there was nae trains, ye see, so ye could walk the line on a Sunday and pick up aw the coal up ye wanted.

	Neil:	Good god.
20	**Joe**:	Aye a whole lot o coal and that.
	Annie:	It was great in they days! And then the puffies came along and all the bankins used tae go on fire . . . ye see?
	Neil:	Aye.
25	**Annie**:	So they had tae beat the fire oot, and the fire-engines used tae hae tae come and put aw the fires oot. There was nae g- overgrown bankings then. It was bare.
	Joe:	Tell Neil aboot yer wee dug eh? 'Cross the railway.
	Annie:	Oh aye the poodle.
	Joe:	Aye.
30	**Annie**:	We'd a wee poodle, and Jean's <--> Jean's poodle, but she went away up the wood on her bike round the road.
	Joe:	'Cross the railway. Ken there was a walkway cross the railway. Ken sleepers how ye walked on them to the signal-box.
	Neil:	Uhuh.
35	**Annie**:	And Cherie was in, and I says, "Don't let Cherie see where ye're goin." Well, Cherie sh- f- <--> got oot and smelt Jean and she crossed the train, and the train was comin and the driver couldnae stop. So, of course, she fell, and she fell in the middle of the track.
	Joe:	It was lucky, aye.
40	**Annie**:	And she was alive. And I rushed her to the vet, but she had holes in her back wae the big stones, and the buffer hit her.
	Joe:	So we rushed her to the vet . . . It was the big chains. No, it was the big chains that hung doun. And the vet s- <--> hit her <--> And the vet said tae me, "If she lives the night, she'll live."
45	**Annie**:	It wasnae the buffer, Neil, it was the snow-plough on the front . . . Oh that hit the wag- <--> that hit the wag- <--> oh aye hit her. Lucky it never killed her!
	Neil:	Mhm.
50	**Annie**:	So she lived, but she was very badly hurt. Well, no many months ago, there was a man came intae the mill and he says tae me, "I often wonder about yer wee poodle."
	Neil:	Aye?
55	**Annie**:	"For," he says, "I noticed that she ran on the railway and you were gonna run efter her and I'm sayin tae mysel, 'Dinnae run on that railway' for I was drivin the train." And he says, "Ye were a young lassie then, and I'm sayin, 'Oh dinnae run on the railway, dinnae run on the railway.'"
	Neil:	Oh he was the driver!
	Annie:	He was the driver!

[Turn over

	Joe:	He was the driver.
60	**Annie**:	And he says, "What happened tae the poodle?" and I says, "The poodle lived, she lived." And I says, "She was badly hurt, but she lived."
	Neil:	Mm.
	Annie:	And he says, "Oh my god, I've often thocht aboot that." And he says, "I was just wonderin if you were gonna move or no tae grab her, because I could never stoapped."
65		
	Neil:	Aye.

Topic I—Variations in the use of Scots among older and younger people

17. *"From at least the first half of the eighteenth century, Scots has always been thought to be 'dying out' as a spoken language."*

Introduction to the Concise Scots Dictionary

Based upon your research into variations in the use of Scots among older and younger people in the 21st century, do **you** think that Scots is *"dying out"* as a spoken language?

18. To what extent has Scots been maintained and adapted for contemporary use (for example, in the home, in the workplace, in the community)?

In answering this question, you should make detailed reference to your own study of the use of Scots among older and younger people.

Topic J—Uses of Scots in the media

19. Choose a television or radio programme or series of programmes which has made significant use of Scots. Describe in detail how Scots is used in the programme or series of programmes you have chosen.

20. *"There's no longer such a thing as BBC English. Voices of all varieties are mainstreamed into broadcast media."*

In the light of this statement, discuss the range of Scots voices heard in broadcast media.

Topic K—Uses of Scots in contemporary literature

21. Analyse and evaluate the use of Scots in the work of **one** or **more than one** novelist or short story writer you have studied.

22. Compare and contrast the use of Scots in the following poem, *Sharleen: Ah'm Shy*, by Janet Paisley, with the use of Scots in the extract from the poem, *Almost Miss Scotland*, by Liz Lochhead.

You should examine vocabulary, grammar, pronunciation, orthography or any other features you think significant.

SHARLEEN: AH'M SHY

Ah'm shy. Aye, ah am. Canny look naebody in the eye.
Ah've seen me go in a shoap an jist hoap naebody wid talk tae me.
Things that happen, likesae—yer oot fur a walk
and some bloke whits never even spoke afore goes by
an he's given ye the eye. See me, ah jist want tae die.
Ah go rid tae the roots o ma hair. Weel it's no fair, is it?
Feel a right twit. See ma Ma. She says it'll pass.
'Ye'll grow oot o it hen.' Aye, aw right. But when?
Ye kin get awfy fed up bein the local beetroot.
So last time I went oot—tae the disco—
ah bought this white make-up. White lightening it said.
Ah thought, nae beamers the night, this stuff'll see me aw right.
Onywey, there ah wis, actin it. Daen ma pale an intrestin bit.
White lightening. See unner them flashin lights
it was quite frightnin. Cause ma face looked aw blue.
See, when a think o it noo, it was mortifyin.
Cause they aw thought ah wis dyin, an they dialled 999.
Fine thing tae be, centre o awbody's attention, me.
They hud me sat oan this chair, bit when they brought stretchers in,
ah slid oantae the flair—an jist lay there.
Ah thought, rule number one, when ye've made a fool o yersell
dinnae let oan, play the game. So ah let oot a groan an lay still.
Until this ambulance fella feels ma wrist,
an then he gies ma neck a twist—an ye'll no believe this.
Bit right there and then—he gies me a kiss.
Blew intae ma mooth, honest. God'strewth ah wis gasping fur breath.
Jist goes tae show yer no safe, naeplace these days.
Onywey ah blew right back, that made him move quick.
Fur he says are you aw right, are ye gaun tae be sick.
That's when ah noticed his eyes—they were daurk broon.
An staring right intae them made ma stomach go roon.
Ah felt kinda queer, an he says, c'mon we'll get ye oot o here.
Bit ah made him take me right hame—though ah'm seein him again,
the morra. Aw the same, how kin ah tell him dae ye suppose,
that when ye kiss a lassie, ye dinnae haud her nose?

Janet Paisley

[**Turn over**

ALMOST MISS SCOTLAND

The night I
Almost became Miss Scotland,
I caused a big stramash
When I sashayed on in my harristweed heathermix onepiece
And my "Miss Garthamlock" sash.

I wis six-fit-six, I wis slinky
(Yet nae skinnymalinky) —
My waist was nipped in wi elastic,
My powder and panstick were three inches thick,
Nails? Long, blood-rid and plastic.
So my big smile'd come across, I'd larded oan lipgloss
And my false eyelashes were mink
With a sky blue crescent that was pure iridescent
When I lowered my eyelids to blink.

Well, I wiggled tapselteerie, my heels were that peerie
While a kinna Jimmy Shandish band
Played "Flower of Scotland"—
But it aw got droont oot wi wolf whistles —
And that's no countin "For These Are My Mountains"
— See I'd tits like nuclear missiles.

Then this familiar-lukkin felly
I'd seen a loat oan the telly
Interviewed me aboot my hobbies —
I says: Macrame, origami,
Being nice tae my mammy —
(Basically I tellt him a loat o jobbies).
I was givin it that
Aboot my ambition to chat
To handicapped and starvin children from other nations
— How I was certain I'd find
Travel wid broaden my mind
As I fulfilled my Miss Scotland obligations.

Liz Lochhead

Topic L—Uses of Scots in specialised fields

23. According to the Scottish Parliament's website, the Cross Party Group on the Scots Language exists to "*promote the cause of Scots, inform members of the culture and heritage of the language and highlight the need for action to support Scots*".

    Discuss how "the culture and heritage" of the Scots language might be promoted in **one** or **more than one** specialised field you have studied.

24. Describe and account for the Scots used in **one** or **more than one** specialised field. You might consider examples from Agriculture, Fishing, the Church, the Law, the Building Trade, Place Names, Street Names or any other specialised field about which you have knowledge.

ADVANCED HIGHER
2007

[BLANK PAGE]

OFFICIAL SQA PAST PAPERS   53   ADVANCED HIGHER ENGLISH 2007

X115/701

NATIONAL
QUALIFICATIONS
2007

FRIDAY, 11 MAY
1.00 PM – 4.00 PM

ENGLISH
ADVANCED HIGHER

There are four sections in this paper.

Section 1—Literary Study	pages	2 – 10
Section 2—Language Study	pages	11 – 22
Section 3—Textual Analysis	pages	23 – 39
Section 4—Reading the Media	pages	40 – 47

Depending on the options you have chosen, you must answer **one** or **two** questions.

If you have submitted a Creative Writing folio, you must answer only **one** question.

Otherwise, you must answer **two** questions.

If you are required to answer only **one question**

- it must be taken from **Section 1—Literary Study**
- you must leave the examination room **after 1 hour 30 minutes**.

If you are required to answer **two questions**

- your first must be taken from **Section 1—Literary Study**
- your second must be taken from **a different section**
- each answer must be written in **a separate answer booklet**
- the maximum time allowed for any question is **1 hour 30 minutes**.

You must identify each question you attempt by indicating clearly

- **the title of the section** from which the question has been taken
- **the number of the question** within that section.

You must also write inside the front cover of your Literary Study answer booklet

- **the topic** of your Specialist Study (Dissertation)
- **the texts** used in your Specialist Study (Dissertation).

LI X115/701 6/4070

Section 1—Literary Study

This section is **mandatory** for all candidates.

You must answer **one question only** in this section.

DRAMA

1. **Bridie**

   "While Bridie stated that his main purpose in his plays was to provide entertainment, we are always aware of a serious moral purpose shaping and informing the entertainment."

   Discuss *The Anatomist* **and** *Mr Bolfry* in the light of this assertion.

2. **Byrne**

   "Byrne's dialogue in **The Slab Boys Trilogy** is characterised by the juxtaposition of earthy vigour and moving lyricism."

   How far do you agree?

3. **Chekhov**

   "Although thrown into close proximity by family or social circumstances, Chekhov's characters remain estranged."

   Taking this statement into account, discuss some of the principal features of Chekhov's characterisation.

   You may base your answer on *Uncle Vanya* **or** on *The Cherry Orchard* **or** on **both** plays.

4. **Glover**

   How effectively, in your view, does Glover dramatise the inner lives of her characters in *Bondagers* **and** in *The Straw Chair*?

5. **Lindsay**

   How effective is *Ane Satyre of the Thrie Estaitis* as satire?

6. **Lochhead**

   EITHER

   (a) Make a close critical evaluation of the dramatic structure of *Mary Queen of Scots Got Her Head Chopped Off* **or** of the dramatic structure of *Dracula*.

   OR

   (b) Make a comparative evaluation of the principal structural features of *Mary Queen of Scots Got Her Head Chopped Off* **and** *Dracula*.

7. **McLellan**

   How important is the interplay between main characters and minor characters in *Jamie the Saxt* **and** in *The Flouers o Edinburgh*?

8. **Pinter**

   "*Pinter's characters often play unsettling, almost ritualistic, mind-games—games in which characters are left confused and sometimes hurt.*"

   Discuss the contribution of such "*games*" to the dramatic impact of **each** of the specified texts.

9. **Shakespeare**

   "*Shakespearean tragedy offers a relentlessly bleak view of mankind, where the ultimate impression is one of profound waste.*"

   Is this view of Shakespearean tragedy consistent with **your** understanding of *Hamlet* **and** of *King Lear*?

10. **Shaw**

    Make a comparative study of Shaw's dramatic exploration of aspects of religion in *Major Barbara* **and** in *St Joan*.

11. **Stoppard**

    Make a comparative study of the dramatic means by which Stoppard explores issues of free will and determinism in *Rosencrantz and Guildenstern are Dead* **and** in *Arcadia*.

12. **Williams**

    The Glass Menagerie and *A Streetcar Named Desire* are set in small apartments in St Louis and New Orleans respectively.

    How do these settings—described by Williams in such vivid detail—contribute to the mood **and** to the meaning of each play?

POETRY

13. **Chaucer**

    Show how, in *The Pardoner's Tale* **and** in any **one** other of the *Canterbury Tales*, Chaucer makes effective use of traditional literary forms (courtly romance, folk-tale, sermon, legend, allegory, fabliau . . .).

14. **Coleridge**

    "*The best of Coleridge's conversation poems arise from a feeling of loneliness, but this feeling is only a starting-point for a developing argument towards a greater unity—of men, of man and nature, of past, present and future.*"

    Analyse the poetic means by which "*a developing argument*" is presented in **two** or **three** of Coleridge's conversation poems.

[Turn over

15. Donne and the metaphysical poets

*Read the following poem carefully and then answer questions (a) **and** (b) that follow it.*

      Oh my blacke Soule! now thou art summoned
      By sicknesse, deaths herald, and champion;
      Thou art like a pilgrim, which abroad hath done
      Treason, and durst not turne to whence hee is fled,
5   Or like a thiefe, which till deaths doome be read,
      Wisheth himselfe delivered from prison;
      But damn'd and hal'd to execution,
      Wisheth that still he might be imprisoned;
      Yet grace, if thou repent, thou canst not lacke;
10 But who shall give thee that grace to beginne?
      Oh make thy selfe with holy mourning blacke,
      And red with blushing, as thou art with sinne;
      Or wash thee in Christs blood, which hath this might
      That being red, it dyes red soules to white.

(a) Identify the features of metaphysical poetry evident in this sonnet by Donne.

(b) Go on to show how characteristic these features are of other metaphysical poems you have studied.

16. Duffy

"*Those poems that explore the deceptiveness of appearances through real-life situations are curiously unsettling.*"

Discuss with reference to **three** or **four** of Duffy's poems.

17. Dunbar

With reference to at least **three** poems, evaluate Dunbar's achievement in **one** or **more than one** poetic style or genre—such as the aureate lyric, the flyting, the allegory, the satire, the complaint, the lament.

18. Dunn

"*In examining the quirks and idiosyncrasies of the individual, Dunn's poetry reveals the essential dignity of the human spirit.*"

Discuss with reference to **three** or **four** of Dunn's poems.

19. Fergusson

"*One of the distinctive features of Fergusson's poetry is his variation of tone—both within individual poems and between poems.*"

Discuss.

20. Heaney

*Read the following poem and then answer questions (a) **and** (b) that follow it.*

BLACKBERRY-PICKING
For Philip Hobsbaum

    Late August, given heavy rain and sun
    For a full week, the blackberries would ripen.
    At first, just one, a glossy purple clot
    Among others, red, green, hard as a knot.
5 You ate that first one and its flesh was sweet
    Like thickened wine: summer's blood was in it
    Leaving stains upon the tongue and lust for
    Picking. Then red ones inked up and that hunger
    Sent us out with milk-cans, pea-tins, jam-pots
10 Where briars scratched and wet grass bleached our boots.
    Round hayfields, cornfields and potato-drills
    We trekked and picked until the cans were full,
    Until the tinkling bottom had been covered
    With green ones, and on top big dark blobs burned
15 Like a plate of eyes. Our hands were peppered
    With thorn pricks, our palms sticky as Bluebeard's.

    We hoarded the fresh berries in the byre.
    But when the bath was filled we found a fur,
    A rat-grey fungus, glutting on our cache.
20 The juice was stinking too. Once off the bush,
    The fruit fermented, the sweet flesh would turn sour.
    I always felt like crying. It wasn't fair
    That all the lovely canfuls smelt of rot.
    Each year I hoped they'd keep, knew they would not.

(a) Make a close study of the poetic means by which Heaney gives significance to the experience he explores in this poem.

(b) How far is Heaney's approach here typical of his exploration of childhood experience in **two** or **three** other poems?

21. Hopkins

An important aspect of Hopkins's poetry, it has been argued, lies in *"its inventiveness, its joy in being a process of language as well as a representation of things in the world."*

Examine **three** or **four** of Hopkins's poems in the light of this assertion.

[Turn over

22. Morgan

Evaluate the effectiveness of Morgan's use of narrative voice in **three** or **four** poems.

23. Plath

"*Plath's poetry is remarkable for its precision—in the detail of its observation and tight control of form.*"

Discuss with reference to **three** or **four** of Plath's poems.

24. The Scottish Ballads

Read the following poems carefully and then answer the question that follows them (Page seven).

THE BONNY EARL OF MURRAY

Ye Highlands, and ye Lawlands,
    Oh where have you been?
They have slain the Earl of Murray
    And they layd him on the green.

5   'Now wae be to thee, Huntly!
    And wherefore did you sae?
I bade you bring him wi you,
    But forbade you him to slay.'

He was a braw gallant,
10   And he rid at the ring;
And the bonny Earl of Murray,
    Oh he might have been a king!

He was a braw gallant,
    And he playd at the ba;
15   And the bonny Earl of Murray
    Was the flower amang them a'.

He was a braw gallant,
    And he playd at the glove;
And the bonny Earl of Murray,
20   Oh he was the Queen's love!

Oh lang will his lady
    Look oer the castle Down,
Eer she see the Earl of Murray
    Come sounding thro the town!
25   Eer she see the Earl of Murray
    Come sounding thro the town!

THE BARON OF BRACKLEY

In Deeside cam Inverey, whistlin an playin,
    An he was at Brackley's yetts ere the day was dawin,
'Oh, are ye there, Brackley, an are ye within?
    There's sherp swords are at your yetts, will gar your bluid spin.'

5   'Then rise up, my baron, an turn back yer kye,
    For the lads frae Drumwharran are drivin them by.'
'Oh, how can I rise up, and how can I gyan,
    For whaur I hae ae man, oh I'm sure they hae ten.

'Then rise up, Betsy Gordon, an gie me ma gun,
10   An though I gyan oot, love, sure I'll never come in.
Come, kiss me, ma Betsy, nor think I'm tae blame,
    But against three-an-thirty, wae is me, what a fame.

When Brackley was mounted, an rade on his horse,
    A bonnier baron ne'er rade owre a close.
15   Twa gallanter Gordons did never sword draw,
    But against three-an-thirty wisnae evens ava.

Wi their dirks an their swords they did him surroond,
    An they've slain bonnie Brackley wi monie's the wound.
Frae the heid o the Dee tae the banks o the Spey,
20   The Gordons shall mourn him an ban Inverey.

'Oh, come ye by Brackley's yetts, or come ye by here?
    An saw ye his lady, a-rivin her hair?'
'Oh, I cam by Brackley's yetts, an I cam by here,
    An I saw his fair lady, she was makkin guid cheer.

25   'She was rantin an dancin an singin for joy
    An she vowed that that nicht she wad feast Inverey.
'She laughed wi him, drank wi him, welcomed him ben;
    She was kind tae the villain had slain her guidman.'

'Through hedges an ditches ye canna be sure,
30   But through the woods o Glenturner you'll slip in an oor.'
Then up spak the babe on the nanny's knee:
    'It's afore I'm a man avengèd I'll be.'

In terms of subject matter and technique, how characteristic are these two poems of the traditional Scottish ballad?

In your answer, you should also make reference to other Scottish ballads.

[Turn over

PROSE FICTION

25. Achebe

"What distinguishes Achebe's fiction is his preoccupation with language, not simply as a communicative device, but as a total cultural experience."

Discuss.

26. Austen

"In Austen's novels, irony is everywhere—in the characterisation, in the narrative voice, in the dialogue, in the situations, in the misreadings of characters and emotions."

Discuss the nature and function of irony in *Emma* **and** in *Persuasion*.

27. Dickens

Discuss Dickens's use of the macabre and the grotesque in *Bleak House* **and** in *Great Expectations*.

28. Forster

"Forster's female protagonists are chaotic and irrational—famously always in a muddle: they don't know what they want or how to get it."

Discuss Forster's characterisation of Helen Schlegel **and** his characterisation of Adela Quested in the light of this assertion.

29. Galloway

"Her protagonists are human to a fault; indeed, far from being heroes, they tend to be victims."

Keeping this quotation in mind, discuss Galloway's characterisation of Joy in *The Trick is to Keep Breathing* **and** her characterisation of Cassie and Rona in *Foreign Parts*.

30. Gray

"It is Gray's blending of the fantasy of other worlds with the identifiable reality of our own world that gives his fiction its distinctive character."

Discuss with reference to *Lanark* **or** with reference to *Lanark* **and** *Poor Things*.

31. Gunn

"Central to Gunn's fiction is the interaction and tension between the individual and the greater social units of family and of community."

Discuss the importance of such interaction and tension in *Highland River* **and** in *The Silver Darlings*.

32. Hardy

"*So do flux and reflux—the rhythm of change—alternate and persist in everything under the sky.*"

[Hardy's narrator in *Tess of the D'Urbervilles*]

In *Tess of the D'Urbervilles*, what effects are created by such "*flux and reflux*"?

How far might it be claimed that *The Mayor of Casterbridge* is also concerned with "*flux and reflux*"?

33. Hogg

Discuss the principal means by which Hogg exposes hypocrisy in *The Private Memoirs and Confessions of a Justified Sinner* **and** in **one** or **more than one** of his short stories.

34. Joyce

"*April 26. Mother is putting my new secondhand clothes in order. She prays now, she says, that I may learn in my own life and away from home and friends what the heart is and what it feels. Amen. So be it. Welcome, O life! I go to encounter for the millionth time the reality of experience and to forge in the smithy of my soul the uncreated conscience of my race.*

April 27. Old father, old artificer, stand me now and ever in good stead."

In *A Portrait of the Artist as a Young Man*, how fitting do you find these two final diary entries as a conclusion to Joyce's earlier exploration of Stephen Dedalus's awareness of himself **and** of his country?

35. Spark

"*Often her novels feature a confined space or setting, and her plots explore the consequences of breaking out of the limitations imposed by that setting.*"

Discuss with reference to *The Prime of Miss Jean Brodie* **and** with reference to *The Girls of Slender Means*.

36. Stevenson

Discuss Stevenson's exploration of questions of identity in *Dr Jekyll and Mr Hyde* **and** in *Weir of Hermiston*.

PROSE NON-FICTION

37. Autobiography

Analyse the means by which any **one** of the specified autobiographies explores the role of women in society.

[Turn over

38. Autobiography

"*There is no formula for writing an autobiography: there are as many approaches to the writing of it as there are to the writing of a novel.*"

Compare and contrast the different approaches taken to the writing of autobiography in any **two** of the specified texts.

39. Travel Writing

"*Good travel books not only tell us the good and bad of the journey, but also let us in on the process of the writer changing as he moves from place to place.*"

Discuss.

40. Travel Writing

"*The traditional genre expectations of travel writing include linearity of narrative, an emphasis on factual detail, sensitive evocation of mood and atmosphere.*"

How far and to what effect do any **two** of the specified texts conform to **or** confound "*traditional genre expectations*"?

41. Writing about Scotland

How effective, in your view, is any **one** of the specified texts as a critique of the Scotland of its time?

42. Writing about Scotland

In presenting images of and ideas about Scotland and its people, what do any **two** of the specified texts have in common **and**, in terms of approach, style and tone, how do they differ?

Section 2—Language Study

You must answer **one question only** in this section.

Topic A—The use of English in a particular geographical area

1. Describe, in detail, from your own research, the linguistic characteristics of the speech used in a particular geographical area.

2. With reference to a particular variety of English you have studied, give a detailed account of the historical development of **at least two** of the following:

   - vocabulary
   - grammar
   - pronunciation
   - spelling.

Topic B—Variations in the use of English related to social class

Consider the following quotation carefully and then answer **either** Question 3 **or** Question 4.

"While attacking people on grounds of race, sex or age is considered politically incorrect, it is still surprisingly common to encounter attacks based on accent, especially if those accents originate in the lower classes. In theory, it ought to be possible to convince fair-minded people that all accents are equally valid, as long as they are mutually intelligible. However, since I and many other linguists have over the past two or three decades failed miserably in our efforts to convince, I have come to the conclusion that we should introduce into our schools 'language awareness programmes' which cover not only the features of Received Pronunciation and local accents, but also the common reactions which the more stigmatised varieties evoke."

[Paul Coggle]

3. Based on your own research into variations in the use of English related to social class, write an essay in which you

   - describe how accent varies according to social class
   - discuss the attitudes that such accents evoke.

4. With reference to your reading and research into Received Pronunciation and your local accent, and the common reactions they evoke, discuss how you might attempt to *"convince fair-minded people that all accents are equally valid, as long as they are mutually intelligible"*.

Topic C—Variations in the use of English related to gender

5. *"In conversations between men and women—because their conversational styles are different—women often find themselves in relatively powerless roles."*

   How far do you agree?

[Turn over

6. Discuss, with illustrations from your own reading and observation, how features of conversation vary according to gender.

You may wish to consider some of the following:
- preferred topics
- taking, holding and giving the floor
- the function of interruptions and overlaps
- the use of questions (eg tag questions)
- the structure and content of stories.

Topic D—The linguistic characteristics of informal conversation

For both questions on this topic you are provided with an extract from a transcript of an informal conversation between an older and a younger woman.

*Read the extract carefully and then answer **either** Question 7 **or** Question 8 (Page thirteen).*

Transcription Key: // // *shows overlap between speakers.*

Older woman:	I *[laugh]* old enough to be at school. I mean, but see, I think Angus and I were pretty inseparable when we were, we were kids //eh//
Younger woman:	//uh-huh//
Older woman:	*[swallow]* oh aye, we were gettin married.
Younger woman:	aw.
Older woman:	When we got bigger, we were gettin married Angus and I. I don't know what happened to them at the blitz. I know his older brother Archie turned out to be a bit of a waster.
Younger woman:	mmhm?
Older woman:	But Angus was nice. They were a really nice family altogether. But the words we learned, the swear-words we learned were beuch.
Younger woman:	*[laugh]*
Older woman:	See, they kept this horse and cart for this old boy that worked for the family, for, and he come back from the First World War
Younger woman:	mmhm?
Older woman:	wi a peg leg from under the knee.
Younger woman:	mmhm?
Older woman:	It was a wooden, a wooden attachment he had, and he used to sit in the cart, and he would dunt the horse, like that wi his
Younger woman:	Wooden leg?
Older woman:	wi his wooden—aye! And then, there was a bit sort of round the corner and there was a s— it was like a garage, but that's where he kept the, the cart

Younger woman:	uh-huh.
Older woman:	and the horse.
Younger woman:	mmhm.
Older woman:	And, we used to watch him as he brought the horse along, and he was backing it in s— in the shafts, and the language was absolutely— my mother was gonnae thump me because, because I learned all these words off by heart. But one day my father was comin home from work, and it was rainin, so we were sittin on the stairs inside, and the game we were playin was to see how many swear-words you could say.
Younger woman:	mmhm.
Older woman:	Before you had to take a breath.
Younger woman:	*[laugh]*
Older woman:	Without repeatin any, and I remember it. There was a hand went down the collar of my coat and I got run up the stairs. *[laugh]* This is my father takin me inside, and I got a penny lecture.
Younger woman:	mmhm.
Older woman:	And, and I says, but we were only playin a game, "Well that's a game I don't want you playin at any more".
Younger woman:	mmhm.
Older woman:	So that was it.

[Source: www.scottishcorpus.ac.uk]

7. Discuss how far the linguistic characteristics of the extract are typical of informal conversation.

8. By making detailed reference to the structure of the extract and to your wider reading and research, discuss the function of personal narratives in informal conversation.

Topic E—The linguistic characteristics of political communication

9. *For this question you are provided with the text of the opening of a speech given by Mr Michael Howard, MP, Leader of the Conservative Party in the run-up to the UK General Election campaign of 2005. The speech was given to a gathering of Conservative party activists and published on the party website. For convenience of reference, each paragraph has been numbered.*

Identify in the text the linguistic characteristics that are typical of political communication.

[1] It's a great pleasure to be here with so many friends.

[2] Two years ago when I launched my leadership election campaign I said "We must look forward not backward".

[3] It was such a good phrase . . . that I repeated the same sentiment again a week later when I became leader.

[4] I believed it then and I believe it now. And it's what I want to talk about this afternoon. Because today I want to share something personal with you: the Britain I believe in, my hopes and aspirations for our country.

[5] The country we should be. The country we can be. The country we must be.

[6] But we need a government that recognises how hard families work and rewards them for their efforts.

[7] Some of you may know that Sandra and I live in Kent. Now our house certainly wouldn't win first prize in a beauty contest. In fact it's quite ugly. But it has one of the most glorious views in Britain.

[8] It looks down over the mysterious beauty of Romney Marsh and out across the Channel. And when I look at that view I think about Britain's history and about her future.

[9] My constituency sent a representative to Simon de Montfort's Parliament, England's first Parliament, in 1265. And it's sent them to every Parliament since.

[10] It was on the Romney coast, some say, that William the Conqueror first tried to land on our shores.

[11] From my kitchen I can see container ships going along the Channel—bearing their cargoes to and from all corners of the world. And it reminds me that Britain's greatness is built on our trade, on our openness, on our integrity, on our companies that can take on and beat the best in the world.

[12] For me, the most moving experience of recent weeks has been learning about the quiet heroism of Private Johnson Beharry VC. And it's not just for his bravery. That humbles all of us who have never served in combat.

[13] That a young man from Grenada, a small island in the Caribbean, with deep and long-standing ties to Britain, should become the first living recipient of the Victoria Cross in 36 years says something remarkable about Britain too.

[14] It reminds us that Britain is bigger than the area bounded by the shores of this island and that for many people beyond our shores British values stand for something in the world.

[15] On a clear day, when the sun's shining, from one corner of our garden, I can even see France. And much though I love France, I always think how intensely grateful I am that I was born on this side of the Channel.

[16] I am deeply proud of being British. I'm proud of our history, our traditions. I'm proud of the contribution our country has made to the world. And I'm confident that Britain can make an even greater contribution in the years ahead. I'm proud of our past and I want to be proud of our future.

[17] Elections, whatever else they may be, are potent reminders of what has kept Britain great. They are the chance for people to hold the powerful to account. And they decide the values which will govern all our futures.

[18] My hopes for Britain are rooted in the values of the hard working families who make our country the best in the world: rewarding enterprise; encouraging individual responsibility; and a pride—no matter what our colour, creed or religion—in being British.

[19] Governments cannot do everything—but if they govern with the right values then they can make a real difference.

[20] The Britain I believe in will reward people who do the right thing: the people who work hard, pay their dues, bring up their children to respect others. The people who don't expect something for nothing.

[21] I want to take this opportunity to do something politicians rarely do—and that is to say thank you.

[22] Politicians often boast about what they themselves have achieved. I want, instead, to pay tribute to the real achievers in our society.

[23] I want to say thank you to all those families who work hard to raise children with the right values.

[24] Bringing up a family in modern Britain isn't easy.

[25] I remember when our first child Nick was born. I was in my thirties and getting going in my career. Like all parents, I wanted to provide them with a secure future.

[26] So I worked hard. And that often meant I didn't get home until very late—or not at all if I was working on a planning inquiry, which I frequently was. And especially in the early years that sometimes made me feel like a bad parent.

[27] So I understand how hard it can be to balance work and home life.

[28] The Britain I believe in will give hard-working families the support they deserve. Those people who play by the rules, pay their taxes, respect others and ask for nothing from the State but good local services need a government which never forgets what a struggle life can be.

[29] A government that cuts bureaucracy so that taxpayers get value for their money.

[30] A government that restores discipline at school so that children get the start in life they deserve.

[31] And a government that delivers cleaner hospitals so that patients can go into hospital secure in the knowledge they'll get better not worse.

[32] As Florence Nightingale once said, "the very first requirement in hospital is that it should do the sick no harm".

[www.conservatives.com]

10. From your own research into political communication, discuss the linguistic means of persuasion used in **at least two** of the following:

- television and radio broadcasts
- websites
- newspaper reports and feature articles
- live debates
- pamphlets and leaflets.

Topic F—The linguistic characteristics of tabloid journalism

11. *For this question you are provided with three articles on the same topic from three different newspapers—**The Daily Record**, **The Sun** and **The Daily Mail**.*

By examining language choice, syntax and presentation of ideas, discuss the extent to which each article is typical of tabloid journalism.

Daily Record
Wednesday, April 27, 2005

Booze doc says start 'em young

CHILDREN should be free to knock back booze just like grown-ups, according to a leading academic.

Dr Paul Skett, a senior lecturer in pharmacology at Glasgow University, wants kids served in pubs to educate them about the dangers of binge drinking.

He has called for new laws that would let barmen serve alcohol to children from the "earliest feasible age".

Dr Skett claims the idea would solve Scotland's binge-drinking culture by normalising alcohol.

He says kids would be better off being served in pubs from an early age rather than sneaking off to drink cheap booze with their mates.

French youngsters can drink legally at the age of 16—and Dr Skett believes the age limit could be even lower in Britain.

He said: "Yes, children in many or most licensed premises would be an improvement—and yes, they should be allowed to consume alcohol there.

"Basically what you have is people being forbidden alcohol in any form until they're 18.

"So for many people, the first experience takes place in very negative circumstances.

"It's going down to the woods with your mates to drink and get drunk and that sets the pace for what happens as you get older.

"Contrast with France, where it's normal for children to be introduced to wine at a very early age—not in any quantity, but diluted with water.

"That way children see that it's part of normal life."

THE SUN
Wednesday, April 27, 2005

Serve our kids drink

CHILDREN should be served booze in pubs to stop them binge-drinking later in life, a top academic claimed yesterday.

Dr Paul Skett, of Glasgow University, said kids should be allowed alcohol from the "earliest feasible age".

And he slammed the Scottish Executive's TV adverts warning about the dangers of drink.

Dr Skett said: "Children in many or most licensed premises would be an improvement."

Daily Mail
Wednesday, April 27, 2005

'Let children drink alcohol in the pub'

CHILDREN should be allowed to drink alcohol in pubs, a leading academic said yesterday.

Dr Paul Skett, of Glasgow University, claimed this would help to educate them about the risks of binge-drinking.

He said that by introducing a "Continental approach" children would be less likely to become problem drinkers in later life.

But critics attacked Dr Skett, a pharmacist, for encouraging under-age drinking after recent figures showed record numbers of Scots are drinking themselves to death.

Children as young as seven are being hospitalised by excessive drinking, while each year nearly 150 youngsters under the age of 17 receive medical treatment for early signs of alcoholism.

Tom Wood, chairman of the Edinburgh Action Team on Alcohol and Drugs, said: "Giving alcohol to a five-year old is not a serious consideration.

"Children need to be given information so they can make quality decisions when it comes to alcohol."

Jack Law, chief executive of Alcohol Focus Scotland, said: "If parents are introducing alcohol to their children, they must be aware children's bodies have not fully developed so offering more than a taste is not advisable."

But Dr Skett, who regularly acts as an expert witness in court cases where alcohol is a factor, said: "Of course I don't want children in pubs where, say, shift workers are drinking a lot.

"But allowing children in many or most licensed premises would be an improvement and they should be allowed to consume alcohol there.

"In France, it's normal for children to be introduced to wine at a very early age—not in any quantity, diluted with water. That way children see and understand that it's a part of normal life.

"Until we address the problem we won't see much change—and we will continue to see the sort of problems you get in a city like Glasgow."

Dr Skett also dismissed Scottish Executive-funded TV ads warning about the effects of drink as "completely useless" and "laughed at" by their target audience.

The Scottish Schools Adolescent Lifestyle and Substance Use Survey found that 38 per cent of 15-year-olds and 17 percent of 13-year-olds drank regularly.

---

12. What have you learned about the nature and function of the linguistic characteristics of tabloid journalism from your study of **at least two** tabloid newspapers?

Topic G—The use of Scots in a particular geographical area

13. Describe in detail, from your own research, the linguistic characteristics of the spoken Scots used in a particular geographical area.

14. With reference to a particular variety of Scots you have studied, give a detailed account of the historical development of **at least two** of the following:
    - vocabulary
    - grammar
    - pronunciation
    - spelling.

[Turn over

Topic H—The linguistic characteristics of Scots as used in informal conversation

15. From your own study and research, what have you discovered about the ways in which people use Scots in informal conversation?

16. Describe and account for the ways in which the **Man** in the following extract uses Scots.

    You should consider the nature and density of his use of Scots terms, Scots syntax and Scots phonology.

    Transcription key: *// // shows overlap between speakers.*

    Woman: Mmhm . . . Ehm, how would you like Scots to be taught then, would it be like a second language like French or German, or would be instead of English? Would it start from primary up to university? I mean,

    Man: Tut—, I think I think the key thing is to hae teachers, I mean even if it is to be taught eh in alang wi Inglis and you would hae tae think it would be taught in alang wi Inglis because if you're //tryin tae//

    Woman: //Mmhm//

    Man: teach twa divergent spellin systems and sets o representation for twa leids that are are gey sib, ane till ither, then ye hae tae think well, [*Cough*] ye know, perhaps in in in that case, unlike the case wi Gaelic it would be sensible that the twa things was aye in in tandem in some sense. But the teachers has tae ken whit they're talkin aboot.

    Woman: Yeah.

    Man: [*Sniff*]. Excuse me, I've got to cough. [*Cough*] I'll poor this tea and we'll just cairrie on //talkin.//

    Woman: //Yeah.// Ehm, your website mentions only the SNP and the Green parties have clear policies on Scots. Ehm, could you tell me what they are and do they fulfil the needs or the wants of Scots enthusiasts?

    Man: No, the Liberal Party eh earlier this year took a fairly clear position on Scots an aw. Eh The Scottish National Party's policy, which A had a hand in pittin through national conference masel, is based on eh the European Chairter for Regional and Minority Languages an an basically says as far as A can mind, A'll f A'll find ye the ful text o that resolution, eh, but basically says that the, ye know, the richts eh set oot in the European Chairter should be the basis of of policy in Scotland and no just in Pairt Twa the wey eh the Government presently accepts but in in relation to Pairt Three o the Chairter, in other words in in ful detail through cultural life in the country. Eh, the other the other rider to that was eh support fur fur Scots medium education in the early scuil in particular.

    Woman: Mmhm.

    Man: Ye know, so that areas whaur the the Scots dialect is is still eh to the fore, the the initial teachin should have a heavy bias towards the retention of that dialect and the the passin it on till the new generations o o bairns.

35	Woman:	So I take it if you're talkin about making teachers more aware of Scots that would mean retraining them so //would that be quite costly and would therefore put a lot of people off.//
40	Man:	//It would mean it would mean teacher trainin, aye, it would mean, it would greatly increase// teacher training. Eh, I mean it would be regarded as an extraordinary proposition in onie other country, in onie other situation, that fowk should be settin oot tae teach a language that they cudnae even speak theirsel.
45	Woman:	Mmhm Well, that's not the problem though. Ehm, defining what Scots is and who speaks it it's quite kind of slippery and difficult to explain I think. Some people speak Scots without realising it, or. So do you think, is that a problem or is the diversity one of the Scots' advantages over other languages?
	Man:	I dinna think that's a problem, I think that's an excuse pitten aboot be folk that eh, ye know, maybe dinna ken [*Laugh*] a lot aboot //Scots an//
	Woman:	Mmhm//
50	Man:	cannae speak it theirsels. I dinnae think there's a lot of difficulty for fowk that does speak it. //Kennin//
	Woman:	//Yeah.//
	Man:	what it is they're speakin or when they're speakin it.
	Woman:	Okay, so that's not a problem for you, it's just
55	Man:	I think it's an excuse brocht up eh by an education system that disna want to be challenged.
	Woman:	Okay.
	Man:	Eh, I've seen, ye know, reaction fae teachers, eh quite adverse to the idea that there's something new that they should learn theirsels.
60	Woman:	Mmhm
	Man:	But others others that are mair honest ken fine that they cannae cannae teach whit they cannae speak.

[www.scottishcorpus.ac.uk]

Topic I—Variations in the use of Scots among older and younger people

17. In a detailed study based on your own research, describe and account for variations in the use of Scots among older and younger people.

18. "*Young people are not losing Scots; they are contributing to its development.*"

    How far do you agree?

    You should support your answer with detailed reference to the research you have done into the use of Scots among older and younger people.

[Turn over

Topic J—Uses of Scots in the Media

19. From your own study of the use of Scots in the media, show how appropriate and effective use is made of Scots in any **one** or **more than one** media genre.

20. *"Nowadays it's in broadcast comedy and drama that the use of Scots really makes an impact."*

How far do you agree?

Topic K—Uses of Scots in contemporary literature

For this topic you are provided with **two** *examples of the use of Scots in contemporary literature:*

- *an extract from a sequence of haiku called* **Glasgow Zen** *by Alan Spence*
- *an extract from* **Da Diary o Gideon Hunter** *by Peter Ratter.*

Read the extracts carefully and then answer **either** *Question 21* **or** *Question 22 (Page twenty-one).*

From *Glasgow Zen* (2002) by Alan Spence

glasgow's full of poets
give it laldy
pure bobo balde

disnae matter
how ye look at it—
ma heid's cauld

New Year—
ma dump ae a hoose,
jist the same

wid ye lookit
the state ae it—
me in ma new jaiket

the full moon shinin
on this buncha heidbangers
(me included)

whit a night, eh?
hey, auld yin!
ye dancing?

see ma feet?
still . . .
no a bad day

the lang dreich night
the bark bark bark
ae that dug

this is me—
nae money nae teeth
nae nothing

From *Da Diary o Gideon Hunter* by Peter Ratter

14th June

I'm no haed a lok o time ta write i me diary fir a braa start. Wir been wirkin datna herd at da haaf, at I'm been ower tired ta budder.

Jim is no been sae seek fir a start, bit he's only geen an gotten himsel brunt wi da sun! On da height of dat, he's bled his fingers on da hooks mair aaft as ony idder body, an he's even managed ta faa ower da side! Ah weel, I'll joost hae ta coont me blissins dit I'm no sae ill-luckit.

15th June

Mebbe I'm no sae lucky as I towt I wis distreen. We wir guttin fish an satin dem. I dunna ken foo it cam tae be, bit me tully slippit, an laid twa inch o skin fae me fore finger. Da saat got inda scrape, an boy, it sweed lik da very ill helt.

I stöd apo da bench sinkin an swearin. Jim sat grinning lik a pent brush, while I wis roarin aa da bad wirds I kent, an twa-tree I towt up joost fir da occasion. Jim lackly deserved a laach fir aa da things it wis happent ta him but whin I saa him sneesterin awaa, I wid a been blyde if every trow in da isle had stucken a fish hook ida sheeck o his backside!

Ony wye, Uncle Rasmie says me hand'll hael ower in a mont or sae. Till dan I'll joost hae ta keep it rowed up, and try no ta swear lood id saat wins on it again. Wir awa tae da haaf da morn.

15th July

I'm in da sixern eenoo while I write dis. It's a most aafil night, da stars ir oot, an da mön is sheenin aff o da waater. Da sea is herdly moving avaa, an aa body's haein a rest. It's bön a lang day, so I'll set doon me book an try an sleep. Da rest o da boys ir been neebin da brucks o a oor noo.

I dunna tink I'll sleep again da nicht! I'm joost haed yon dream again, da wan wi da cloods an da corbie. I saa yon fellow it lookit laek me again. Dis time, he raise up an raekit oot a hand tae me. I wok up sweatin. Dir suntan aafil fey aboot yon dream.

21. How effective do you find **either** Alan Spence's use of Glaswegian Scots **or** Peter Ratter's use of Shetlandic Scots?

    You should support your answer to this question with detailed reference to choice of vocabulary, grammar, spelling, idiom or any other feature you consider relevant.

22. **Either** compare Alan Spence's use of Scots with Peter Ratter's use of Scots **or** compare the use of Scots by either writer with the use of Scots by any other writer you have studied.

Topic L—Uses of Scots in specialised fields

The following entry appeared on the Scottish Parliament's official website in 2005.

*Read the entry carefully and then answer **either** Question 23 **or** Question 24 (Page twenty-two).*

VISITIN THE SCOTTISH PAIRLAMENT IN EDINBURGH

You are walcome tae visit the Pairlament tae hae a keek roon or find oot aboot whit wey the Pairlament warks.

Gin ye decide tae visit, please think on whit ye wid like tae see and dae, as the biggin is gey popular and can get gey thrang:

- Gin it is important for ye tae see Pairlament at its darg, ye'll be wantin tae visit on a business day when ye'll can gang til the public galleries for tae watch a comatee meetin or a meetin o the fu Pairlament in progress. It is aye better tae book aheid for a gallery ticket. Tickets tae see Pairlament in action is free.

- Gin ye're wantin tae see the biggin an learn mair aboot the Pairlament in general, ye micht prefer a visit on a non-business day when ye will can explore at yer leisure or enjoy a guidit tour wi a professional tour guide (there a chairge for the guidit tour).

The Scottish Pairlament walcomes official visits fae folk fae Pairlaments in ither countries and aw. Gin ye're wantin tae arrange an official visit for a group o folk fae anither Pairlament, please request hit as faur aheid as possible. Normally, we'll no can arrange thir official visits while the Scottish Pairlament is in recess or wi less nor sax weeks' notice.

We want tae mak siccar that awbody is able tae visit the Scottish Pairlament biggin. Wir premises is awready designit tae be as accessible as possible. Hooanever, gin ye are disablit and hae ony specific requirements, ye're gey walcome tae contact us afore yer visit.

Follae this link for
Contactin the Scottish Pairlament

> Gin ye wid like mair information anent the Scottish Pairlament, ye can scrieve til us, in ony leid, by post, email or fax.
>
> Wir contact details is:
>
> **Address:**
>
> The Scottish Pairlament
> Edinburgh
> EH99 1SP
>
> **Email:** sp.info@scottish.parliament.uk
>
> **Fax:** 0131 348 5601
>
> Forby yon, ye can telephone the Scottish Pairlament on 0845 278 1999 (or fae ootwith the UK dial +44 131 348 5000).
>
> Hooanever, at present we can tak telephone and textphone caws in English and Gaelic juist.
>
> Forby yon, gin ye're deif or speech impairit and a textphone uiser, ye can contact the Pairlament's textphone nummer. Yon nummer is 0845 270 0152. Ye're walcome tae contact us uisin the RNID Typetalk service and aw.

23. Examine in detail the vocabulary, the grammar and the density of Scots used in this entry on the official Scottish Parliamentary website.

    Go on to discuss the issues involved in using Scots in this specialised field.

24. Compare the variety and range of Scots used on the official Scottish Parliamentary website with the variety and range of Scots used in another specialised field you have studied.

    In your answer, you should take into account the expected "audiences" or readers of Scots in such fields.

Section 3—Textual Analysis

You must answer **one question only** in this section.

1. **Prose fiction** [*Pages twenty-three to twenty-seven*]

   Read carefully the short story **Poker Night** *(1987) by John Updike and then answer the question that follows it (Page twenty-seven).*

   The plant has been working late, with the retailers hustling to get their inventories up for Christmas even though this is only August, so I grabbed a bite on the way to the doctor's and planned to go straight from there to poker. The wife in fact likes my not coming home now and then; it gives her a chance to skip dinner and give her weight
5 problem a little knock.

   The doctor has moved from his old office over on Poplar to one of these medical centers, located right behind the mall, where for years when I was a kid there was a field where I can remember the Italians growing runner beans on miles and miles of this heavy brown string. The new center is all recessed ceiling lighting and there's
10 wall-to-wall carpet everywhere and Muzak piped into the waiting room, but if you look at their doors you could put a fist through them easily and can hear the other doctors and patients through the walls, everything they say, including the breathing.

   What mine said to me wasn't good. In fact, every time I tried to get a better grip on it it seemed to get worse.

15 He provided a lot of cheerful energetic talk about the treatments they have now, the chemotherapy and then cobalt and even something they can do with platinum, but at my age I've seen enough people die to know there's no real stopping it, just a lot of torment on the way. If it wasn't for company insurance and Medicaid you wonder how many of these expensive hospitals would still be in business.

20 I said at least I was glad it hadn't been just my imagination. I asked if he thought it could have been anything to do with any of the chemicals they have to use over at the plant, and he said with his prim mouth how he really couldn't venture any opinion about that.

   He was thinking lawsuit, but I had just been curious. Me, I've always figured if it
25 isn't going to be one thing it'll be another; in this day and age you can stand out on a street corner waiting for a light to change and inhale enough poison to snuff out a rat.

   We made our future appointments and he gave me a wad of prescriptions to get filled. Closing the door, I felt somebody could have put a fist through me pretty easily, too.

30 But drugstores are bright places, and while waiting I had a Milky Way and leafed through a *People*, and by the time the girl behind the counter had the medicine ready you could tell from her smile and the way the yellow Bic-click stuck out of her smock pocket that nothing too bad was going to happen to me, ever. At least at a certain level of my mind this seemed the case.

[Turn over

35   Moths were thick as gnats under the streetlights and there was that old sound of summer happiness in the swish of car tires on sticky tar and the teen-agers inside the cars calling out even to people they didn't know. I got into my own car and after some thinking about it drove in the Heights direction to poker.

     I wanted to be sharing this with the wife but then they were counting on me to be
40 the sixth and a few hours couldn't make much difference. Bad news keeps: isn't that what the old people used to say?

     The group has been meeting every other Wednesday for thirty years, with some comings and goings, people moving away and coming back. We've even had some deaths, but up to now none of the regulars, just substitutes—brother-in-laws or
45 neighbors called in to round out the table for just that one night.

     It was at Bob's tonight. Bob's a framer, in his own shop downtown: it's amazing what those guys get now, maybe forty, fifty bucks for just some little watercolor somebody's aunt did as a hobby, or some kid's high-school diploma.

     Jerry does mechanical engineering for an outfit beyond the new mall, Ted's a
50 partner in a downtown fruit store, Greg manages the plumbing business his father founded way back. Rick's a high-school guidance counsellor believe it or not, and Arthur's in sales for Doerner's Paints and Stains. Arthur had to be on the road tonight, which is why they needed me to make six.

     It all began when we were newlyweds more or less starting up our families in the
55 neighborhood between Poplar and Forrest, on the side of the avenue away from what used to be the great old Agawam Wallpaper factory, before they broke it up into little commercial rental units. One April night I got this call from Greg, a guy I hardly knew except everybody knew his old man's truck.

     I thought Alma would make resistance: both Jimmy and Grace must have been
60 under two at the time and she was still trying to give piano lessons in the evenings. But she said go ahead, I'd been working pretty hard and she thought I could use the relaxation.

     Now none of us live in the neighborhood except me and Ted, and he talks about moving to a condo now that the kids are out of the house, except he hates the idea of
65 fighting the traffic into town every day. From where he is now he can walk to the fruit store in a blizzard if he has to, and that crazy Josie of his never did learn how to drive.

     For years Arthur has been over on the Heights too, about three of these curving streets away from Bob's place, and Rick is over on the other side of town toward the lake, and Jerry has gone and bought himself some run-down dairy farm south of the
70 mall; he's fixing up the barn as a rental property, doing most of the work himself on weekends. Also over the years there have been a few changes as to wives and business situations.

     But the stakes haven't changed, and with inflation and our moving more or less up in the world the dimes and quarters and even the dollar bills look like chips, flipping
75 back and forth. It really *is* pretty much relaxation now, with winning more a matter of feeling good than the actual profit.

I arrived maybe ten minutes late because of the wait in the drugstore. The little paper bags in the pocket rattled when I threw my jacket on the sofa and the sound scraped in my stomach, reminding me.

80 Did you ever have the strong feeling that something *has* to be a dream, and that tomorrow you'll wake up safe? It used to come to me as a kid, whenever I'd be in real trouble, like the time Lynn Pechilis said she was pregnant or when they caught us stealing the comic books from Woolworth's.

I got a beer and settled in at the table between Ted and Rick. The five faces, all lit
85 up already with beer and the flow of the cards, looked like balloons, bright pink balloons in that overhead light Bob has rigged up in his den, a naked 100-watt bulb on an extension cord propped up there among the exposed two-by-eights.

He's been working on his den for years, bringing the ceiling down and the walls in for better insulation. But the framing business keeps him downtown Saturdays as well
90 as evenings, and the plasterboard sheets and lumber and rolls of insulation have been leaning around so long in this den it always gives us something to rib him about.

I thought, *I'll never see this room finished*. The thought hit me like lead in the gut; but I figured if I sat perfectly quiet and drank the first beer fast the balloons of their faces would slowly take me up with them, to where I could forget my insides.

95 And it worked, pretty well. The cards began to come to me, under the naked bulb, the aces and deuces and the queens with their beautiful cold faces, and I really only made two mistakes that night.

The one was, I hung on with two pair, jacks and eights, all the way into the dollar-raise stage of a game of seven-card high-low when Jerry had four cards of a straight
100 showing and only two of the nines, the card he needed, were accounted for. But I figured he would *have* to bet as if he had it whether he did or not; as it turned out, he *did* have it, and I wasn't even second best, since Greg had been sitting there sandbagging with three kings.

The other was, in the last round, when what with the beer the pots really build, I
105 folded a little full house, five and treys, in a game of Twin Beds, because so many pairs were already out there on the board I figured somebody had to have me beat. I was wrong: Rick won it with an ace-high heart flush.

Can you imagine, winning Twin Beds with a flush? It's in my character to feel worse about folding a winner than betting a loser; it seems less of a sin against God or
110 Nature or whatever.

Maybe my concentration was off; it did seem silly, at moments, sitting here with these beered-up guys (it gets pretty loud towards the end) playing a game like kids killing a rainy Sunday afternoon when I'd just been told my number was up. The cards at these moments when I thought about it looked incredibly thin: a kind of silver
115 foil beaten to just enough of a thickness to hide the numb reality that was under everything.

My cards as it happened were generally pretty dull, so I had time to look around. The guys' faces looked like pink balloons but their hands as they reached on the table were another story altogether: they were old guys' hands, withered long wrinkled
120 white claws with spots and gray hair and stand-up veins.

[*Turn over*

We had grown old together. We were all drawing near to death, and I guess that was the comfort of it, the rising up with them.

Ted spilled his beer as he tends to do as the evening wears on, reaching for some cards or the popcorn basket or his bifocals (it's an awkward length: you can see your own cards fine with the short vision but the cards in the middle tend to blur, and vice versa) and everybody howled and kidded him as they always do, and my throat began to go rough, they were all so damn sweet, and I'd known them so damn long, without ever saying much of anything except this clowning around and whose deal was it; maybe that was the sweetness. Their faces blurred and came up in starry points like that out-of-focus thing they do with television cameras now—the false teeth and glasses and the shiny high foreheads where hair had been—and the crazy thought came to me that people wouldn't mind which it was so much, heaven or hell, as long as their friends went with them.

Ted has these slightly swollen-looking hands, nicked around the fingers and fat at the sides of the palms, from handling the crates I suppose, and you would think, deft as he must have to be every day in the fruit store, picking out plums and tomatoes for the lady customers, he would be the last one of us to be knocking his beer glass over. But he's always the one, just like Rick is the one to hang in there with junk and Jerry the one to catch that one card in the deck he needs.

I wound up about five dollars down. If I'd had the guts to stay with that little full house I might have been five dollars ahead.

I put on my jacket and the rustling in the pocket reminded me again of the prescriptions and the doctor. Woolworth's didn't prosecute, and it turned out Lynn just wanted to give me a scare.

The wife wasn't up. I didn't expect her to be, at quarter to twelve.

But she wasn't asleep, either. She asked me from the bed in the dark how I did.

I said I broke about even. She asked me what the doctor had said.

I asked her if she'd like to come down to the kitchen and talk. I don't know exactly why I didn't want anything said in the bedroom, but I didn't.

She said she'd love to, she had skipped supper tonight and was starving. There was some leftover lasagna in the fridge she could warm in the microwave in a minute; she'd been lying there in the dark thinking about it.

Alma isn't fat exactly; solid is more how I think of it. When you're with her in bed, you can feel she still has a waist.

We went downstairs and turned on the light and she in her bathrobe heated the Pyrex dish half full of lasagna and I thought about one more beer and decided against it. Then the lasagna was so hot—amazing, how those microwaves do it; from the inside out, they say, vibrating the molecules—I went and got the beer just to soothe my mouth.

I told her everything as much like the doctor had told me as I could. His exact words, his tone of voice as if it wasn't him saying this but a kind of pre-recorded announcement; the look of the recessed lights about his examining table and his steel desk and of his fake hardboard wood-grained wainscoting all revived in me as if I'd just come from there, as if I hadn't been to poker at all.

165　　Alma did and said all the right things, of course. She cried but not so much I'd panic and came up with a lot of sensible talk about second opinions and mysterious remissions and modern medicine and how we'd take it a day at a time and had to have faith.

But she wasn't me. I was me.

170　　While we were talking across the kitchen table there was a barrier suddenly that I was on one side of and she was on the other, overweight and over fifty as she was, a middle-aged tired woman up after midnight in a powder-blue bathrobe but with these terribly alive dark eyes, suddenly. I had handed her this terrible edge.

You could see it in her face, her mind working. She was considering what she had 175　been dealt; she was thinking how to play her cards.

Question

Early in this story, the central character visits his doctor, from whom he receives significant news.

How effectively, in your view, does John Updike convey the character's changed perception of himself and his world after this visit?

2. **Prose non-fiction** [*Pages twenty-seven to thirty*]

The following essay by Andro Linklater is the foreword to a biography of his father, Eric Linklater.

Read the essay carefully and then answer the question that follows it (Page thirty).

　　When I was a child in the 1950s, my father's reputation as a writer had passed its peak. He was one year older than the century and his great fame had come in the 1930s and 1940s with a succession of best-selling novels beginning with *Juan in America* and ending with *Private Angelo*. Nevertheless his reputation remained sufficiently powerful 5　to breed in me a distinct expectancy of recognition. In the company of strangers voices above my head would say "This is Eric Linklater's boy" or a face would duck down to my level and assert brightly, "So you're the great man's son", and I would feel the spread of a wider penumbra than a small boy could throw. To be Eric Linklater's son then seemed no hardship.

10　　With my father on hand, however, the expectancy was shot through by a fearful apprehension that something might go wrong. Like some infant Duke of Norfolk superintending a coronation, I felt it imperative that his importance be acknowledged by those around him. My worries reached a peak when he appeared in public—on a local "Matter of Opinion" panel where he was bound to be contradicted, or on the 15　radio where the interviewer would surely fail to catch his jokes, or on television where the camera would reveal him, as indeed it did, with his flies undone. To be his son in those circumstances was to feel his dignity threatened at every turn.

　　To some extent these were the natural misgivings of any child seeing his parent perform in public, but they also had a source in Eric's own apprehensions. One of the 20　many merits of Michael Parnell's biography is his recognition that beneath his subject's exuberant exterior ran a layer of uncertainty. My father disliked his physical appearance and emotional inhibition, and from adolescence had fought to overcome these shortcomings, as he perceived them to be. Anything which reminded him of them was liable to provoke a fury quite disproportionate to its overt cause. There was a manner in which people *should* behave and a way in which things *should* be done, and it was crucial that the people or things around him should measure up to the standards he had set himself. Thus my Norfolk-like concern for appearances echoed in some degree that of the monarch.

From our different standpoints we were both familiar with the ideal. It came when he was in the company of men he admired, for the most part those who added writing to other accomplishments: soldiers, such as Robert Henriques or Bernard Fergusson; a doctor such as O. H. Mavor (James Bridie); and above all Compton Mackenzie whose additional guises defy brief description. With them he became the person he wanted to be, extravagant in affection, hospitality and discourse.

When they came to stay the house swelled in sympathetic grandeur. The dining-room table grew in length, the cellar was harvested of bottles, and dark corners of the hall sprouted sheaves of roses, lupins or gladioli. From a mingled sense of drama and terror the butcher produced his best mutton, my mother her best cooking, and the four children their best behaviour. It was a pleasure to be present on such occasions, and to offer a second helping of carrots was to stand on the edge of glory.

Eric then made a splendid companion. His conversation was served by a Jacobean wit and a prodigious memory crammed with reading and experience, but most importantly admiration unstoppered his feelings so that his friends were bathed in their warmth. Driven by the gale of his personality their talk grew boisterous and its direction unpredictable. Allusion served for explanation, personal experience stood in for definition. A quotation from Racine comprehended France and war was caught in the memory of a battle. Like wizards they leapt from one conversational peak to another, and wherever they landed an entire mountain of knowledge was assumed to stand beneath their feet.

There was something of Cinderella in this gaiety and the departure of the guests represented the chimes of midnight. Then the saddle of mutton turned to rissoles, the claret bottles became a water-jug, and in place of the glittering talkers sat four bespectacled, unattractive children. I surmise that nothing reminded Eric more forcibly of his secret faults than his children, for he strove repeatedly and angrily to mould us to a less irritating form.

In memory these attempts have their focus on the long-polished table in the dining-room from one end of which he sat facing the window so that its westerly light illuminated the pink, imperial dome of his bald head and made his spectacles gleam like mirrors. Meals took place in an atmosphere which I recall as being so charged the squeal of a knife on china or the slurrup of soup on lip could trigger an explosion. "If you can't eat like a civilised human being," he bellowed, "you can finish your meal at the bottom of the garden." At his most irritable, he had a habit of addressing us through my mother as though she were the NCO of a slovenly platoon he had to inspect. "Marjorie! Have you seen this boy's tie? Does he have to come to table looking like a slum child?" or, on the occasion I first tried to carve a chicken, "Marjorie! What's that bloody boy been doing? The bird looks as though it's been attacked with a Mills grenade."

When he shouted, his voice had a percussive force at which I usually cried, as much for my own failure as his anger. Despite straining every Norfolk nerve, things could not be prevented from going wrong. There were sudden unannounced purges against the smell of peeled oranges or grapes pulled from the stalk, and if these were avoided paralysing interrogations exposed my ignorance about people, places and dates.

The other children, being older, had presumably run this gauntlet before me, and our collective failings must have seemed part of a conspiracy against him. For all his shouting, deficiencies continued to appear on every side. Plates were served cool when they should have been hot, drinking water was tepid instead of cold, and spoons were dull instead of sparkling. There was, in consequence, no mistaking who was at the centre of the conspiracy—the woman responsible for plates, spoons, children and, most infuriatingly of all, for boiled potatoes which either dissolved to flour or split as crisply as apples. "Good God, woman, look at this!" he bawled in disbelief. "After twenty-three years of married life you *still* haven't learned to boil a potato." And despite the years, he would still be goaded into slinging the potato at my mother, though either because she was only a silhouette against the light, or out of good manners, he usually missed.

The emotional drama left no one untouched, and viewed on the distorting screen of memory, meal-times have a decidedly operatic quality. Conversations are shouted arguments, unforgivable accusations are hurled across the table, people break down and cry, exits are made to the sound of slammed doors—my elder sister once exited with a slam which dislodged a full-length portrait of my maternal grandmother from the wall and two painted plates from the sideboard. Acknowledging a force as elemental as himself, my father relapsed briefly into silence.

I do not present this as the whole truth—the sunnier moods are absent, and as we grew older and tougher, and thus more acceptable, they often predominated—but it is accurate as to the intemperate quality of his frustration. For a child it was impossible to understand that the violence of his emotions was inseparable from his writing, and that what enraged him in life could become comedy in fiction. In fact I remember my embarrassment at the age of seven when I first read *The Pirates in the Deep Green Sea*, a book which he wrote for my brother Magnus and me. There for all to see was my father in the person of the ferocious pirate, Dan Scumbril, who terrified half the North Atlantic with his blazing temper and loud voice. "Split my liver with a brass harpoon," thundered Dan Scumbril, and I quailed, not with fright but shame that my father's rages should now be known to everyone. When, so far from being thought the worse of, he was congratulated on the creation of an exceptionally comic character, I logged it as one more of those bewildering quirks of existence which had to be accepted even though they made no sense.

As it happens, it is more complex than most childhood matters to understand how fiction transforms reality. In my adolescence and early twenties, I found—as did most of my contemporaries to judge by reviews and comments—a lack of sensitivity in his resort to comedy. It was too obviously the right thing to do, not to take the world very seriously—even his nightmare of service on the Western Front in the First World War was presented in *The Man on My Back* in comic form.

Yet, when I read his books today it seems to me that what underlies his writing is not an absence but an excess of feeling. Michael Parnell illustrates with admirable clarity the violent sentiment which runs through his most extravagant comedy so that it dances on the edge of blackness or slips abruptly into tragedy. The variety of his approaches to fiction which once irritated his critics—the rollicking *Juan in America* followed by the gut-spilling *Men of Ness*, the macaroni jollity of *Private Angelo* and the sombre *Roll of Honour*—now appear much more of a piece. A word which he liked was inenarrable, or untellable, and what strikes me is the persistent attempt to convey the inenarrable exorbitance of his feelings.

Had he been born with a poet's head, with tragic brows and an aquiline nose, he would have had a mask to suit his inner being. As it was, the sergeant-major's jaw was surmounted by a massive skull and a nose which he explained as the outcome of eight hundred years of peasant ancestry exposed to the bulbous gales of Orkney. The physical ideal was subverted before he began, and his spirit met a similar stumbling-block in the weighty Victorian values instilled by his parents. It was little wonder that he raged so furiously, sometimes to be free of the encumbrances, sometimes to make sense of them.

They bred in him a lust for beauty—for the sense of liberation which it conferred and for the model which it offered of the way things should be. No moment exposes him more clearly than when in wartime he found himself alone in the room where Botticelli's *Primavera* had been stored for protection, and stretching up on tiptoe he pressed his lips to those of Spring. He married a beautiful wife, he built and bought houses for their views rather than their suitability as homes, and he purchased pictures even faster than poverty required him to sell them. He kept Highland cattle for their shaggy grandeur, and allowed a succession of elegant, self-possessed Siamese cats to step with impunity across his writing-paper. Even the aggressive pattern of his tweed jackets I suspect of answering some aspiration which he felt to be bold and carefree.

His laugh was always loud and in old age his tears grew copious. He cried at memories of soldiering, at a pipe tune or a reading of *Danny Deever*. Perhaps they sprang in part from an old man's sentimentality, but I also remember the remark made by a neighbour, Donald MacGillivray, a supreme piper and teacher of piping. When he played *The Lament for the Children* Eric was not the only one moved to tears, but it was for him in particular that the piece was performed. "I always like playing for your father," Donald said. "You see, he has the soul for it."

Andro Linklater

Question

How effectively in this essay does Andro Linklater convey his perceptions of his father?

3. **Poetry** [*Page thirty-one*]

Read carefully the poem **The Sunlight on the Garden** *(1938) by Louis MacNeice and then answer the question that follows it.*

THE SUNLIGHT ON THE GARDEN

    The sunlight on the garden
    Hardens and grows cold,
    We cannot cage the minute
    Within its nets of gold,
5 When all is told
    We cannot beg for pardon.

    Our freedom as free lances
    Advances towards its end;
    The earth compels, upon it
10 Sonnets and birds descend;
    And soon, my friend,
    We shall have no time for dances.

    The sky was good for flying
    Defying the church bells
15 And every evil iron
    Siren and what it tells:
    The earth compels,
    We are dying, Egypt, dying

    And not expecting pardon,
20 Hardened in heart anew,
    But glad to have sat under
    Thunder and rain with you,
    And grateful too
    For sunlight on the garden.

Note: line 18 echoes Antony's words to Cleopatra in Act 4 of Shakespeare's *Antony and Cleopatra*.

Question

Write a critical response to this poem taking into consideration **some** or **all** of the following:

- the framing image of "sunlight on the garden" (lines 1 and 24)
- other key images and symbols
- shifts in tense and tone
- the patterning of internal and end rhyme
- other sound patterns—assonance, alliteration, repetition
- any other aspects of the poem you think significant.

[*Turn over*

4. **Drama** [*Pages thirty-two to thirty-nine*]

The extracts that follow are taken from Alan Bennett's play **The History Boys** *(2004). In the play, set in the 1980s in a grammar school in the north of England, a group of boys is being prepared for scholarship examinations for Oxford and Cambridge.*

The characters in the extracts are:

The Boys	The Staff
AKTHAR	HECTOR
CROWTHER	IRWIN
DAKIN	THE HEADMASTER
LOCKWOOD	MRS LINTOTT
POSNER	
RUDGE	
SCRIPPS	
TIMMS	

Read the extracts carefully and then answer the question that follows them (Page thirty-nine).

EXTRACTS FROM *THE HISTORY BOYS*

Though the general setting is a sixth-form classroom in a boys' school in the eighties in the north of England, when Hector first comes in, a figure in motor-cycle leathers and helmet, the stage is empty.

His sixth-formers, eight boys of seventeen or eighteen, come briskly on and take Hector out
5 *of his motor-cycle gear, each boy removing an item and as he does so presenting it to the audience with a flourish.*

LOCKWOOD: (*with gauntlets*) Les gants.

AKTHAR: (*with a scarf*) L'écharpe.

RUDGE: Le blouson d'aviateur.

10 *Finally the helmet is removed.*

TIMMS: Le casque.

The taking-off of the helmet reveals Hector (which is both his surname and his nickname) as a schoolmaster of fifty or so.

Dakin, a handsome boy, holds out a jacket.

15 DAKIN: Permettez-moi, monsieur.

Hector puts on the jacket.

HECTOR: Bien fait, mes enfants. Bien fait.

Hector is a man of studied eccentricity. He wears a bow tie.

* * * *

Classroom.

20 HECTOR: Now fades the thunder of the youth of England clearing summer's obligatory hurdles.
Felicitations to you all. Well done, Scripps! Bravo, Dakin! Crowther, congratulations. And Rudge, too. Remarkable. All, all

		deserve prizes. All, all have done that noble and necessary thing, you
25		have satisfied the examiners of the Joint Matriculation Board, and now, proudly jingling your A Levels, those longed-for emblems of your conformity, you come before me once again to resume your education.
	RUDGE:	What were A Levels, then?
30	HECTOR:	Boys, boys, boys.
		A Levels, Rudge, are credentials, qualifications, the footings of your CV. Your Cheat's Visa. Time now for the bits in between. You will see from the timetable that our esteemed Headmaster has given these periods the euphemistic title—
35		*Posner looks up the word in the dictionary.*
		—of General Studies.
	POSNER:	"Euphemism . . . substitution of mild or vague or roundabout expression for a harsh or direct one."
	HECTOR:	A verbal fig-leaf. The mild or vague expression being General Studies. The harsh or direct one, Useless Knowledge. The otiose—
40		(*Points at Posner.*)—the trash, the department of why bother?
	POSNER:	"Otiose: serving no practical purpose, without function."
	HECTOR:	If, heaven forfend, I was entrusted with the timetable, I would call these lessons A Waste of Time.
45		Nothing that happens here has anything to do with getting on, but remember, open quotation marks, "All knowledge is precious whether or not it serves the slightest human use," close quotation marks.
		Who said? Lockwood? Crowther? Timms? Akthar?
		Pause.
50		"Loveliest of trees the cherry now."
	AKTHAR:	A. E. Housman, sir.
	HECTOR:	"A. E. Housman, sir." (*He hits him on the head with an exercise book.*)
	CROWTHER:	You're not supposed to hit us, sir. We could report you, sir.
	HECTOR:	(*despair*) I know, I know. (*an elaborate pantomime, all this*)
55	DAKIN:	You should treat us with more respect. We're scholarship candidates now.
		We're all going in for Oxford and Cambridge.
		There is a silence and Hector sits down at this table, seemingly stunned.
	HECTOR:	"Wash me in steep-down gulfs of liquid fire."
60		I thought all that silliness was finished with.
		I thought that after last year we were settling for the less lustrous institutions . . . Derby, Leicester, Nottingham. Even my own dear Sheffield. Scripps. You believe in God. Believe also in me: forget Oxford and Cambridge.
65		Why do you want to go there?
	LOCKWOOD:	Old, sir. Tried and tested.

HECTOR:	No, it's because other boys want to go there. It's the hot ticket, standing room only. So I'll thank you (*hitting him*) if nobody mentions Oxford (*hit*) or Cambridge (*hit*) in my lessons. There is a world elsewhere.
DAKIN:	You're hitting us again, sir.
HECTOR:	Child, I am your teacher. Whatever I do in this room is a token of my trust. I am in your hands. It is a pact. Bread eaten in secret. "I have put before you life and death, blessing and cursing; therefore choose life, that both thou and thy seed may live." Oxford and Cambridge!

He sits with his head on the desk, a parody of despair.
[*The boys begin to speak Shakespeare's King Lear.*]

POSNER:	(*Edgar*) "Look up, My Lord."
TIMMS:	(*Kent*) "Vex not his ghost. O let him pass. He hates him That would upon the rack of this tough world Stretch him out longer."
POSNER:	(*Edgar*) "O, he is gone indeed."
TIMMS:	(*Kent*) "The wonder is he hath endured so long. He but usurped this life."

Bell goes. Hector sits up.

HECTOR:	"I have a journey, sir, shortly to go; My master calls me, I must not say no."
POSNER:	(*Edgar*) "The weight of this sad time we must obey Speak what we feel, not what we ought to say."
TIMMS:	The hitting never hurt. It was a joke. None of us cared. We lapped it up.

* * * *

SCRIPPS:	I'd been on playground duty, so I saw Irwin on what must have been his first morning waiting outside the study. I thought he was a new boy, which of course he was, so I smiled. Then the Headmaster turned up.

Irwin is a young man, about twenty-five or so.

HEADMASTER:	You are?
IRWIN:	Irwin.
HEADMASTER:	Irwin?
IRWIN:	The supply teacher.
HEADMASTER:	Quite so.

He beckons Irwin cagily into the study.

110	SCRIPPS:	Hector had said that if I wanted to write I should keep a notebook, and there must have been something furtive about Irwin's arrival because I wrote it down. I called it clandestine, a word I'd just learnt and wasn't sure how to pronounce.
115	HEADMASTER:	The examinations are in December, which gives us three months at the outside . . . Well, you were at Cambridge, you know the form.
	IRWIN:	Oxford, Jesus.
	HEADMASTER:	I thought of going, but this was the fifties. Change was in the air. A spirit of adventure.
	IRWIN:	So, where did you go?
120	HEADMASTER:	I was a geographer. I went to Hull.
	IRWIN:	Oh. Larkin.
125	HEADMASTER:	Everybody says that. "Hull? Oh, Larkin." I don't know about the poetry . . . as I say, I was a geographer . . . but as a librarian he was pitiless. The Himmler of the Accessions Desk. And now, we're told, women in droves. Art. They get away with murder. They are a likely lot, the boys. All keen. One oddity. Rudge. Determined to try for Oxford and Christ Church of all places. No hope. Might get in at Loughborough in a bad year. Otherwise all bright. But they need polish. Edge. Your job. We are low in the league. I want to see us up there with Manchester Grammar School, Haberdashers' Aske's. Leighton Park. Or is that an open prison? No matter. *Pause.*
130		
135		There is a vacancy in history.
	IRWIN:	(*thoughtfully*) That's very true.
	HEADMASTER:	In the school.
	IRWIN:	Ah.
140	HEADMASTER:	Get me scholarships, Irwin, pull us up the table, and it is yours. I am corseted by the curriculum, but I can find you three lessons a week.
	IRWIN:	Not enough.
145	HEADMASTER:	I agree. However, Mr Hector, our long-time English master, is General Studies. There is passion there. Or, as I prefer to call it, commitment. But not curriculum-directed. Not curriculum-directed at all. In the circumstances we may be able to filch an hour. (*going*) You are very young. Grow a moustache. I am thinking classroom control.

* * * *

150 *Classroom.*

	IRWIN:	So we arrive eventually at the less-than-startling discovery that so far as the poets are concerned, the First World War gets the thumbs-down. We have the mountains of dead on both sides, right . . . "hecatombs", as you all seem to have read somewhere . . .
155		

	Anybody know what it means?
POSNER:	"Great public sacrifice of many victims, originally of oxen."
DAKIN:	Which, sir, since Wilfred Owen says men were dying like cattle, is the appropriate word.
IRWIN:	True, but no need to look so smug about it. What else? Come on, tick them all off.
CROWTHER:	Trench warfare.
LOCKWOOD:	Barrenness of the strategy.
TIMMS:	On both sides.
AKTHAR:	Stupidity of the generals.
TIMMS:	Donkeys, sir.
DAKIN:	Haig particularly.
POSNER:	Humiliation of Germany at Versailles. Re-drawing of national borders.
CROWTHER:	Ruhr and the Rhineland.
AKTHAR:	Mass unemployment. Inflation.
TIMMS:	Collapse of the Weimar Republic. Internal disorder. And . . . The Rise of Hitler!
IRWIN:	So. Our overall conclusion is that the origins of the Second War lie in the unsatisfactory outcome of the First.
TIMMS:	(*doubtfully*) Yes. (*with more certainty*) Yes.
	Others nod.
IRWIN:	First class. Bristol welcomes you with open arms. Manchester longs to have you. You can walk into Leeds. But I am a fellow of Magdalen College, Oxford, and I have just read seventy papers all saying the same thing and I am asleep . . .
SCRIPPS:	But it's all true.
IRWIN:	What has that got to do with it? What has that got to do with anything? Let's go back to 1914 and I'll put you a different case. Try this for size. Germany does not want war and if there is an arms race it is Britain who is leading it. Though there's no reason why we should want war. Nothing in it for us. Better stand back and let Germany and Russia fight it out while we take the imperial pickings. These are facts. Why do we not care to acknowledge them? The cattle, the body count. We still don't like to admit the war was even partly our fault because so many of our people died. A photograph on every mantelpiece. And all this mourning has veiled the truth. It's not so much lest we forget, as lest we remember. Because you should realise that so far as the Cenotaph and the Last Post and all that stuff is concerned, there's no better way of forgetting something than by commemorating it. And Dakin.

	DAKIN:	Sir?
	IRWIN:	You were the one who was morally superior about Haig.
	DAKIN:	Passchendaele. The Somme. He was a butcher, sir.
205	IRWIN:	Yes, but at least he delivered the goods. No, no, the real enemy to Haig's subsequent reputation was the Unknown Soldier. If Haig had had any sense he'd have had him disinterred and shot all over again for giving comfort to the enemy.
	LOCKWOOD:	So what about the poets, then?
210	IRWIN:	What about them? If you read what they actually say as distinct from what they write, most of them seem to have enjoyed the war. Siegfried Sassoon was a good officer. Saint Wilfred Owen couldn't wait to get back to his company. Both of them surprisingly bloodthirsty. Poetry is good up to a point. Adds flavour.
215		But if you want to relate the politics to the war, forget Wilfred Owen and try Kipling:
	AKTHAR:	Thanks a lot.
220	IRWIN:	"If any question why we died, Tell them because our fathers lied." In other words . . .
	TIMMS:	Oh no, sir. With respect, can I stop you? No, with a poem or any work of art we can never say "in other words". If it is a work of art there are no other words.
225	LOCKWOOD:	Yes, sir. That's why it is a work of art in the first place. You can't look at a Rembrandt and say "in other words", can you, sir?
		Irwin is puzzled where all this comes from but is distracted by Rudge.
	RUDGE:	So what's the verdict then, sir? What do I write down?
230	IRWIN:	You can write down, Rudge, that "I must not write down every word that teacher says." You can also write down that the First World War was a mistake. It was not a tragedy. And as for the truth, Scripps, which you were worrying about: truth is no more at issue in an examination than thirst at a wine-tasting or fashion at a striptease.
235	DAKIN:	Do you really believe that, sir, or are you just trying to make us think?
	SCRIPPS:	You can't explain away the poetry, sir.
	LOCKWOOD:	No, sir. Art wins in the end.
		The bell goes.

[Turn over

	SCRIPPS:	What about this, sir?
240		"Those long uneven lines Standing as patiently As if they were stretched outside The Oval or Villa Park, The crowns of hats, the sun
245		On moustached archaic faces Grinning as if it were all An August Bank Holiday lark . . ."
		The others take up the lines of Larkin's poem, maybe saying a couple of lines each through to the end, as they go—but matter of factly.
250	LOCKWOOD:	"Never such innocence, Never before or since, As changed itself to past Without a word—
255	AKTHAR:	"—the men Leaving the gardens tidy,
	POSNER:	"The thousands of marriages Lasting a little while longer:
	TIMMS:	"Never such innocence again."
260	IRWIN:	How come you know all this by heart? (*Baffled, shouts.*) Not that it answers the question. (*He goes.*)

* * * *

Staffroom
Irwin and Hector.

	IRWIN:	It's just that the boys seem to know more than they're telling.
265	HECTOR:	Don't most boys? Diffidence is surely to be encouraged.
	IRWIN:	In an examination? They seem to have got hold of the notion that the stuff they do with you is off-limits so far as the examination is concerned.
270	HECTOR:	That's hardly surprising. I count examinations, even for Oxford and Cambridge, as the enemy of education. Which is not to say that I don't regard education as the enemy of education, too. However, if you think it will help, I will speak to them.
275	IRWIN:	I'd appreciate it. For what it's worth, I sympathise with your feelings about examinations, but they are a fact of life. I'm sure you want them to do well and the gobbets you have taught them might just tip the balance.
280	HECTOR:	What did you call them? Gobbets? Is that what you think they are, gobbets? Handy little quotes that can be trotted out to make a point? Gobbets? Codes, spells, runes—call them what you like, but do not call them *gobbets*.

	IRWIN:	I just thought it would be useful . . .
285	HECTOR:	Oh, it would be useful . . . every answer a Christmas tree hung with the appropriate gobbets. Except that they're learned *by heart*. And that is where they belong and like the other components of the heart not to be identified by being trotted out to order.
290	IRWIN:	So what are they meant to be storing them up for, these boys? Education isn't something for when they're old and grey and sitting by the fire. It's for now. The exam is next month.
	HECTOR:	And what happens after the exam? Life goes on. Gobbets!

* * * *

Headmaster and Irwin.

295	HEADMASTER:	How are our young men doing? Are they "on stream"?
	IRWIN:	I think so.
	HEADMASTER:	You think so? Are they or aren't they?
	IRWIN:	It must always be something of a lottery.
300	HEADMASTER:	A lottery? I don't like the sound of that, Irwin. We have been down that road too many times before.
	IRWIN:	I'm not sure the boys are bringing as much from Mr Hector's classes as they might.
305	HEADMASTER:	You're lucky if they bring anything at all, but I don't know that it matters. Mr Hector has an old-fashioned faith in the redemptive power of words. In my experience, Oxbridge examiners are on the lookout for something altogether snappier.
		After all, it's not how much literature that they know. What matters is how much they know *about* literature.
310		Chant the stuff till they're blue in the face, what good does it do? Dorothy.

Mrs Lintott has appeared and the Headmaster goes.

315	MRS LINTOTT:	One thing you will learn if you plan to stay in this benighted profession is that the chief enemy of culture in any school is always the Headmaster. Forgive Hector. He is trying to be the kind of teacher pupils will remember. Someone they will look back on. He impinges.

Question

Make a detailed study of the dramatic means by which, in these extracts, Alan Bennett raises questions about education and its purposes.

[*Turn over*

Section 4—Reading the Media

You must answer **one question only** in this section.

Category A—Film

1. *"Central to the language of film is the moving image."*

   How far do you agree?

   In support of your answer you should analyse and evaluate the language of **two** or **three** key sequences from **one** or **more than one** film.

2. *"Hollywood requires of film narrative that it be readily comprehensible and a model of classic narrative structure."*

   Discuss **two** or **more than two** Hollywood films in the light of this assertion.

Category B—Television

3. *"Both the content and the presentation of non-fiction television are determined by the need to satisfy the audience's craving for drama."*

   Discuss the truth of this claim with detailed reference to **one** or **more than one** of the non-fiction genres of television—news, current affairs, documentary, sport.

4. In what ways and how effectively does television drama engage with serious social issues?

Category C—Radio

5. *"The relationship we have with radio is closer, more intimate, than the relationship we have with any other medium."*

   Discuss some of the means by which radio achieves this intimacy.

   In your discussion, you may wish to refer to aspects such as mode of address, channel identity and content, ways in which listeners use radio.

6. Discuss and evaluate some of the ways in which character is created in **one** or **more than one** radio drama.

Category D—Print journalism

7. *"The press seems to assume that the only way we can comprehend large-scale disasters is if our attention is focused on individual victims and on poignant scenarios."*

   Discuss **one** newspaper's coverage of a recent large-scale disaster in the light of this assertion.

8. For this question you are provided with extracts from the front page coverage in two newspapers, *The Times* (*Page forty-two*) and *The Guardian* (*Page forty-three*), of the inauguration for a second term of George W. Bush as US President.

Compare and contrast the means employed by the newspapers to present their views on the event and on the implications of President Bush's second term in office.

In your comparison and contrast, you should pay close attention to the content and effect of:

- the images
- the headlines
- the texts.

[**Turn over**

8. (continued)

THE TIMES

No. 68290 ■ FRIDAY JANUARY 21 2005 ■ www.timesonesline.co.uk ■ 50p

His second-term mission: to end tyranny on earth

From Gerard Baker
in Washington

FOUR years ago he was the Accidental President, scion of a ruling family propelled into the highest office more by genetics and duty than by political zeal and ideological mission.

Victor, sort of, after a messy constitutional scrum left him in charge of a divided nation and holding a flimsy legitimacy, this apparently callow and unengaged President seemed to match the times. America in January 2001 was fat, happy and self-absorbed with the trivia of the post-Cold War world.

Yesterday the transformation of George W. Bush from frat-boy-made-good to solemn champion of an urgent messianic mission to transform the world was completed.

In his second inaugural address, delivered to tens of thousands in front of a snowy Capitol building in Washington, but pointedly directed at friends and enemies around the world, President Bush dedicated himself and the next four years to no less than the ending of tyranny on Earth.

President Bush and his wife, Laura, and daughters, Barbara, far left, and Jenna leave the White House before his inauguration.

Invoking the ghosts of Abraham Lincoln, Franklin D. Roosevelt and John F. Kennedy, and at times borrowing their rhetorical voices, Mr Bush placed the current war in Iraq, and the wider War on Terror, as the natural successor to the struggles those predecessors fought to advance liberty—the Civil War, the Second World War and the Cold War. Indeed, he promised to match or even exceed those victories.

"America, in this young century, proclaims liberty throughout all the world, and to all the inhabitants thereof. Renewed in our strength—tested, but not weary—we are ready for the greatest achievements in the history of freedom."

Acknowledging that he and his country had been called to duty by the "day of fire" in September 2001 that woke the US from its post-Cold War torpor, Mr Bush said that the task of promoting freedom was not just some worthy ideal. It was a goal on which America's very existence depended. "We are led, by events and common sense, to one conclusion: the survival of liberty in our land increasingly depends on the success of liberty in other lands. The best hope for peace in our world is the expansion of freedom in all the world."

The Guardian

Smiles for the family, a fiery warning for the world

George Bush with wife Laura, left, and daughters Barbara and Jenna at his inauguration.

Photograph: Alex Wong/Getty

Julian Borger in Washington

George Bush yesterday began his second presidential term with a call to American action abroad, committing the United States to the spread of global democracy and "ending tyranny in our world".

In arguably the most combative inauguration speech for a half a century, President Bush made clear that the Afghan and Iraqi conflicts had not diminished his determination to take the "war on terror" to America's enemies. He saw them as only part of a much broader mission, which he phrased in almost messianic terms.

"By our efforts, we have lit . . . a fire in the minds of men. It warms those who feel its power, it burns those who fight its progress, and one day this untamed fire of freedom will reach the darkest corners of our world," Mr Bush said on the steps of the Capitol building.

The speech, much of it couched in religious language, was addressed first to the rest of the world and only secondly to the American people. In it, the president portrayed a planet consumed by the struggle between liberty and tyranny, in which the US would not stand aside.

"So it is the policy of the United States to seek and support the growth of democratic movements and institutions in every nation and culture, with the ultimate goal of ending tyranny in our world," he said.

The confrontations to come would not necessarily be "the task of arms", Mr Bush insisted, but at a time of rising speculation over this second-term plans for Iran, the newly re-elected president did not exclude the possibility of further conflict.

He said "We will defend ourselves and our friends by force of arms when necessary."

To the American people, concerned at the US death toll in Iraq, he argued that the only way to defend the country was to promote democracy overseas and thus uproot the source of threats to the homeland.

"The survival of liberty in our land increasingly depends on the success of liberty in other lands," America's 43rd president told the crowds on a cool, bright Washington day. "The best hope for peace in our world is the expansion of freedom in all the world."

Mr Bush also suggested the struggle against global oppression was ordained by God, exporting the ideas enshrined in the US constitution that all people have God-given inalienable rights.

"History has an ebb and flow of justice, but history also has a visible direction set by liberty and the author of liberty," the president said. The deliberate use of language, familiar to evangelical Christians, won more cheers from the crowd than any other phrase in the speech.

With this radical address, President Bush nailed his colours once and for all to the "neoconservative" mast, committing himself to an activist foreign policy. He went out of his way to reject the more traditional "realist" Republican philosophy associated with his father, which argues that democracy cannot be exported to regions like the Middle East and that US foreign policy should be guided by narrowly defined national self-interest.

Burning Bush brandishes Dostoevsky

Given the Biblical language in which George Bush and his speechwriters are steeped, it is not surprising that the US president should have invoked the imagery of fire yesterday, *writes James Meek*.

One of the models of American leadership is that of Moses, leading God's chosen people—then the Jews, now the Americans—toward a promised land, following a pillar of fire. At one point, according to the Bible, Moses was shown a sign: "Behold, the bush burned with fire, and the bush was not consumed."

But the key fire passage in the Burning Bush speech—"We have lit a fire as well; a fire in the minds of men"—actually has its origins in a novel by the 19th century Russian novelist Fyodor Dostoevsky, The Devils, about a group of terrorists' ineffectual struggles to bring down the tyrannical Tsarist regime.

One of the characters declares that it is pointless to try to put out a fire started by terrorists: "The fire is in the minds of men and not in the roofs of houses," he says.

The novel belongs to a period in Dostoevsky's life which the White House might find attractive, after he had been sent by the Tsar to a kind of Russian Guantánamo and enraged a deeply religious conservative.

Nonetheless, it is not clear whether Bush is identifying here with the terrorists—or the tyrants.

Category E—Advertising

9. *"Advertising assumes that the objects we use and consume carry information about the kind of people we are or would like to be."*

    To what extent do you agree?

    In your answer you should make detailed reference **either** to a range of advertisements **or** to an advertising campaign.

    NB You may not use the materials provided for Question 10 in order to answer Question 9.

10. Examine carefully the following **three** advertisements for PULSAR watches:

    Poise Collection—*Glamour Magazine* (August 2004) (*Page forty-five*)
    Performance Collection—*The Guardian Weekend Magazine* (November 2004) (*Page forty-six*)
    Prestige Collection—*The Guardian Weekend Magazine* (December 2004) (*Page forty-seven*).

    How effectively does each advertisement convey the message *"**it's all in the detail**"* to its target audience?

    In your answer you should consider:

    - the construction of each image—camera angle and distance, composition, cropping and framing
    - the cultural codes which establish the representation of the subjects
    - the role of the written texts (content **and** typography)
    - the stereotyping of gender in establishing the brand identity of each product.

From SEIKO WATCH CORPORATION
pulsarwatches.com

Loves Mondays
Collects teapots
Only goes out with Scorpios
Has 7 brothers
Doesn't own a mobile phone
Watches ice hockey
Plays the banjo
Cries watching E.T.
Wears a Pulsar.

it's all in the detail

- 3 bar water resistant • curved mineral crystal
- stainless steel case and bracelet
- quick-release clasp • **Poise Collection**

PULSAR

Loves horror movies. Drinks Tequila. Owns a kilt. Supports Dundee United. 80s music. 70s decor. Addicted to The Simpsons. Grows sunflowers. Favourite colour is dark grey. Talks to plants. Wears a Pulsar.

it's all in the detail

alarm chronograph • dual time capability • stainless steel case and bracelet • 10 bar water resistant • Performance Collection

PULSAR

Plays the bagpipes
Owns a pet snake
Loves Hitchcock films
Owns 15 pairs of jeans
Only needs 5 hours sleep
Still uses a typewriter
Reads Sci-fi
Wears a Pulsar.

it's all in the detail

alarm chronograph • dual time capability • tachymeter • 10 bar
water resistant • all titanium • Prestige Collection

PULSAR

[END OF QUESTION PAPER]

ADVANCED HIGHER SQP
2008

[C115/SQP308]

English
Advanced Higher
Specimen Question Paper
for use in and after 2008

Time: 1 hour 30 minutes
or 3 hours

NATIONAL
QUALIFICATIONS

Note: The questions in the Literary Study and Language Study sections of this paper reflect the new specified lists for use in and after session 2007–2008 and in and after the 2008 examination.

There are four sections in this paper.

Section 1—Literary Study	pages 2–10
Section 2—Language Study	pages 11–16
Section 3—Textual Analysis	pages 17–28
Section 4—Reading the Media	pages 29–31

Depending on the options you have chosen, you must answer **one** or **two** questions.

If you have submitted a Creative Writing folio, you must answer only **one** question.

Otherwise you must answer **two** questions.

If you are required to answer only **one question**

- it must be taken from **Section 1—Literary Study**
- you must leave the examination room **after 1 hour 30 minutes**.

If you are required to answer **two questions**

- your first must be taken from **Section 1—Literary Study**
- your second must be taken from **a different section**
- each answer must be written in **a separate answer booklet**
- the maximum time allowed for any question is **1 hour 30 minutes**.

You must identify each question you attempt by indicating clearly

- **the title of the section** from which the question has been taken
- **the number of the question** within that section.

You must also write inside the front cover of your Literary Study answer booklet

- **the topic** of your Specialist Study (Dissertation)
- **the texts** used in your Specialist Study (Dissertation).

Section 1—Literary Study

This section is **mandatory** for all candidates.

You must answer **one question only** in this section.

DRAMA

1. **Beckett**

   "*The basic questions posed in Beckett's plays seem to be these: Who are we? What is the true nature of self? What does a human being mean when he says 'I?'.*"

   How effectively, in your view, does Beckett address such questions in *Waiting for Godot* and in *Endgame*?

2. **Byrne**

   "*. . . brilliant social commentary . . .*"

   "*. . . biting satire . . .*"

   "*. . . a powerful blend of comedy and pathos . . .*"

   Taking into account **one** or **more than one** of the above critical comments, outline your own response to *The Slab Boys Trilogy*.

3. **Chekhov**

   "*Chekhov knows what it is for people to yearn for self-realisation and self-fulfilment . . . and knows the negative side of these ideals, where yearning produces only continuing frustration and pain.*"

   What indications are there in the plays that Chekhov sees **more** in human life than yearning, frustration and pain?

4. **Friel**

   "*Friel's later plays deal with the inadequacy of language and move towards an exchange beyond rational thought, beyond language . . .*"

   How far, in your view, does this assertion apply to *Translations* **and** to *Dancing at Lughnasa*?

5. **Lindsay**

   Discuss the contribution of pageantry to *Ane Satyre of The Thrie Estaitis*.

6. **Lochhead**

   "*Liz Lochhead's principal dramatic talent is to find the ordinary in the apparently grand.*"

   Discuss.

7. **Pinter**

   Speaking of his plays, Pinter has said, "*We cannot understand other people; we cannot even understand ourselves; the truth of any situation is almost always beyond our grasp.*"

   Discuss the relevance of this statement to Pinter's treatment of character and situation in **each** of the specified plays.

8. **Shakespeare**

   EITHER

   (a) ***Othello* and *Antony and Cleopatra***

   "***Othello** is a simple domestic tragedy with a black male protagonist; the tragedy of **Antony and Cleopatra** derives from the clash of opposing worlds at a key moment of world history.*"

   Discuss the nature of the tragedy of both plays in the light of this assertion.

   OR

   (b) ***The Winter's Tale* and *The Tempest***

   Analyse the principal means by which Shakespeare dramatises the struggle between good and evil **either** in *The Winter's Tale* **or** in *The Tempest* **or** in **both** plays.

9. **Stoppard**

   Read the following extract from ***Rosencrantz and Guildenstern are Dead*** and then answer the question that follows it:

	ROS:	[*At footlights*] How very intriguing! [*Turns*] I feel like a spectator—an appalling prospect. The only thing that makes it bearable is the irrational belief that somebody interesting will come on in a minute . . .
	GUIL:	See anyone?
5	ROS:	No. You?
	GUIL:	No. [*At footlights*] What a fine persecution—to be kept intrigued without ever quite being enlightened . . . [*Pause.*] We've had no practice.
	ROS:	We could play at questions.
	GUIL:	What good would that do?
10	ROS:	Practice!
	GUIL:	Statement! One-love.
	ROS:	Cheating!
	GUIL:	How?
	ROS:	I hadn't started yet.
15	GUIL:	Statement. Two-love.
	ROS:	Are you counting that?
	GUIL:	What?
	ROS:	Are you counting that?

	GUIL:	Foul! No repetitions. Three-love. First game to . . .
20	ROS:	I'm not going to play if you're going to be like that.
	GUIL:	Whose serve?
	ROS:	Hah?
	GUIL:	Foul! No grunts. Love-one.
	ROS:	Whose go?
25	GUIL:	Why?
	ROS:	Why not?
	GUIL:	What for?
	ROS:	Foul! No synonyms! One-all.
	GUIL:	What in God's name is going on?
30	ROS:	Foul! No rhetoric. Two-one.
	GUIL:	What does it all add up to?
	ROS:	Can't you guess?
	GUIL:	Were you addressing me?
	ROS:	Is there anyone else?
35	GUIL:	Who?
	ROS:	How would I know?
	GUIL:	Why do you ask?
	ROS:	Are you serious?
	GUIL:	Was that rhetoric?
40	ROS:	No.
	GUIL:	Statement! Two-all. Game point.
	ROS:	What's the matter with you today?
	GUIL:	When?
	ROS:	What?
45	GUIL:	Are you deaf?
	ROS:	Am I dead?
	GUIL:	Yes or no?
	ROS:	Is there a choice?
	GUIL:	Is there a God?
50	ROS:	Foul! No non sequiturs, three-two, one game all.
	GUIL:	[*Seriously*] What's your name?
	ROS:	What's yours?
	GUIL:	I asked first.
	ROS:	Statement. One-love.
55	GUIL:	What's your name when you're at home?
	ROS:	What's yours?
	GUIL:	When I'm at home?
	ROS:	Is it different at home?
	GUIL:	What home?
60	ROS:	Haven't you got one?
	GUIL:	Why do you ask?

	ROS:	What are you driving at?
	GUIL:	[*With emphasis*] What's your name?!
	ROS:	Repetition. Two-love. Match point to me.
65	GUIL:	[*Seizing him violently*] WHO DO YOU THINK YOU ARE?
	ROS:	Rhetoric! Game and match! [*Pause.*] Where's it going to end?
	GUIL:	That's the question.
	ROS:	It's all questions.
	GUIL:	Do you think it matters?
70	ROS:	Doesn't it matter to you?
	GUIL:	Why should it matter?
	ROS:	What does it matter why?
	GUIL:	[*Teasing gently*] Doesn't it matter why it matters?
	ROS:	[*Rounding on him*] What's the matter with you?
75		[*Pause.*]
	GUIL:	It doesn't matter.
	ROS:	[*Voice in the wilderness*] . . . What's the game?
	GUIL:	What are the rules?

How characteristic is this extract of Stoppard's dramatic approach, not only in *Rosencrantz and Guildenstern are Dead*, but also in *Arcadia*?

10. Wilde

To what extent, in your view, can Wilde's plays be considered to be critiques of Victorian values?

In your answer you should refer to all **three** of the specified texts.

11. Williams

Discuss Williams's treatment of loneliness in *Sweet Bird of Youth* and in *A Streetcar Named Desire*.

POETRY

12. Burns

EITHER

(a) Make a close comparative study of the poetic means by which, in **three** or **four** poems, Burns criticises aspects of the society of his day.

OR

(b) "*The typical Burns lyric is almost beyond criticism; it is transparent and artless. And yet it speaks of intense emotion, it is powerful, it resonates.*"

Account for the lasting emotional impact of a number of Burns's "transparent and artless" songs.

13. Chaucer

With reference to the *General Prologue* and to **either** or to **both** of the specified *Canterbury Tales*, illustrate what you consider to be the subtlety of Chaucer's characterisation.

14. Donne

"*It is a characteristic of the metaphysical poets that profound emotion stimulates their powers of intellectual analysis and argument.*"

Examine in detail the relationship between profound emotion and intellect in **three** or **four** poems by Donne.

15. Duffy

By making reference to both content and technique in a range of her poems, evaluate the extent to which Duffy could be termed "a poet for our times".

16. Heaney

Read the following poem from the sequence *Clearances* and answer the question that follows it.

In Memoriam M.K.H., 1911–1984

When all the others were away at Mass
I was all hers as we peeled potatoes.
They broke the silence, let fall one by one
Like solder weeping off the soldering iron:
5   Cold comforts set between us, things to share
Gleaming in a bucket of clean water.
And again let fall. Little pleasant splashes
From each other's work would bring us to our senses.
So while the parish priest at her bedside
10 Went hammer and tongs at the prayers for the dying
And some were responding and some crying
I remembered her head bent towards my head,
Her breath in mine, our fluent dipping knives --
Never closer the whole rest of our lives.

It has been said that Heaney "*never allows elegy to sentimentalise actual, intractable human difficulty*".

How far is this statement true of **this** poem and of **two** or **three** other elegies on the death of friends or family members?

17. Henryson

EITHER

(a) *"I have pietie thou suld fall sic mischance."*

By what means does Henryson communicate his compassion for Cresseid and her plight?

OR

(b) What do you consider to be the principal poetic features of Henryson's *Morall Fabillis*?

18. Keats

*"In **Ode to a Nightingale** Keats presents the speaker's engagement with the fluid music of the bird's song; in **Ode on a Grecian Urn** with the static immobility of sculpture."*

Make a comparative study of the poet's use of key images and symbols to express his principal thematic concerns in **both** of these poems.

19. MacDiarmid

EITHER

(a) Do you find *A Drunk Man Looks at the Thistle* a satisfying poetic unity?

OR

(b) Read the following poem and answer the questions that follow it.

THE EEMIS STANE

    I' the how-dumb-deid o' the cauld hairst nicht
    The warl' like an eemis stane
    Wags i' the lift;
    An' my eerie memories fa'
5 Like a yowdendrift.

    Like a yowdendrift so's a couldna read
    The words cut oot i' the stane
    Had the fug o' fame
    An' history's hazelraw
10 No' yirdit thaim.

(i) Make a close critical appreciation of this poem.

(ii) To what extent can this poem be taken as representative of the themes and techniques of MacDiarmid's lyrics?

20. Muir

Discuss in detail the means by which, in **three** or **four** poems, Muir explores the relationship between mankind and nature.

21. Plath

"*The reading of Sylvia Plath's poetry is a disturbing . . . even frightening experience.*"

How far has this been your experience of reading her poetry?

You should make detailed reference to **three** or **four** poems in your answer.

22. Yeats

Discuss the principal poetic means by which, in *Sailing to Byzantium* **and** in *Byzantium*, Yeats explores the relationship between nature and art.

PROSE FICTION

23. Atwood

"*Her female protagonists are forced to remake themselves, to achieve courage and self-reliance in their attitudes and relationships with others and with the world around them.*"

Make a close evaluative study of the characterisation of **either** Elaine **or** Grace in the light of this assertion.

24. Austen

Discuss the scope and function of irony in *Pride and Prejudice* and in *Persuasion*.

25. Dickens

Dickens has often been described as the most dramatic of our novelists.

Illustrate what you consider to be the essentially dramatic qualities of *Great Expectations* and *Hard Times*.

26. Fitzgerald

To what extent is Fitzgerald concerned with exposing the destructive power of wealth and materialism in *The Beautiful and Damned* and in *Tender is the Night*?

27. Galloway

How effectively does Galloway explore alienation in *The Trick is to Keep Breathing* and in *Foreign Parts*?

28. Gray

Gray has been described as "*a master of the playful nightmare*".

With reference to *Lanark* and *Poor Things*, discuss the validity of this description.

29. Hardy

"There are no innocent victims in Hardy's mature novels. What is innocent or fine is tragically linked with what is sentimental, blind, or self-injuring."

How far is this true of the central characters in *The Return of the Native* **and** *Tess of the d'Urbervilles*?

30. Hogg

Discuss the presentation of the duality of human nature in *The Private Memoirs and Confessions of a Justified Sinner* and in **one** of the specified short stories.

31. Joyce

Read the following extract from *A Portrait of the Artist as a Young Man* and then answer the question that follows it.

Publisher's note. In the original exam paper, an extract from the final few pages of chapter 4 of *A Portrait of the Artist as a Young Man* was supplied. However, due to copyright restrictions, we are unable to publish this extract and apologise for any inconvenience caused. We would therefore advise you to use a copy of the book alongside this question.

Comment on some of the literary and linguistic means by which Joyce makes Stephen's vision of the girl seem special.

Go on to discuss in some detail the significance of this episode in the novel as a whole.

32. Stevenson

Compare and contrast Stevenson's treatment of moral conflict in *The Master of Ballantrae* **and** in **two** of the specified short stories.

33. Waugh

". . . *no new mad thing brought to his notice could add a jot to the all-encompassing chaos that shrieked about his ears.*"

A Handful of Dust

". . . *man had deserted his post and the jungle was creeping back into its old strongholds.*"

Brideshead Revisited

To what extent can these two novels be regarded as elegies for the passing of a way of life?

PROSE NON-FICTION

34. "*The heart of any place is the relationships you have there. Geography is people.*"

(William McIlvanney)

Discuss any **two** of the specified texts in the light of this comment.

35. It has been suggested that we "*turn to autobiography to see how others have managed to secure their sense of a self*".

Examine the means by which a sense of the author's "self" has emerged from your reading of **one** or **more than one** of the specified autobiographies.

Section 2—Language Study

You must answer **one question only** in this section.

> **N.B.** *This Specimen Paper contains only **one** question on each of the specified Language Study topics.*
>
> *The actual examination paper will contain **two** questions on each topic.*
>
> *One (or even both) of these questions may be text-based—as in Question 4, Question 6 and Question 7 of this Specimen Paper.*

TOPIC A—VARIETIES OF ENGLISH OR SCOTS

1. Describe the principal linguistic features of **one** particular variety of English **or** Scots you have studied and go on to discuss
   - who uses it
   - the contexts in which it is used
   - its relationship to other varieties of English or Scots.

TOPIC B—THE HISTORICAL DEVELOPMENT OF ENGLISH OR SCOTS

2. Show how **two** or **three** key historical events or movements or writers or texts have influenced the development of contemporary English **or** Scots.

TOPIC C—MULTILINGUALISM IN CONTEMPORARY SCOTLAND

3. What evidence is there in the conversation of contemporary Scottish multilingual speakers **either** of the structural and functional patterns associated with codeswitching **or** of the ongoing process of language shift?

TOPIC D—THE USE OF SCOTS IN CONTEMPORARY LITERATURE

4. Comment in detail on the linguistic characteristics of **two** of the following extracts.

Extract 1

"Gie's a bottle o vodka an twa o Eddie's peels," he spiered o a loon ower bi the kitchie. "I dinna ken fit's in Eddie's peels," the loon telt him. "They could be Smarties, or E's, or onythin."

"So?" quo Derek. "It's just fur a lauch. I'm gonna spike yon Laurie's punch, the wee scrubber. It'll be funny . . . wyte an see."

He cowped some o the punch frae Laurie's glaiss inno the bowl, syne tappit it up wi vodka an twa peels. Syne he gaed ower tae the CD player, tae pit on a rave album.

Dauncin made Laurie droothy. Efter twa tracks o the album, she teemed her glaissie ina wunner. Efter, she gied a bit grue. "It disna taste richt," quo she. Steven dippit the ladle inno the punch bowl, takkin a sup o the reid bree. "It tastes aaricht tae me," he replied. "Ach, forget it, an come up fur anither daunce."

Hauf ben the dance, she sterted tae feel shuggily. Ferlies bleared an furled. The room gaed tapsalteerie. Music skirled. Lichts grew skyrie. Her heid stooned. Her een played trickes. Faces aroon her ran an dreepit like meltin wax, like a widdendreme.

Her pulse quickened, her braith grew ticht, her moo dried. Fleg, set bricht reid roses in her chikks. "Fit's adee wi me Steven?" she cried. "Fit's adee? Ah'm needin hame. An'm wantin ma. Ah want tae lie doon . . ."

Wi a sough, she slippit doon tae the fleer, like an auld cloot. "Fit's gaun on here?" cried Sarah Broon. "Fit neep-heid spiked the puir quine's drink?"

Naebody spukk fur a meenit, syne a loon clypit.

"It's Derek's wyte . . . speir at him."

(from *Leddy-Bird, Leddy-Bird* by Sheena Blackhall)

Extract 2

"Hallo, Sandy," she smilit, as if it wis nae mair than ten days instead o ten years sin they'd seen ane anither. "A'm sorry A wisnae right wakin when A seen ee in the toon."

"Sorry?" He wis slow in the uptak.

"It wis yow, wis eet no, that gien iz a light? A wis walkin the dog in the High Street."

"Wis it yow, then?" He wis thunnerstruck. He'd seen his childhood sweethairt an thocht it wis some dreich, ill-faured, nameless woman he micht hae seen somewhaur afore. Whit wis wrang wi him?

"A'm no at my best early in the mornin," she chirmed.

May didnae jine in the joke. Her face wis wan an dowie.

"Sandy," she said. "Mum's gey hard up. She'll hev ti gaun ti the hospital."

"When did it happen?" Sandy wis bumbazed. He'd been up the hill for nae mair nor an oor.

"Oh, she can tak a bad turn gey quick," May said. "She's been hingin on jist ti see ee. Now ee're here, she's happy."

They gae intil the bedroom whaur his mother was white as the bedsheets unner the blue quilt.

"She's hed her pille, an the doctor'll gie her an injection. She's in nae pain. The ambulance'll no be lang."

Luikin doun at her face, he kent she wis deein. A terrible knot o dule fankled his kist, forcin oot his raith. Toronto seemed no jist thoosans, but millions o miles away fae him noo.

(from *The Hamecomin* by Sheila Douglas)

Extract 3

He goat the idea offy the telly. Heard oan the news this Chinese boy hud ritten 2000 characters oan a singul grainy rice. Well o coarse, he kidny rite Chinese an he dooted if thur wiz any rice in the hoose (unless mebby in the chinky cartons fi last nite). Butty liked the idea. Whit wi the asbestos fi wurk damajin his lungs an him oan the invalidity an that. Well, he hudda loatty time tay himsel an no much munny ti day anyhin wi it. Anny didny reckon he hud long tay go noo. It wid be nice, yi ken, jist tay day sumhin, tay leeve sumhin behind that peepul wid mebby notice. Jist a wee thing.

So wunce the bairnz wur offty skule an the wife wiz offty wurk, he cleared the kitchin table an hud a luke in the cubburds. Rite enuff, nay rice. He foond sum tattys but. Thottyd better scrub thum furst. So he did. Then he took thum back tay the table. He picked the smollist wun soze it wizny like he wiz cheatin too much, anny began tay rite aon it wi a byro. He stied ther aw day. Kept on gawn, rackiniz brains an straynin tay keepiz hand fi shakin.

Efter 7 oors o solid con-sen-tray-shun, he ran ooty space. Heed manijd tay rite 258 swayr wurds oan the wee tatty. He sat back tae huv a luke. Even tho heed scrubd it, it wiz still a bit durty-lukin an it wuz that fully ize yi kidny see the ritin very well. Bit still. He felt heed acheeved sumhin.

(from *The Wee Tatty* by Alison Kermack)

TOPIC E—LANGUAGE AND SOCIAL CONTEXT

5. *"People's perception of linguistic differences across social classes, genders or age-groups has more to do with their prejudices than with any substantial variations in vocabulary, grammar and pronunciation."*

   How far do you agree?

TOPIC F—THE LINGUISTIC CHARACTERISTICS OF INFORMAL CONVERSATION

6. The following short text is an extract from a transcript of an informal interview with a father of two children (Stephen and Sally) about his attitudes to parenthood.

   It contains the following transcription codes:
   - { indicates overlapping speech
   - (.) indicates minor pauses.

   Written punctuation, such as full stops and commas, has been avoided.

   Read the extract carefully and then answer the question that follows it.

INTERVIEWER:	what about erm Stephen do you s
FATHER:	{he comes to Aikido with me now
INTERVIEWER:	oh yeh
FATHER:	I try to er encourage him to do it (.)
	I've tried the painting on 'em all
INTERVIEWER:	yeh

FATHER: tried to find if there's anything there you know
anything that's been passed on (.)
Sally's quite good (.) for her age like you know
INTERVIEWER: mm
FATHER: erm she seems to be able to put things in the right place (.)
which is the main thing really (.)
and er (.) I try and get them to do the things you know
but (.) they sort of go their own way (.) you know

In what ways do you consider the linguistic characteristics of this extract to be typical of informal conversation?

In answering this question, you should make a detailed analysis of the lexical, grammatical, syntactical and structural features of the extract.

TOPIC G—THE LINGUISTIC CHARACTERISTICS OF POLITICAL COMMUNICATION

7. The following text has been transcribed from a televised party election broadcast made by the Conservative Party in the run-up to the 1997 General Election. At the time of the broadcast, the Conservative Party was the party of government, but Labour, the main opposition party, had a strong lead in the opinion polls.

The broadcast presented viewers with a representation, set in the future, of what life would be like (in the opinion of the Conservative Party) under a future Labour government. In the representation, actors, using carefully scripted dialogue, took the role of unidentified speakers in everyday settings talking directly to camera.

The transcript includes pauses, indicated by (.); and each spoken sentence or clause complex has been numbered [1,2,3 etc]. Material which has been difficult to transcribe is enclosed within parentheses: for example, (the). "Er" and "erm" are vocalised pause fillers. Written punctuation, such as commas and capital letters, has been avoided.

Read the transcript carefully and then answer the question that follows it.

CONSERVATIVE PARTY ELECTION BROADCAST: 1997

Voice One:
[1] she said (.) you don't know what it's like living under a Labour Government
[2] you haven't experienced it
[3] you're too young to remember (.)
[4] and (.) you know I mean obviously that was true
[5] but (.) I just thought well (.) I mean nobody believes their mother do they
[6] you know I just wanted to (.) see it for myself (.) basically (.)
[7] and (.) well I certainly have

Voice Two:
[8] it's affected me personally much more than I would have expected (.)
[9] erm I mean for example talk about unemployment figures
[10] well it's just numbers
[11] it doesn't mean anything to you
[12] but when you actually when I actually lost my job a few weeks ago cos I was made redundant (.) erm then it's a whole different story
[13] it was a difficult decision (.) cos I'd voted Tory before (.)
[14] but (.) I thought they really had learned their lesson the Labour Party
[15] erm (.) Tories had that slogan erm (.) Britain's booming don't let Labour mess it up (.)
[16] and I thought (.) you know they won't do that Blair won't do that (.)
[17] erm (.) but they have (.) hheh

Voice Three:
[18] things were nice and calm (.)
[19] I mean (.) how much damage can you do eh (.)
[20] interest rates have gone up (.)
[21] unemployment's rising (.)
[22] I'm having to pay an extra thirty or forty pounds a week now because of them

Voice Four:
[23] yeh well they('ve) had their chance
[24] and they made a complete mess of it
[25] me mortgage has gone through the roof
[26] and they've put tax up (.) almost straight after they got in when they promised they wouldn't
[27] you know don't worry they said (.) we're different
[28] now I suppose it was our fault for trusting them in the first place
[29] but basically we're back in recession aren't we

Voice Five:
[30] my son is looking for a job for over a year now
[31] he can't get one because of minimum wage
[32] nobody can afford to take him on
[33] I don't know how long he'll have to wait

Voice Six:
[34] well (ob) it's democracy you know (.)
[35] Tories had had their day
[36] we thought maybe somebody else (.)
[37] see what they've done
[38] I mean it's just been a total downhill total downhill for three years
[39] but what gets to me you see I went for it
[40] we all went for it
[41] we thought you know a change equals something better (.)
[42] course it wasn't (.)
[43] something heck of a lot worse

Voice Seven:
[44] we voted Labour
[45] and (.) you know like most people thought fresh blood you know (.)
[46] er (.) and we believed all that stuff about (.) government running out of steam and sleaze
[47] and (.) well (.) it seems the further we get into the Labour term the more it was just (.) change for change sake (.)
[48] you know look at us now I mean weren't badly informed
[49] we (.) most of us we (.) you know read decent newspapers
[50] and we kept up with the news
[51] but I mean we knew about we knew about erm the the great state the economy was in
[52] and we knew about government's record on employment and inflation all that
[53] but (.) well we knew it but I suppose we didn't value it

Voice Eight:
[54] every time you open the newspaper there's more bad news things going wrong (.)
[55] every time I go to the shops prices gone up again
[56] inflation's just going through the roof (.)

Voice Nine:
[57] so I had a good job (.) had a low mortgage (.)
[58] and (the) inflation was low (.)
[59] an(d) I was stupid enough to vote for Blair (.)
[60] whew (.) those were the good days
[61] d'you know I never thought I'd say that

Voice Ten:
[62] I'm here in the future (.)
[63] I know what it's like (.)
[64] don't do this to Britain (.)
[65] that's my advice

Make a detailed analysis of the above transcript, evaluating its effectiveness as a piece of political communication in terms of as many of the following as you think appropriate:

- its overall style and tone
- its orientation to audience
- the ways in which its discourse is structured and organised
- the effects created by the linguistic characteristics of its various "voices"
- any other aspects of it you consider significant.

Section 3—Textual Analysis

You must answer **one question only** in this section.

1. **Prose fiction (*Pages seventeen to nineteen*)**

   The following extract is the first part of the opening chapter of Elizabeth Gaskell's novel **Wives and Daughters** *(1866).*

   Read the extract carefully and then answer the question that follows it (*Page twenty*).

   To begin with the old rigmarole of childhood. In a country there was a shire, and in that shire there was a town, and in that town there was a house, and in that house there was a room, and in that room there was a bed, and in that bed there lay a little girl; wide awake and longing to get up, but not daring to do so for fear of the unseen
5 power in the next room; a certain Betty, whose slumbers must not be disturbed until six o'clock struck, when she wakened of herself 'as sure as clockwork', and left the household very little peace afterwards. It was a June morning, and early as it was, the room was full of sunny warmth and light.

   On the drawers opposite to the little white dimity bed in which Molly Gibson lay, was
10 a primitive kind of bonnet-stand on which was hung a bonnet, carefully covered over from any chance of dust with a large cotton handkerchief; of so heavy and serviceable a texture that if the thing underneath it had been a flimsy fabric of gauze and lace and flowers, it would have been altogether 'scomfished' (again to quote from Betty's vocabulary). But the bonnet was made of solid straw, and its only trimming was a
15 plain white ribbon put over the crown, and forming the strings. Still, there was a neat little quilling inside, every plait of which Molly knew, for had she not made it herself the evening before, with infinite pains? and was there not a little blue bow in this quilling, the very first bit of such finery Molly had ever had the prospect of wearing?

   Six o'clock now! the pleasant, brisk ringing of the church bells told that; calling every
20 one to their daily work, as they had done for hundreds of years. Up jumped Molly, and ran with her bare little feet across the room, and lifted off the handkerchief and saw once again the bonnet; the pledge of the gay bright day to come. Then to the window, and after some tugging she opened the casement, and let in the sweet morning air. The dew was already off the flowers in the garden below, but still rising
25 from the long hay-grass in the meadows directly beyond. At one side lay the little town of Hollingford, into a street of which Mr Gibson's front door opened; and delicate columns, and little puffs of smoke were already beginning to rise from many a cottage chimney where some housewife was already up, and preparing breakfast for the bread-winner of the family.

30 Molly Gibson saw all this, but all she thought about it was, 'Oh! it will be a fine day! I was afraid it never never would come; or that, if it ever came, it would be a rainy day!' Five-and-forty years ago, children's pleasures in a country town were very simple, and Molly had lived for twelve long years without the occurrence of any event so great as that which was now impending. Poor child! it is true that she had lost her
35 mother, which was a jar to the whole tenour of her life; but that was hardly an event in the sense referred to; and besides, she had been too young to be conscious of it at the time. The pleasure she was looking forward to to-day was her first share in a kind of annual festival in Hollingford.

The little straggling town faded away into country on one side close to the entrance-lodge of a great park, where lived my Lord and Lady Cumnor: 'the earl' and 'the countess', as they were always called by the inhabitants of the town; where a very pretty amount of feudal feeling still lingered, and showed itself in a number of simple ways, droll enough to look back upon, but serious matters of importance at the time. It was before the passing of the Reform Bill, but a good deal of liberal talk took place occasionally between two or three of the more enlightened freeholders living in Hollingford; and there was a great Whig family in the county who, from time to time, came forward and contested the election with the rival Tory family of Cumnor. One would have thought that the above-mentioned liberal-talking inhabitants of Hollingford would have, at least, admitted the possibility of their voting for the Hely-Harrison who represented their own opinions. But no such thing. 'The earl' was lord of the manor, and owner of much of the land on which Hollingford was built; he and his household were fed, and doctored, and, to a certain measure, clothed by the good people of the town; their fathers' grandfathers had always voted for the eldest son of Cumnor Towers, and following in the ancestral track, every man-jack in the place gave his vote to the liege lord, totally irrespective of such chimeras as political opinion.

This was no unusual instance of the influence of the great landowners over their humbler neighbours in those days before railways, and it was well for a place where the powerful family, who thus overshadowed it, were of so respectable a character as the Cumnors. They expected to be submitted to, and obeyed; the simple worship of the townspeople was accepted by the earl and countess as a right; and they would have stood still in amazement, and with a horrid memory of the French *sansculottes* who were the bugbears of their youth, had any inhabitant of Hollingford ventured to set his will or opinions in opposition to those of the earl's. But, yielded all that obeisance, they did a good deal for the town, and were generally condescending, and often thoughtful and kind in their treatment of their vassals. Lord Cumnor was a forbearing landlord; putting his steward a little on one side sometimes, and taking the reins into his own hands from time to time, much to the annoyance of the agent, who was, in fact, too rich and independent to care greatly for preserving a post where his decisions might any day be overturned by my lord's taking a fancy to go 'pottering' (as the agent irreverently expressed it in the sanctuary of his own home), which, being interpreted, meant that occasionally the earl asked his own questions of his own tenants, and used his own eyes and ears in the management of the smaller details of his property. But his tenants liked my lord all the better for this habit of his. Lord Cumnor had certainly a little turn for gossip, which he contrived to combine with the failing of personal intervention between the old land-steward and the tenantry. But, then, the countess made up by her unapproachable dignity for this weakness of the earl's. Once a year she was condescending. She and the ladies, her daughters, had set up a school; not a school after the manner of schools now-a-days, where far better intellectual teaching is given to the boys and girls of labourers and work-people than often falls to the lot of their betters in worldly estate; but a school of the kind we should call 'industrial', where girls were taught to sew beautifully, to be capital housemaids, and pretty fair cooks, and, above all, to dress neatly in a kind of charity uniform devised by the ladies of Cumnor Towers;—white caps, white tippets, check aprons, blue gowns, and ready curtseys, and 'please, ma'ams', being *de rigueur*.

Now, as the countess was absent from the Towers for a considerable part of the year, she was glad to enlist the sympathy of the Hollingford ladies in this school, with a view to obtaining their aid as visitors during the many months that she and her daughters were away. And the various unoccupied gentlewomen of the town responded to the call of their liege lady, and gave her their service as required; and along with it, a great deal of whispered and fussy admiration. 'How good of the countess! So like the dear countess—always thinking of others!' and so on; while it was always supposed that no strangers had seen Hollingford properly, unless they had been taken to the countess's school, and been duly impressed by the neat little pupils, and the still neater needlework there to be inspected. In return, there was a day of honour set apart every summer, when with much gracious and stately hospitality, Lady Cumnor and her daughters received all the school visitors at the Towers, the great family mansion standing in aristocratic seclusion in the centre of the large park, of which one of the lodges was close to the little town. The order of this annual festivity was this. About ten o'clock one of the Towers' carriages rolled through the lodge, and drove to different houses, wherein dwelt a woman to be honoured; picking them up by ones or twos, till the loaded carriage drove back again through the ready portals, bowled along the smooth tree-shaded road, and deposited its covey of smartly-dressed ladies on the great flight of steps leading to the ponderous doors of Cumnor Towers. Back again to the town; another picking up of womenkind in their best clothes, and another return, and so on till the whole party were assembled either in the house or in the really beautiful gardens. After the proper amount of exhibition on the one part, and admiration on the other, had been done, there was a collation for the visitors, and some more display and admiration of the treasures inside the house. Towards four o'clock, coffee was brought round; and this was a signal of the approaching carriage that was to take them back to their own homes; whither they returned with the happy consciousness of a well-spent day, but with some fatigue at the long-continued exertion of behaving their best, and talking on stilts for so many hours. Nor were Lady Cumnor and her daughters free from something of the same self-approbation, and something, too, of the same fatigue; the fatigue that always follows on conscious efforts to behave as will best please the society you are in.

For the first time in her life, Molly Gibson was to be included among the guests at the Towers. She was much too young to be a visitor at the school, so it was not on that account that she was to go; but it had so happened that one day when Lord Cumnor was on a 'pottering' expedition, he had met Mr Gibson, *the* doctor of the neighbourhood, coming out of the farm-house my lord was entering; and having some small question to ask the surgeon (Lord Cumnor seldom passed any one of his acquaintance without asking a question of some sort—not always attending to the answer; it was his mode of conversation), he accompanied Mr Gibson to the out-building, to a ring in the wall of which the surgeon's horse was fastened. Molly was there too, sitting square and quiet on her rough little pony, waiting for her father. Her grave eyes opened large and wide at the close neighbourhood and evident advance of 'the earl'; for to her little imagination the grey-haired, red-faced, somewhat clumsy man, was a cross between an archangel and a king.

'Your daughter, eh, Gibson?—nice little girl, how old? Pony wants grooming though,' patting it as he talked. 'What's your name, my dear? He is sadly behindhand with his rent, as I was saying, but if he is really ill, I must see after Sheepshanks, who is a hardish man of business. What's his complaint? You'll come to our school-scrimmage on Thursday, little girl—what's-your-name? Mind you send her, or bring her, Gibson; and just give a word to your groom, for I'm sure that pony was not singed last year, now, was he? Don't forget Thursday, little girl—what's-your-name?—it's a promise between us, is it not?' And off the earl trotted.

Question

How successfully in this first part of the opening chapter of the novel has Elizabeth Gaskell engaged the reader in her narrative?

In answering this question, you should examine the narrative and linguistic means by which she

- introduces the main characters
- creates an impression of the community of Hollingford
- encourages the reader to read further.

2. **Prose non-fiction** *(Pages twenty-one to twenty-two)*

The following extract is from **Moon Country** *(1996), an account by Simon Armitage and Glyn Maxwell of their travels in Iceland. In this extract, on the last day of their visit, Simon Armitage reflects upon the place and upon himself as a writer.*

Read the extract carefully and then answer the question that follows it (*Page twenty-two*).

I'm sitting way above the farm, high up at the back of the bay. This is Europe's most westerly point; set out from here and you finish up on the tip of Greenland or the coast of America, the way the Vikings did. It's two in the afternoon. A headland at either side curves out into the ocean, like two arms protecting everything within reach—the track uncoiling out of the hills, the boulders and rocks in the middle distance, the strip of grassland that makes up the apron of the beach, then a mile or so of sand, and then the sea. I can count seven buildings down there, all of them huddled together under the hill for shelter, beginning with the farm itself, a rectangular white bungalow, connected to a three-storey dormitory or bunk-house that looks like a lunatic asylum imported from Eastern Europe. Close by, there are two free-standing wooden sheds, a breeze-block garage, and a long-by-narrow greenhouse with polythene instead of glass, most of it shredded by the wind. And then there's the church. Anywhere else, it probably wouldn't be much more than a pigeon loft or a dovecote, but it does well for itself here, its miniature spire taking whatever elements the Atlantic can throw at it, and the metal cross on top making its point. To the left, a chain-gang of telegraph poles lines up across the hillside, tethered by a single cable.

Glyn's gone wandering off along the coast, around the peninsula, out of sight. I've come inland, turning stones over and following paths that dry up after a couple of hundred yards or go to ground like hunted animals. Behind me there's a steep valley leading to higher ground, but I think I've come far enough. I've lost all sense of perspective and scale this last week, and every time I look over my shoulder towards the horizon I can't decide if it's two miles away or twenty, if it's a walk I can make before dark or not. In and amongst the rocks I can make out a couple of rooks or ravens or crows, scavenging on the ground, and another one just launching itself into mid-air, more like a pair of big black gloves in the shape of a bird than a bird itself, throwing a huge feathered shadow against the side of the hill.

This is the last day and these are the last hours. I should be writing but haven't managed a single word as yet, and I'm hovering with a pen about an inch above a notebook, like the teleprinter in the old sports reports, waiting for the results to come in. On the opposite page, I can just about decipher a few scribbled lines from a piece I once wrote about my sister, and for some reason I'm more interested in that than in all this epic geography going on in the foreground. Maybe I'm just homesick at the moment, but even back at home I don't seem to be able to make anything of anything until it's gone down in history, until it's been transmuted into memory. And the fact that I've written nothing doesn't surprise me, because I'm very slowly coming to the conclusion that all writing comes from the past, from childhood or innocence or naivety, and from loss, lost lives and lives gone by, even the loss of only eight, nine, ten, eleven seconds ago.

Maybe there's some unwritten rule of inversion, to do with distance, a rule that makes the spaceman think of his house, and a room in his house, and a box in that room, and inside that box his most treasured possession, a rule that makes him open the box and look inside it, while orbiting the Earth. It's the rule that brings out the *there and then* from the *here and now*, a rule that I'm very much aware of this precise minute, from the *here and now*, a rule that I'm very much aware of this precise minute, because this is the sort of place where you rub noses with yourself, catch up with yourself, meet yourself coming back the other way; this is the place where your own face looks back at you, where the days happen in real time, where every moment is simultaneous to itself, synchronised, and where all actions are true to life, unimaginary, right now. This is actuality, the present, and according to the rule I have to get as far away from it as possible.

Question

How effectively does this piece of writing enable you to understand why Simon Armitage feels he has "to get as far away from it as possible"?

You should support your answer to this question by detailed reference to the language, imagery, structural features and patterning of ideas in the extract.

3. Poetry (*Page twenty-three*)

*Read the poem **At Marsden Bay** by Peter Reading and then answer the question that follows it.*

AT MARSDEN BAY

    Arid hot desert stretched here in the early
    Permian Period—sand dune fossils
    are pressed to a brownish bottom stratum.
    A tropical saline ocean next silted
5   calcium and magnesium carbonates
    over this bed, forming rough Magnesian
    Limestone cliffs on the ledges of which
    Rissa tridactyla colonizes—
    an estimated four thousand pairs
10 that shuttle like close-packed tracer bullets
    against dark sky between nests and North Sea.
    The call is a shrill "kit-e-wayke, kit-e-wayke",
    also a low "uk-uk-uk" and a plaintive
    "ee-e-e-eeh, ee-e-e-eeh".

15 Four boys about sixteen years old appear
    in Army Stores combat-jackets, one wearing
    a Balaclava with a long narrow eye-slit
    (such as a rapist might find advantageous),
    bleached denims rolled up to mid calf, tall laced boots
20 with bright polished toe-caps, pates cropped to stubble.
    Three of the four are crosseyed, all are acned.
    Communication consists of bellowing
    simian ululations between
    each other at only a few inches range:
25 "Gibbo, gerrofforal getcher yaffuga",
    also a low "lookadembastabirdsmon".

    Gibbo grubs up a Magnesian Limestone
    chunk and assails the ledges at random,
    biffing an incubating kittiwake
30 full in the sternum—an audible slap.
    Wings facing the wrong way, it thumps at the cliff base,
    twitching, half closing an eye. Gibbo seizes
    a black webbed foot and swings the lump joyously
    round and round his head. It emits
35 a strange wheezing noise. Gibbo's pustular pal
    is smacked in the face by the flung poultry, yowls,
    and lobs it out into the foam. The four
    gambol euphoric like drunk chimps through rock pools.
    Nests are dislodged, brown-blotched shells crepitate
40 exuding thick rich orange embryo goo
    under a hail of hurled fossilized desert
    two hundred and eighty million years old.

Question

How do you react to the poem *At Marsden Bay*?

In answering this question, you should consider the effectiveness of the poetic techniques used in the presentation of

- the place and the birds
- the boys and their actions.

4. Drama (*Pages twenty-four to twenty-eight*)

*The following extract is taken from the end of Arthur Miller's play **All My Sons** (1947). The play not only exposes the evils of wartime profiteering, but also confronts the ideological conflict between father and son, and its tragic consequences.*

The characters who appear in the extract are listed below, with some of Miller's own introductory description of them. Larry does not actually appear in the extract, but plays an important part in the play.

Joe Keller: *nearly sixty, "a business man, with the imprint of the machine-shop worker and boss still upon him . . . a man whose judgements must be dredged out of him". His firm manufactured parts for aircraft.*

Kate (Mother *in the script): early fifties, Keller's wife, "a woman of uncontrolled inspirations and an overwhelming capacity for love".*

Chris: *thirty-two, Keller's son, "capable of immense affection and loyalty".*

Larry: *Keller's other son, presumed dead, except by his mother, who cannot accept that he is dead.*

Ann: *twenty-six, "gentle, but despite herself capable of holding fast to what she knows". She was Larry's girl when he was alive—but is now in love with Chris.*

At this point in the play, Keller is struggling to face up to the fact that those close to him (Chris in particular) have discovered that he knowingly allowed his firm to fit faulty cylinder heads into fighter planes. As a direct consequence, many pilots died—but up to this point Keller has always managed to avoid taking responsibility. Having just had a showdown with Chris, who has recently found out about the cylinder heads, Keller is with Kate bemoaning the family's inability to understand that his business decisions were driven by the importance of providing for the family.

Keller and Kate are just outside the Keller house. Chris has run off in despair. The time is 2 a.m. Ann enters from the house. Her first words refer to Chris.

Read the extract carefully and then answer questions (a), (b) and (c) that follow it (Page twenty-seven).

	ANN:	Why do you stay up? I'll tell you when he comes.
	KELLER	[*rises, goes to her*]: You didn't eat supper, did you? [*To* MOTHER] Why don't you make her something?
	MOTHER:	Sure, I'll—
5	ANN:	Never mind, Kate, I'm all right. [*They are unable to speak to each other.*] There's something I want to tell you. [*She starts, then halts.*] I'm not going to do anything about it.
	MOTHER:	She's a good girl! [*To* KELLER] You see? She's a—
	ANN:	I'll do nothing about Joe, but you're going to do something for me. [*Directly to* MOTHER] You made Chris feel guilty with me. Whether you wanted to or not, you've crippled him in front of me. I'd like you to tell him that Larry is dead and that you know it. You understand me? I'm not going out of here alone. There's no life for me that way. I want you to set him free. And then I promise you, everything will end, and we'll go away, and that's all.
	KELLER:	You'll do that. You'll tell him.
	ANN:	I know what I'm asking, Kate. You had two sons. But you've only got one now.
	KELLER:	You'll tell him.

Page twenty-four

20	ANN:	And you've got to say it to him so he knows you mean it.
	MOTHER:	My dear, if the boy was dead, it wouldn't depend on my words to make Chris know it . . . The night he gets into your bed, his heart will dry up. Because he knows and you know. To his dying day he'll wait for his brother! No, my dear, no such thing. You're going in the morning and you're going alone. That's your life, that's your lonely life. [*She goes to porch, and starts in.*]
25		
	ANN:	Larry is dead, Kate.
	MOTHER	[—*she stops*]: Don't speak to me.
30	ANN:	I said he's dead. I know! He crashed off the coast of China November twenty-fifth! His engine didn't fail him. But he died, I know . . .
	MOTHER:	How did he die? You're lying to me. If you know, how did he die?
	ANN:	I loved him. You know I loved him. Would I have looked at anyone else if I wasn't sure? That's enough for you.
35	MOTHER:	[*moving on her*]: What's enough for me? What're you talking about? [*She grasps* ANN's *wrists.*]
	ANN:	You're hurting my wrists.
	MOTHER:	What are you talking about! [*Pause. She stares at* ANN *a moment, then turns and goes to* KELLER.]
	ANN:	Joe, go in the house.
40	KELLER:	Why should I—
	ANN:	Please go.
	KELLER:	Lemme know when he comes. [KELLER *goes into house.*]
	MOTHER	[*as she sees* ANN *taking a letter from her pocket*]: What's that?
45	ANN:	Sit down. [MOTHER *moves left to chair, but does not sit.*] First you've got to understand. When I came, I didn't have any idea that Joe—I had nothing against him or you. I came to get married. I hoped . . . So I didn't bring this to hurt you. I thought I'd show it to you only if there was no other way to settle Larry in your mind.
	MOTHER:	Larry? [*Snatches letter from* ANN's *hand.*]
50	ANN:	He wrote it to me just before he—[MOTHER *opens and begins to read letter.*] I'm not trying to hurt you, Kate. You're making me do this, now remember you're—Remember. I've been so lonely, Kate . . . I can't leave here alone again. [*A long, low moan comes from* MOTHER's *throat as she reads.*] You made me show it to you. You wouldn't believe me. I told you a hundred times, why wouldn't you believe me!
55		
	MOTHER:	Oh, my God . . .
	ANN	[*with pity and fear*]: Kate, please, please . . .
	MOTHER:	My God, my God . . .
	ANN:	Kate, dear, I'm so sorry . . . I'm so sorry.
60		[CHRIS *enters from driveway. He seems exhausted.*]
	CHRIS:	What's the matter—?
	ANN:	Where were you? . . . You're all perspired. [MOTHER *doesn't move.*] Where were you?
	CHRIS:	Just drove around a little. I thought you'd be gone.
65	ANN:	Where do I go? I have nowhere to go.

	CHRIS	[to MOTHER]: Where's Dad?
	ANN:	Inside lying down.
	CHRIS:	Sit down, both of you. I'll say what there is to say.
	MOTHER:	I didn't hear the car . . .
70	CHRIS:	I left it in the garage. Mother . . . I'm going away. There are a couple of firms in Cleveland, I think I can get a place. I mean, I'm going away for good. [To ANN alone] I know what you're thinking, Annie. It's true. I'm yellow. I was made yellow in this house because I suspected my father and I did nothing about it, but if I knew that night when I came home what I know now, he'd be in the district attorney's office by this time, and I'd have brought him there. Now if I look at him, all I'm able to do is cry.
75		
	MOTHER:	What are you talking about? What else can you do?
	CHRIS:	I could jail him! I could jail him, if I were human any more. But I'm like everybody else now. I'm practical now. You made me practical.
80	MOTHER:	But you have to be.
	CHRIS:	The cats in that alley are practical, the bums who ran away when we were fighting were practical. Only the dead ones weren't practical. But now I'm practical, and I spit on myself. I'm going away. I'm going now.
	ANN	[going up to him]: I'm coming with you.
85	CHRIS:	No, Ann.
	ANN:	Chris, I don't ask you to do anything about Joe.
	CHRIS:	You do, you do.
	ANN:	I swear I never will.
	CHRIS:	In your heart you always will.
90	ANN:	Then do what you have to do!
	CHRIS:	Do what? What is there to do? I've looked all night for a reason to make him suffer.
	ANN:	There's reason, there's reason!
	CHRIS:	What? Do I raise the dead when I put him behind bars? Then what'll I do it for? We used to shoot a man who acted like a dog, but honour was real there, you were protecting something. But here? This is the land of the great big dogs, you don't love a man here, you eat him! That's the principle; the only one we live by—it just happened to kill a few people this time, that's all. The world's that way, how can I take it out on him? What sense does that make? This is a zoo, a zoo!
95		
100		
	ANN	[to MOTHER]: You know what he's got to do! Tell him!
	MOTHER:	Let him go.
	ANN:	I won't let him go. You'll tell him what he's got to do . . .
	MOTHER:	Annie!
105	ANN:	Then I will!
		[KELLER enters from house. CHRIS sees him, goes down near arbour.]
	KELLER:	What's the matter with you? I want to talk to you.
	CHRIS:	I've got nothing to say to you.
	KELLER:	[taking his arm]: I want to talk to you!
110	CHRIS	[pulling violently away from him]: Don't do that, Dad. I'm going to hurt you if you do that. There's nothing to say, so say it quick.

KELLER: Exactly what's the matter? What's the matter? You got too much money? Is that what bothers you?

CHRIS: [*with an edge of sarcasm*]: It bothers me.

KELLER: If you can't get used to it, then throw it away. You hear me? Take every cent and give it to charity, throw it in the sewer. Does that settle it? In the sewer, that's all. You think I'm kidding? I'm tellin' you what to do, if it's dirty then burn it. It's your money, that's not my money. I'm a dead man, I'm an old dead man, nothing's mine. Well, talk to me! What do you want to do!

CHRIS: It's not what I want to do. It's what you want to do.

KELLER: What should I want to do? [CHRIS *is silent*.] Jail? You want me to go to jail? If you want me to go, say so! Is that where I belong? Then tell me so! [*Slight pause*.] What's the matter, why can't you tell me? [*Furiously*] You say everything else to me, say that! [*Slight pause*.] I'll tell you why you can't say it. Because you know I don't belong there. Because you know! [*With growing emphasis and passion, and a persistent tone of desperation*] Who worked for nothin' in that war? When they work for nothin', I'll work for nothin'. Did they ship a gun or a truck outa Detroit before they got their price? Is that clean? It's dollars and cents, nickels and dimes; war and peace, it's nickles and dimes, what's clean? Half the goddam country is gotta go if I go! That's why you can't tell me.

CHRIS: That's exactly why.

KELLER: Then . . . why am *I* bad?

CHRIS: *I* know you're no worse than most men but I thought you were better. I never saw you as a man. I saw you as my father. [*Almost breaking*] I can't look at you this way, I can't look at myself!

[*He turns away, unable to face* KELLER. ANN *goes quickly to* MOTHER, *takes letter from her and starts for* CHRIS. MOTHER *instantly rushes to intercept her.*]

MOTHER: Give me that!

ANN: He's going to read it! [*She thrusts letter into* CHRIS's *hand*.] Larry. He wrote it to me the day he died.

KELLER: Larry!

MOTHER: Chris, it's not for you. [*He starts to read*.] Joe . . . go away . . .

KELLER [*mystified, frightened*]: Why'd she say, Larry, what—?

MOTHER [*desperately pushes him towards alley, glancing at* CHRIS]: Go to the street, Joe, go to the street! [*She comes down beside* KELLER.] Don't, Chris . . . [*Pleading from her whole soul*] Don't tell him.

CHRIS [*quietly*]: Three and one half years . . . talking, talking. Now you tell me what you must do . . . This is how he died, now tell me where you belong.

KELLER [*pleading*]: Chris, a man can't be a Jesus in this world!

CHRIS: I know all about the world. I know the whole crap story. Now listen to this, and tell me what a man's got to be! [*Reads*.] 'My dear Ann: . . .' You listening? He wrote this the day he died. Listen, don't cry . . . Listen! 'My dear Ann: It is impossible to put down the things I feel. But I've got to tell you something. Yesterday they flew in a load of papers from the States and I read about Dad and your father being convicted. I can't express myself. I can't tell you how I feel—I can't bear to live any more. Last night I circled the base for twenty minutes before I could bring myself in. How

160		could he have done that? Every day three or four men never come back and he sits back there doing business . . . I don't know how to tell you what I feel . . . I can't face anybody . . . I'm going out on a mission in a few minutes. They'll probably report me missing. If they do, I want you to know that you mustn't wait for me. I tell you, Ann, if I had him there now
165		I could kill him—' [KELLER *grabs letter from* CHRIS's *hand and reads it. After a long pause*] Now blame the world. Do you understand that letter?
	KELLER	[*speaking almost inaudibly*]: I think I do. Get the car. I'll put on my jacket. [*He turns and starts slowly for the house.* MOTHER *rushes to intercept him.*]
	MOTHER:	Why are you going? You'll sleep, why are you going?
170	KELLER:	I can't sleep here. I'll feel better if I go.
	MOTHER:	You're so foolish. Larry was your son too, wasn't he? You know he'd never tell you to do this.
	KELLER	[*looking at the letter in his hand*]: Then what is this if it isn't telling me? Sure, he was my son. But I think to him they were all my sons. And I guess
175		they were, I guess they were. I'll be right down. [*Exits into house.*]
	MOTHER	[*to* CHRIS, *with determination*]: You're not going to take him!
	CHRIS:	I'm taking him.
	MOTHER:	It's up to you, if you tell him to stay he'll stay. Go and tell him!
	CHRIS:	Nobody could stop him now.
180	MOTHER:	You'll stop him! How long will he live in prison? Are you trying to kill him?
	CHRIS	[*holding out letter*]: I thought you read this!
	MOTHER	[*of Larry, the letter*]: The war is over! Didn't you hear? It's over!
	CHRIS:	Then what was Larry to you? A stone that fell into the water? It's not enough for him to be sorry. Larry didn't kill himself to make you and Dad sorry.
185	MOTHER:	What more can we be!
	CHRIS:	You can be better! Once and for all you can know there's a universe of people outside and you're responsible to it, and unless you know that, you threw away your son because that's why he died.
190		[*A shot is heard in the house. They stand frozen for a brief second.* CHRIS *starts for porch, pauses a step, turns to* ANN. *He goes on into the house and* ANN *runs up driveway.* MOTHER *stands alone, transfixed.*]
	MOTHER	[*softly, almost moaning*]: Joe . . . Joe . . . Joe . . . Joe . . .
		[CHRIS *comes out of the house, down to* MOTHER's *arms.*]
	CHRIS	[*almost crying*]: Mother, I didn't mean to—
195	MOTHER:	Don't dear. Don't take it on yourself. Forget now. Live. [CHRIS *stirs as if to answer.*] Shhh . . . [*She puts his arms down gently and moves towards porch.*] Shhh . . . [*As she reaches porch steps she begins sobbing.*]

CURTAIN

Questions

(a) Trace the role of Mother in the above extract from *All My Sons*.

(b) Discuss the dramatic significance of the letter in the extract.

(c) Imagine you are directing a performance of the play. How would you advise the actors to deliver their lines in the final part of the extract (from "MOTHER [*to* CHRIS, *with determination*]: You're not going to take him!" to the end)? You should base your answer on a detailed exploration of the language of lines 176 to 197.

Section 4—Reading the Media

*N.B. This section of the specimen paper contains only **one question** on each of the five specified media categories. The actual examination paper will contain **two questions** on each category.*

You must answer **one question only** in this section.

Category A—Film

1. *"Genre films allow little scope for innovation."*

   With reference to **at least two** films, from **one** or **more than one** genre, indicate to what extent you agree or disagree that genre inhibits innovation.

Category B—Television

2. *"Modern television drama equals cops, docs or frocks."* [crime, medical or costume]

   Discuss the potential of **one** or **more than one** of the above categories to provide the audience with challenging television drama. You should support your discussion with evidence drawn from **at least two** television dramas.

Category C—Radio

3. Discuss, with detailed reference to **a range** of programmes, how radio responds to the challenge of communicating purely through sound.

Category D—Print journalism

4. With reference to **a range** of examples from **one** or **more than one** newspaper, consider how journalists employ the devices of narrative and representation to create news stories out of real life events.

Category E—Advertising

5. In this question you are provided with **two** advertisements (*Pages thirty and thirty-one*).

   How effectively, in your judgement, do these advertisements convey the message(s) of the advertisers?

   You should support your answer to this question by making detailed reference to:
   - the use of technical codes (camera, lighting, black and white film, composition)
   - the cultural codes which establish the representation of each woman
   - how the written text (caption and copy) contributes to our interpretation of each woman
   - the cultural assumptions—and social expectations—that underlie both written text and image in each advertisement
   - any other features of the advertisements you consider significant.

Such a lot of history behind it and still full of fire.
Now that I call inspiring.
THE KAREN HUGHES DIAMOND.
Karen's diamond has had more birthdays than anyone can count. A geologist would say at least 3 billion. Yet its inner fire burns as brightly as ever. Karen, two of whose birthdays have been described as Big Ones, finds this most encouraging. Phone 0115 919 2240 for a brochure on solitaires from £750. It has been compiled for you by De Beers, the world's experts in diamonds since 1888.
DE BEERS
A DIAMOND IS FOREVER

*As he put it on my finger he just said, 'Forever.'
It takes a diamond solitaire to make a man that romantic.*

THE SARAH WESSON DIAMOND.

Sarah's diamond is a beautiful example of the hardest known substance. Diamond. It has a melting point two and a half times greater than that of steel. Yet, as a diamond solitaire engagement ring, it can melt the heart of a man who has just spent a little over a month's salary. Phone 0115 919 2240 for a brochure on solitaires from £750. It has been compiled for you by De Beers, the world's experts in diamonds since 1888.

DE BEERS
A DIAMOND IS FOREVER

[END OF QUESTION PAPER]

[BLANK PAGE]

ADVANCED HIGHER
2008

[BLANK PAGE]

X115/701

NATIONAL
QUALIFICATIONS
2008

THURSDAY, 15 MAY
1.00 PM – 4.00 PM

ENGLISH
ADVANCED HIGHER

There are four sections in this paper.

Section 1—Literary Study	pages	2 – 6
Section 2—Language Study	pages	7 – 12
Section 3—Textual Analysis	pages	13 – 33
Section 4—Reading the Media	pages	34 – 35 (plus Insert)

Depending on the options you have chosen, you must answer **one** or **two** questions.

If you have submitted a Creative Writing folio, you must answer only **one** question.

Otherwise, you must answer **two** questions.

If you are required to answer only **one question**

- it must be taken from **Section 1—Literary Study**
- you must leave the examination room **after 1 hour 30 minutes**.

If you are required to answer **two questions**

- your first must be taken from **Section 1—Literary Study**
- your second must be taken from **a different section**
- each answer must be written in **a separate answer booklet**
- the maximum time allowed for any question is **1 hour 30 minutes**.

You must identify each question you attempt by indicating clearly

- **the title of the section** from which the question has been taken
- **the number of the question** within that section.

You must also write inside the front cover of your Literary Study answer booklet

- **the topic** of your Specialist Study (Dissertation)
- **the texts** used in your Specialist Study (Dissertation).

Section 1—Literary Study

This section is **mandatory** for all candidates.

You must answer **one question only** in this section.

DRAMA

1. **Beckett**

   "In a Beckett play, the audience is often tricked into laughter at situations which are bleak, anguished, desperate."

   Keeping this statement in mind, discuss the uses Beckett makes of humour in *Waiting for Godot* **and** in *Endgame*.

2. **Byrne**

   "While the three plays exist as compelling works in their own right, **The Slab Boys Trilogy** is best appreciated as a dramatic whole."

   How far do you agree?

3. **Chekhov**

   Discuss the dramatic means by which Chekhov gives significance to the effects of change in *The Cherry Orchard* **and** in *Uncle Vanya*.

4. **Friel**

   How effectively in *Translations* **and** in *Dancing at Lughnasa* does Friel dramatise the impact on the individual of large-scale social change?

5. **Lindsay**

   According to one critic, "*Lindsay's great play has endured the passage of time not for the strength of its themes or the universal appeal of its subject matter but for its grand theatrical effect.*"

   Why, in your view, has *Ane Satyre of the Thrie Estaitis* endured the passage of time?

6. **Lochhead**

   Make a detailed study of the nature and function of characterisation in *Mary Queen of Scots Got Her Head Chopped Off*.

7. **Pinter**

   Discuss the means by which an atmosphere of menace is created in *The Homecoming*, *One for the Road* and *Mountain Language*.

8. **Shakespeare**

   EITHER

   (a) **Othello and Antony and Cleopatra**

   "In these plays, what finally gives the protagonists tragic stature is their power to transcend—even in defeat—the forces ranged against them."

   How far, in your view, does this assertion apply to *Othello* **or** to *Antony and Cleopatra* **or** to both plays?

   OR

   (b) **The Winter's Tale and The Tempest**

   Make a detailed study of Shakespeare's treatment of reconciliation and forgiveness in *The Winter's Tale* **or** in *The Tempest* **or** in both plays.

9. **Stoppard**

   EITHER

   (a) Make a detailed study of the uses Stoppard makes of *Hamlet* in *Rosencrantz and Guildenstern are Dead*.

   OR

   (b) Make a detailed study of the dramatic effects created by Stoppard's juxtaposition of different historical periods in *Arcadia*.

10. **Wilde**

    With close reference to *The Importance of Being Earnest* **and** to **one** of the other specified plays, discuss the principal dramatic means by which Wilde explores some of the serious issues and conflicts that existed within Victorian society.

11. **Williams**

    "For Williams, Time is the enemy: things go; things fade; things end. And yet, in the face of these certainties, there emerges a sense of nobility in his characters."

    Discuss *A Streetcar Named Desire* **and** *Sweet Bird of Youth* in the light of this statement.

POETRY

12. **Burns**

    EITHER

    (a) Discuss the techniques of satire employed by Burns in *The Twa Dogs* **and** in *The Holy Fair*.

    OR

    (b) "Whether a love song or a political song or a melancholy song, what marks it out is Burns's mastery of tone and idiom to express deep feeling."

    Discuss a range of Burns's songs in the light of this statement.

13. Chaucer

Discuss the principal means by which, in the General Prologue **and** in **either** or **both** of the specified Tales, Chaucer exposes the *"sinne of Pryde"*.

14. Donne

"Donne's love poetry reveals an obsession with the darker aspects of love—its dissatisfactions, resentments and pains."

Discuss Donne's treatment of "the darker aspects of love" in **three** or **four** poems.

15. Duffy

Make a study of **three** or **four** poems in which Duffy makes use of dramatised voices—in monologue and/or in dialogue. In your study, you should examine the poetic techniques Duffy uses to create these voices and consider the effects achieved.

16. Heaney

Referring to the outbreak of sectarian violence in 1969 that led to The Troubles, Heaney wrote: *". . . from that moment the problems of poetry moved . . . to being a search for images and symbols adequate to our predicament."*

(*Feelings into Words*, 1974)

How successful, in your view, was Heaney in finding images and symbols to convey the effects of The Troubles on society and on the individual?

17. Henryson

EITHER

(a) Analyse the means by which Henryson explores Cresseid's spiritual and psychological development following her abandonment by Diomede.

OR

(b) *"Henryson is a master of the beast-fable: his mastery is based on the relationship he creates between the world of beasts and the world of men."*

Discuss the means by which, in **two** or **three** of the *Morall Fabillis*, Henryson creates a relationship between *"the world of beasts"* and *"the world of men"*.

18. Keats

*"Far from being merely an amiable parody of a medieval court romance, **The Eve of St Agnes** is a complex exploration of the relationship between poetic vision and real life."*

How far do you agree?

19. **MacDiarmid**

    EITHER

    (a) Discuss MacDiarmid's use of the symbol of the thistle in *A Drunk Man Looks at the Thistle*.

    OR

    (b) "MacDiarmid's early poems constitute perfectly crafted examples of the capacity of the short lyric to address themes of profound significance."

    Discuss with reference to **three** or **four** of MacDiarmid's early lyrics.

20. **Muir**

    Discuss the uses Muir makes of elements of religion in **three** or **four** poems.

21. **Plath**

    Discuss the uses Plath makes of aspects of the natural world in **three** or **four** poems.

22. **Yeats**

    Make a detailed study of *The Stolen Child*, *The Host of the Air* and *The Song of Wandering Aengus* in which you identify those aspects of theme and technique that characterise Yeats's early poetry.

PROSE FICTION

23. **Atwood**

    Discuss Atwood's use of narrative voice in *Cat's Eye* **and** in *Alias Grace*.

24. **Austen**

    "A key aspect of Austen's narrative technique is her use of contrast—in characters, in situations, in setting."

    Discuss with reference to *Pride and Prejudice* **and** to *Persuasion*.

25. **Dickens**

    Discuss Dickens's treatment of issues of social class in *Hard Times* **or** in *Great Expectations* **or** in both novels.

26. **Fitzgerald**

    "In Fitzgerald's depiction of marriage, failure and waste are given a tragic grandeur of their own."

    Keeping this statement in mind, make a detailed study of Fitzgerald's depiction of the relationship between Anthony and Gloria in *The Beautiful and Damned* **and** of the relationship between Dick and Nicole in *Tender is the Night*.

27. Galloway

Analyse and evaluate Galloway's treatment of gender issues in *The Trick is to Keep Breathing* **and** in *Foreign Parts*.

28. Gray

Discuss the function of the dual narrative in *Lanark*.

29. Hardy

EITHER

(*a*) Discuss the significance of Egdon Heath in *The Return of the Native*.

OR

(*b*) Blackmoor Vale . . . Talbothays . . . Flintcomb-Ash . . . Stonehenge.

Discuss the uses Hardy makes of these settings in *Tess of the D'Urbervilles*.

30. Hogg

Discuss Hogg's treatment of moral issues in *The Private Memoirs and Confessions of a Justified Sinner* **and** in **one** or **more than one** of the other specified texts.

31. Joyce

Discuss the fictional means by which Joyce explores the individual's response to the condition of Ireland in *A Portrait of the Artist as a Young Man* **and** in any **two** of the stories in *Dubliners*.

32. Stevenson

Discuss Stevenson's portrayal of evil in *The Master of Ballantrae* **and** in **one** or **two** of the specified short stories.

33. Waugh

Discuss the importance of religion in *A Handful of Dust* **and** in *Brideshead Revisited*.

PROSE NON-FICTION

34. How successful, in your view, are any **two** of the specified texts in their reconstruction of childhood experience?

35. How effectively do any **two** of the specified texts convey a sense of the distinctive identity of Scotland **or** of a part (or parts) of Scotland?

Section 2—Language Study

You must answer **one question only** in this section.

Topic A—Varieties of English or Scots

1. Describe and account for some of the principal features of the English **or** Scots used in a particular geographical area.

2. From your research, discuss how the use of a particular variety of English **or** Scots contributes to the creation of a distinct regional and/or cultural identity.

Topic B—The historical development of English or Scots

3. Which language do you consider to have had the greatest influence on the historical development of English **or** Scots? Give reasons for your decision.

4. Discuss some of the ways in which English **or** Scots words have changed over time. You may wish to consider some or all of the following:

   - changes in meaning
   - changes in word-formation patterns
   - the effects of borrowing from other languages
   - the effects of standardisation.

Topic C—Multilingualism in contemporary Scotland

5. In what ways can minority languages in Scotland be protected and encouraged?

6. What issues about multilingualism in contemporary Scotland are raised in the following extract from the novel *Bhudda Da* by Anne Donovan?

Ah started tae edge oot towards the door. Ah kind of wanted tae say ah was sorry too but didnae want tae interrupt. Then he started speakin even lower, in a language ah didnae understaund but mixed up wi English words and Nisha was answerin him in the same way. Ah stood just outside the room till Nisha came oot and shut the door behind her. She never said a word, just made a face, crossin her eyes and stickin her tongue oot at me. Ah managed tae haud in the laughter till we went through tae Nisha's room, then the two of us collapsed on the bed, gigglin.

"Ah don't believe it—he's never home at this time. Just ma luck."

"Was he really mad? What were yous sayin? Do yous speak Punjabi in the hoose then?"

"No really. When ma da was alive we used tae – he wanted us to speak the mother tongue – but Kamaljit and me just speak English maist of the time. Even my ma doesnae really speak it tae us a lot. But Gurpreet likes tae mix it in, especially when he's DJin. Thinks it makes him a bit different fae the others."

Nisha looked oot the windae. "It's rainin. Chuckin it doon. Don't want tae go oot in that."

"Naw."

"Fancy watchin a video?"

Topic D—The use of Scots in contemporary literature

For both questions on this topic, you are provided with three poems written in Scots: *SOS SOS* by Sheena Blackhall, *A Manifesto for MSPs* by James Robertson and *"The Corrie" Sailin* by John Law.

Read the poems carefully and then answer **either** Question 7 **or** Question 8.

7. Make a detailed study of the ways in which Scots is used in any **two** or in all **three** of the poems.

    In your study, you should consider features such as vocabulary, grammar, orthography, implied pronunciation.

8. Compare the use of Scots in any **one** of the poems provided with the use of Scots in the work of **one** other writer you have studied.

SOS SOS

SOS SOS I am a phone box in distress!
Jeannie Murphy's quine wis greetin,
Said she catched her boyfreen cheatin.
Big Joe Christie's giro's tint,
Phoned the Broo tae say he's skint.
Auld Ma Sangster's neebor telt her
Vandals smashed the new bus shelter.
Jocky Todd is stottin fu,
Baxter's laddie's sniffin glue.

SOS SOS I am a phone box in distress!
If the news I gie is bad,
Ten tae wan the fowk get mad,
And they catch me by the lug,
Gie ma wires and heid a rug.
Tak me Lord, frae cooncil scheme
Tae be a phone box on the meen!

A Manifesto for MSPs

Dinna be glaikit, dinna be ower smert,
dinna craw croose, dinna be unco blate,
dinna breenge in, dinna be ayewis late,
dinna steek yer lugs, dinna steek yer hert.
Dinna be sleekit, dinna be a sook,
dinna creesh nae loof for future favour,
dinna swick nor swither, hash nor haiver,
dinna be soor o face, and dinna jouk.
Open yer airms and minds tae folk in need,
hain frae fylin and skaith the land and sea,
tak tent o justice and the commonweal,
ding doon hypocrisy, wanthrift and greed,
heeze up the banner o humanity,
seek oot the truth and tae the truth be leal.

"The Corrie" Sailin
(Owreset frae Siubhal a' Choire, bi George Campbell Hay)

Up an awa oot wi us on the green sea machairs liftit
an we pit past dour Garvel o the gurlin storms –
lowps on us syne a sair blast wast bi sooth, an hard rain.
Up wi her heid, prow fornent cauld wave-heids
stoondin an stunnin, a slim dark lassie,
up wi her sang an surgin forrit.

She streikit her lee sheet ticht as steel
she streikit her hainch til the thies o the brekkers
she streikit her gait til the gait o the ocean
she gaed dunt wi her gunnel gin yaw
an dunt wi the seam of her shouther gaed she
an ryvit the wave wi her beak at the pitch.

Come Eilean Aoidh she raired oot joyfu
Ardlamont haerd her prood bellin
bi Inchmarnock she crooned a douce air.
Oorsels wappit in her smeik – smoorit-nane –
that stang in oor een frae the ram-stam o her
in a spelder o speindrift an saut spray
an nocht cuid we hear but the pulse o her pechin.

Topic E—Language and social context

9. Why is knowledge of the social context of language use important for our understanding of linguistic variation?

10. Using evidence from your own reading and research, illustrate some of the ways in which studies of language and social context reveal people's attitudes towards language variation.

[Turn over

Topic F—The linguistic characteristics of informal conversation

11. Discuss some of the functions of interruptions in informal conversation.

12. For this question, you are provided with an extract from a transcript of an informal conversation between three adolescent males, Andrew, Adrian and Mashuk, and two anonymous females, Anon F and Anon F2, who are discussing some homework they have to do.

Read the extract carefully and then answer the question that follows it.

Transcription Key:

The lines have been numbered individually.

[	overlapping turns
(.)	pause of less than one second
( )	speech inaudible
(text)	speech hard to discern: the analyst's guess is provided as text, as in (ished) in line 9

Extract

```
1   Anon F:    what lesson have we got last
2   Andrew:    ma  ⌈ths
3   Adrian:        ⌊we got maths
4   Anon F:    oh cor
5   Andrew:    the assignment
6   Anon F:    I know but um- I haven't finished my- task one yet
7   Andrew:    ain't you
8   Anon F:    no
9   Andrew:    I ain't fin(ished) my task four
10  Anon F:    I ain't (started on) task one and ( ) two  (I
11             haven't finished) task three and I havent done task
12             four
13  Mashuk:    ain't you done none of the tasks
14  Anon F:    no ⌈ no we've got 'em but I ain't done 'em
15  Adrian:       ⌊ I've done all of 'em I've done all of 'em
16             ⌈ I'm on task six
17  Mashuk:    ⌊ have you got 'em in rough
18  Anon F:    yeh- no (.) I ain't done anything
19  Anon F2:   I've done it in rough
20  Mashuk:    when does it have to be in by this-
21             ⌈ this Monday init
22  Anon F2:   ⌊ Monday
```

(Source: Rampton, Ben (1995) *Crossing: language and ethnicity among adolescents.* London: Longman. Pages 210–211.)

To what extent do you consider the linguistic characteristics of this exchange to be typical of informal conversation?

Topic G—The linguistic characteristics of political communication

13. Below is a transcript of part of President George W. Bush's State of the Union address to the American Congress in 2002. For ease of reference, the paragraphs have been numbered.

    Make a detailed analysis of the linguistic characteristics of political communication evident in this speech. In your analysis, you should examine as many of the following as you consider appropriate:

    - the degree of formality
    - the choice of vocabulary
    - grammatical complexity
    - the use of figurative language.

[1] Our nation will continue to be steadfast, and patient, and persistent, in the pursuit of two great objectives. First, we will shut down terrorist camps, disrupt terrorist plans and bring terrorists to justice. And second, we must prevent the terrorists and regimes who seek chemical, biological or nuclear weapons from threatening the United States and the world.

[2] Our military has put the terror training camps of Afghanistan out of business, yet camps still exist in at least a dozen countries. A terrorist underworld – including groups like Hamas, Hezbollah, Islamic Jihad and Jaish-i-Mohammed – operates in remote jungles and deserts, and hides in the centres of large cities.

[3] While the most visible military action is in Afghanistan, America is acting elsewhere. We now have troops in the Philippines helping to train that country's armed forces to go after terrorist cells that have executed an American and still hold hostages. Our soldiers, working with the Bosnian government, seized terrorists who were plotting to bomb our embassy. Our Navy is patrolling the coast of Africa to block the shipment of weapons and the establishment of terrorist camps in Somalia. My hope is that all nations will heed our call and eliminate the terrorist parasites who threaten their countries and our own.

[4] Many nations are acting forcefully. Pakistan is now cracking down on terror, and I admire the strong leadership of President Musharraf. But some governments will be timid in the face of terror. And make no mistake about it: if they do not act, America will.

[5] Our second goal is to prevent regimes that sponsor terror from threatening America or our friends and allies with weapons of mass destruction. Some of these regimes have been pretty quiet since September 11, but we know their true nature. North Korea is a regime arming with missiles and weapons of mass destruction, while starving its citizens. Iran aggressively pursues these weapons and exports terror, while an unelected few repress the Iranian people's hope for freedom. Iraq continues to flaunt its hostility toward America and to support terror. The Iraqi regime has plotted to develop anthrax and nerve gas and nuclear weapons for over a decade. This is a regime that has already used poison gas to murder thousands of its own citizens, leaving the bodies of mothers huddled over their dead children. This is a regime that agreed to international inspections then kicked out the inspectors. This is a regime that has something to hide from the civilized world.

[6] States like these, and their terrorist allies, constitute an axis of evil, arming to threaten the peace of the world. By seeking weapons of mass destruction, these regimes pose a grave and growing danger. They could provide these arms to terrorists, giving them the means to match their hatred. They could attack our allies or attempt to blackmail the United States. In any of these cases, the price of indifference would be catastrophic.

14. David Crystal has suggested that political debate is conducted in "a style of language which is at times opaque, inspecific, or empty". Does your own reading and research suggest that this is true of political communication generally?

Justify your answer.

Section 3—Textual Analysis

You must answer **one question only** in this section.

1. **Prose fiction [*Pages thirteen to nineteen*]**

   Read carefully the short story **Soldier's Home** *(1939) by Ernest Hemingway and then answer the question that follows it (Page nineteen).*

   KREBS went to the war from a Methodist college in Kansas. There is a picture which shows him among his fraternity brothers, all of them wearing exactly the same height and style collar. He enlisted in the Marines in 1917 and did not return to the United States until the second division returned from the Rhine in the summer of 1919.

   There is a picture which shows him on the Rhine with two German girls and another corporal. Krebs and the corporal look too big for their uniforms. The German girls are not beautiful. The Rhine does not show in the picture.

   By the time Krebs returned to his home town in Oklahoma the greeting of heroes was over. He came back much too late. The men from the town who had been drafted had all been welcomed elaborately on their return. There had been a great deal of hysteria. Now the reaction had set in. People seemed to think it was rather ridiculous for Krebs to be getting back so late, years after the war was over.

   At first Krebs, who had been at Belleau Wood, Soissons, the Champagne, St Mihiel, and in the Argonne, did not want to talk about the war at all. Later he felt the need to talk but no one wanted to hear about it. His town had heard too many atrocity stories to be thrilled by actualities. Krebs found that to be listened to at all he had to lie, and after he had done this twice he, too, had a reaction against the war and against talking about it. A distaste for everything that had happened to him in the war set in because of the lies he had told. All of the times that had been able to make him feel cool and clear inside himself when he thought of them; the times so long back when he had done the one thing, the only thing for a man to do, easily and naturally, when he might have done something else, now lost their cool, valuable quality and then were lost themselves.

   His lies were quite unimportant lies and consisted in attributing to himself things other men had seen, done, or heard of, and stating as facts certain apocryphal incidents familiar to all soldiers. Even his lies were not sensational at the pool-room. His acquaintances who had heard detailed accounts of German women found chained to machine guns in the Argonne forest and who could not comprehend, or were barred by their patriotism from interest in, any German machine-gunners who were not chained, were not thrilled by his stories.

   Krebs acquired the nausea in regard to experience that is the result of untruth or exaggeration, and when he occasionally met another man who had really been a soldier and they talked a few minutes in the dressing-room at a dance he fell into the easy pose of the old soldier among other soldiers: that he had been badly, sickeningly frightened all the time. In this way he lost everything.

   [Turn over

During this time, it was late summer, he was sleeping late in bed, getting up to walk down town to the library to get a book, eating lunch at home, reading on the front porch until he became bored, and then walking down through the town to spend the hottest hours of the day in the cool dark of the pool-room. He loved to play pool.

In the evening he practised on his clarinet, strolled down town, read, and went to bed. He was still a hero to his two young sisters. His mother would have given him breakfast in bed if he had wanted it. She often came in when he was in bed and asked him to tell her about the war, but her attention always wandered. His father was non-committal.

Before Krebs went away to the war he had never been allowed to drive the family motor-car. His father was in the real-estate business and always wanted the car to be at his command when he required it to take clients out into the country to show them a piece of farm property. The car always stood outside the First National Bank building where his father had an office on the second floor. Now, after the war, it was still the same car.

Nothing was changed in the town except that the young girls had grown up. But they lived in such a complicated world of already defined alliances and shifting feuds that Krebs did not feel the energy or the courage to break into it. He liked to look at them, though. There were so many good-looking young girls. Most of them had their hair cut short. When he went away only little girls wore their hair like that or girls that were fast. They all wore sweaters and shirt waists with round Dutch collars. It was a pattern. He liked to look at them from the front porch as they walked on the other side of the street. He liked to watch them walking under the shade of the trees. He liked the round Dutch collars above their sweaters. He liked their silk stockings and flat shoes. He liked their bobbed hair and the way they walked.

When he was in town their appeal to him was not very strong. He did not like them when he saw them in the Greek's ice-cream parlour. He did not want them themselves really. They were too complicated. There was something else. Vaguely he wanted a girl but he did not want to have to work to get her. He would have liked to have a girl but he did not want to have to spend a long time getting her. He did not want to get into the intrigue and the politics. He did not want to have to do any courting. He did not want to tell any more lies. It wasn't worth it.

He did not want any consequences. He did not want any consequences ever again. He wanted to live along without consequences. Besides he did not really need a girl. The army had taught him that. It was all right to pose as though you had to have a girl. Nearly everybody did that. But it wasn't true. You did not need a girl. That was the funny thing. First a fellow boasted how girls meant nothing to him, then a fellow boasted that he could not get along without girls, that he had to have them all the time, that he could not go to sleep without them.

That was all a lie. It was all a lie both ways. You did not need a girl unless you thought about them. He learned that in the army. Then sooner or later you always got one. When you were really ripe for a girl you always got one. You did not have to think about it. Sooner or later it would come. He had learned that in the army.

80　　　Now he would have liked a girl if she had come to him and not wanted to talk. But here at home it was all too complicated. He knew he could never get through it all again. It was not worth the trouble. That was the thing about French girls and German girls. There was not all this talking. You couldn't talk much and you did not need to talk. It was simple and you were friends. He thought about France and then
85　he began to think about Germany. On the whole he had liked Germany better. He did not want to leave Germany. He did not want to come home. Still, he had come home. He sat on the front porch.

　　　He liked the girls that were walking along the other side of the street. He liked the look of them much better than the French girls or the German girls. But the world
90　they were in was not the world he was in. He would like to have one of them. But it was not worth it. They were such a nice pattern. He liked the pattern. It was exciting. But he would not go through all the talking. He did not want one badly enough. He liked to look at them all, though. It was not worth it. Not now when things were getting good again.

95　　　He sat there on the porch reading a book on the war. It was a history and he was reading about all the engagements he had been in. It was the most interesting reading he had ever done. He wished there were more maps. He looked forward with a good feeling to reading all the really good histories when they would come out with good detail maps. Now he was really learning about the war. He had been a good soldier.
100　That made a difference.

　　　One morning after he had been home about a month his mother came into his bedroom and sat on the bed. She smoothed her apron.

　　　"I had a talk with your father last night, Harold," she said, "and he is willing for you to take the car out in the evenings."

105　　　"Yeah?" said Krebs, who was not fully awake. "Take the car out? Yeah?"

　　　"Yes. Your father has felt for some time that you should be able to take the car out in the evenings whenever you wished, but we only talked it over last night."

　　　"I'll bet you made him," Krebs said.

　　　"No. It was your father's suggestion that we talk the matter over."

110　　　"Yeah. I'll bet you made him," Krebs sat up in bed.

　　　"Will you come down to breakfast, Harold?" his mother said.

　　　"As soon as I get my clothes on," Krebs said.

　　　His mother went out of the room and he could hear her frying something downstairs while he washed, shaved, and dressed to go down into the dining-room for
115　breakfast. While he was eating breakfast his sister brought in the mail.

　　　"Well, Hare," she said. "You old sleepy-head. What do you ever get up for?"

　　　Krebs looked at her. He liked her. She was his best sister.

"Have you got the paper?" he asked.

She handed him the *Kansas City Star* and he shucked off its brown wrapper and opened it to the sporting page. He folded the *Star* open and propped it against the water pitcher with his cereal dish to steady it, so he could read while he ate.

"Harold," his mother stood in the kitchen doorway, "Harold, please don't muss up the paper. Your father can't read his *Star* if it's been mussed."

"I won't muss it," Krebs said.

His sister sat down at the table and watched him while he read.

"We're playing indoor over at school this afternoon," she said. "I'm going to pitch."

"Good," said Krebs. "How's the old wing?"

"I can pitch better than lots of the boys. I tell them all you taught me. The other girls aren't much good."

"Yeah?" said Krebs.

"I tell them all you're my beau. Aren't you my beau, Hare?"

"You bet."

"Couldn't your brother really be your beau just because he's your brother?"

"I don't know."

"Sure you know. Couldn't you be my beau, Hare, if I was old enough and if you wanted to?"

"Sure. You're my girl now."

"Am I really your girl?"

"Sure."

"Do you love me?"

"Uh, huh."

"Will you love me always?"

"Sure."

"Will you come and watch me play indoor?"

"Maybe."

"Aw, Hare, you don't love me. If you loved me, you'd want to come over and watch me play indoor."

Krebs's mother came into the dining-room from the kitchen. She carried a plate of
two fried eggs and some crisp bacon on it and a plate of buckwheat cakes.

"You run along, Helen," she said. "I want to talk to Harold."

She put the eggs and bacon down in front of him and brought in a jug of maple syrup for the buckwheat cakes. Then she sat down across the table from Krebs.

"I wish you'd put down the paper a minute, Harold," she said.

Krebs took down the paper and folded it.

"Have you decided what you are going to do yet, Harold?" his mother said, taking off her glasses.

"No," said Krebs.

"Don't you think it's about time?" His mother did not say this in a mean way. She seemed worried.

"I hadn't thought about it," Krebs said.

"God has some work for everyone to do," his mother said. "There can be no idle hands in His Kingdom."

"I'm not in His Kingdom," Krebs said.

"We are all of us in His Kingdom."

Krebs felt embarrassed and resentful as always.

"I've worried about you so much, Harold," his mother went on. "I know the temptations you must have been exposed to. I know how weak men are. I know what your own dear grandfather, my own father, told us about the Civil War, and I have prayed for you. I pray for you all day long, Harold."

Krebs looked at the bacon fat hardening on his plate.

"Your father is worried, too," his mother went on. "He thinks you have lost your ambition, that you haven't got a definite aim in life. Charley Simmons, who is just your age, has a good job and is going to be married. The boys are all settling down; they're all determined to get somewhere; you can see that boys like Charley Simmons are on their way to being really a credit to the community."

Krebs said nothing.

"Don't look that way, Harold," his mother said. "You know we love you and I want to tell you for your own good how matters stand. Your father does not want to hamper your freedom. He thinks you should be allowed to drive the car. If you want to take some of the nice girls out riding with you, we are only too pleased. We want you to enjoy yourself. But you are going to have to settle down to work, Harold. Your father doesn't care what you start in at. All work is honourable as he says. But you've got to make a start at something. He asked me to speak to you this morning and then you can stop in and see him at his office."

"Is that all?" Krebs said.

"Yes. Don't you love your mother, dear boy?"

"No," Krebs said.

His mother looked at him across the table. Her eyes were shiny. She started crying.

190 "I don't love anybody," Krebs said.

It wasn't any good. He couldn't tell her, he couldn't make her see it. It was silly to have said it. He had only hurt her. He went over and took hold of her arm. She was crying with her head in her hands.

"I didn't mean it," he said. "I was just angry at something. I didn't mean I didn't 195 love you."

His mother went on crying. Krebs put his arm on her shoulder.

"Can't you believe me, mother?"

His mother shook her head.

"Please, please, mother. Please believe me."

200 "All right," his mother said chokily. She looked up at him. "I believe you, Harold."

Krebs kissed her hair. She put her face up to him.

"I'm your mother," she said. "I held you next to my heart when you were a tiny baby."

Krebs felt sick and vaguely nauseated.

205 "I know, Mummy," he said. "I'll try to be a good boy for you."

"Would you kneel and pray with me, Harold?" his mother asked.

They knelt down beside the dining-room table and Krebs's mother prayed.

"Now, you pray, Harold," she said.

"I can't," Krebs said.

210 "Try, Harold."

"I can't."

"Do you want me to pray for you?"

"Yes."

So his mother prayed for him and then they stood up and Krebs kissed his mother
and went out of the house. He had tried so to keep his life from being complicated.
Still, none of it had touched him. He had felt sorry for his mother and she had made
him lie. He would go to Kansas City and get a job and she would feel all right about it.
There would be one more scene maybe before he went away. He would not go down to
his father's office. He would miss that one. He wanted his life to go smoothly. It had
just gotten going that way. Well, that was all over now, anyway. He would go over to
the schoolyard and watch Helen play indoor baseball.

Question

In what ways in this short story does Hemingway explore the state of mind of the soldier returned from war?

2. **Prose non-fiction [*Pages nineteen to twenty-three*]**

   *Read carefully **The Old Silk Route** (1989) by Colin Thubron and then answer the question that follows it (Page twenty-three).*

   The trees were neither living nor dead: a Grimm forest of willows convulsed by vanished winds. Their roots sank so deep that they found moisture which never reached the surface, but the thinning sap had desiccated their leaves, and their bark had loosened and split. Behind them a grey piedmont gravel, pushed down from the Tianshan snows, was smeared across hundreds of square miles of sand. In front, the true desert began.

   Our spirits rose, as if the weight of eastern China, which lay far behind us, was suddenly lifted. For a moment, I think, my companions too wanted to be alone. As for me, solitude seemed the natural condition of travel. Alone, I was at once more vulnerable and more sensitized, and even China appeared no longer precisely a strange land. I was just a stranger in it, my identity thinned. And this solitude carried an inner excitement, which has been perfectly distinct to me since childhood.

   But now the company of my own people—a television camera team—filled me with misgiving. In a film, the lone traveller's windfalls—the chance intimacies and impulses—are gone. Solitude can only be recreated. Yet our film aimed to record the Chinese Silk Road through my eyes, and I nursed a fantasy that our journey would somehow bifurcate. I would experience it, and they would shoot it. The two processes could be decently separated, just as the writing of a travel book is separate from the journey it records.

   Such a daydream must have belonged to a time of innocence twenty-five years before, when I made freelance documentaries alone, wandering about Morocco and Japan with a cine-camera and a tape-recorder slung over my back. The films' ideas, script, shooting had all been mine, and their technical naivety had been balanced, I suppose, by some raw freshness.

   But now I was only the visual tip of a corporate iceberg. Behind me trudged a two-man camera crew, a sound-recordist, the director, his assistant, a Mandarin interpreter, a Turkic interpreter, two camel-drivers and seven camels loaded with cameras, tripods and stock-boxes.

Yet for the screen we were fabricating solitude.

30 We journeyed in the unnatural silence of huge beasts treading in softness. The wind had dropped to nothing. The camels' hooves left dim circles in the powdery earth. Once or twice we crossed the tracks of intermittent rivers, now dry. Their starved reeds splintered at our touch; our feet crunched through their beds. Then the forest gave way to stunted red willows until even these had reverted to dust—ancient-
35 looking mounds of roots and crumbled wood littered over the sand.

If I had charted the most landlocked spot on earth, the arms of my compass would have intersected here, in China's far north-west. Its heart is a howling wilderness, 600 miles wide, where the winds have buried and mummified whole caravans. The native Uighurs call it Taklimakan, "You enter and you never return." Aurel Stein thought
40 Arabia tame by comparison. Sven Hedin called it the world's most dangerous desert. Its dunes rise to 300 feet, and in sudden temperature changes the moving sands make hallucinatory noises, as if caravans or troupes of musicians were passing nearby. So at night, wrote Marco Polo, "the stray traveller will hear as it were the tramp and hum of a great cavalcade of people away from the real line of march, and taking this to be their
45 own company they will follow the sound; and when day breaks they find that a cheat has been put on them and that they are in an ill plight. Even in daytime one hears those spirits talking . . ."

But I could hear nobody talking, except my own countrymen—shared gossip, jokes, assumptions. We sheltered in our own culture. We plodded across the sand in
50 disparate groups, complaining about Chinese bureaucracy and the cameleers. Nobody else seemed to be missing a lonely fraternization with the land. Perhaps, I thought, the habit of living alone had paradoxically exacerbated my awareness of people: until their presence obliterated everything else. But it seemed now that this companionship enfolded us all in a balloon of Britishness: amiable, safe, uncreative.

55 We intruded on the desert like a regiment. Only in the lens were some of us—three select camels, my guide and I—effortlessly, romantically isolated. We five moved in the borrowed glory of Lawrence and Doughty. Even my guide, in his flat cap and loose trousers, was touched by a shambling glamour. As we went, the horizon was closed by shallow hills stubbled with tamarisk, and in front of us range upon range of stark
60 dunes came beating in out of emptiness. The land was simplifying itself, shedding its stones first, then its trees, then its shrubs. Horses were useless in this terrain—their hooves burned in the sand—and donkeys slowly weakened. Only the twin-humped Bactrian camel, which can go waterless for two weeks, travelled the wastes at all. Its long, slender legs lift its body as if on stilts above the surface heat, and its spatular feet
65 dissipate the impact of its tread. It only starts to sweat—mildly—in a temperature at which a man would be dead.

I watch these three sauntering in train behind us. They carried plastic water-containers, bedding, tent-poles, food-boxes. (They carried film equipment too, but it was concealed under a native rug.) They were like emissaries of the desert's
70 strangeness. Their rhythmic swaying echoed the surge of its dunes. Shaggy fringes dribbled down the underside of their necks like inverted manes, and each head rose to a punkish tuft far back on the forehead, above long-lashed eyes and vain lips. They shared an air of randy contempt.

Before us the desert wrinkled to the horizon in a tumult of ghostly curves. The deepening silence, the intensifying heat, the ever-purer slopes, suggested that we were approaching some presence—or primal absence—in the wastes. Was this, the viewer might have wondered, a paradigm of the ultimate journey, the paring away of everything essential, little by little, as we advanced into the heart of Nothing?

But no. We were conscious mainly of mild boredom and an unheroic thirst (we had plenty of water). Our glamour rested only in the eyes of others. It is uncertain if we were really journeying at all. We were creating the likeness of a journey.

In fact, we were undergoing not one voyage, but two. The first of these was real but stayed unfilmed—the director's battle for transport and locations, the crew's struggling with light and angles; whereas the second—the imaginary journey which it produced—was a celluloid narrative of premeditated images, the voyage whose destination was always known (since everything had to be prepared in advance), fostered in an illusion of naturalness by camera-shots repeated over and over. This was the ghost-journey, in which I was an actor. It was produced only for the screen.

So I became nostalgic for writing. A travel-book is an account: it records the real. A travel-film is an illusion: it reconstructs it. And the confusion of this harassed both the director and me. He was an austerely sensitive man, who instinctively wanted to mould the film to a travel-writer's energies. But travelling like this, I could only imagine those energies. I could not feel them. So while he tried to envisage our journey through the eyes of a writer, I perversely began to see it through the lens of a film director.

But this was obscured by more brutal confusions. We were at the mercy of four Uighurs, local Turkomen more volatile than the native Chinese, who dwindle to a minority in this far north-west. The Uighur had once made the Silk Road work: opportunists trading between the static hierarchies of China and the empires to the west. But as far as our film was concerned, only one Uighur (my guide) existed. The other three—two camel herdsmen and an interpreter—accompanied us invisibly: part of the true journey which lurked beneath the film. They belonged to the chaos of real travel. They split into factions. The guide and interpreter came from one village, the cameleers from another. They wrangled, and fell into bitter silences.

The camels, too, were not what they seemed. They had been assembled in advance from different regions of the province, but were less beasts of burden than herd animals. They bellowed resentment at their loads, and suddenly broke loose and rampaged over the desert, scattering boxes and blankets in their wake. It was a star performance. But we could not film it: because our cameras were on their backs. The cameleers followed them, mutinously. And all afternoon we marched on south, looking for sand unblemished by any speck of scrub, ranges which would say to the camera: this is the harshest desert on earth.

The camera, after its fashion, was demanding truth.

[Turn over

At last, by evening, we arrived. Long, virgin dunes curved photogenically in front of us, and the camels were back in harness. We had reconvened the mythic elements of our journey. The three most filmic beasts, their loads reassembled for continuity, paraded along the dune-lips behind the guide and me. But we were, of course, going nowhere in particular. We were completing patterns of backlit beauty for the lens, creating compositions, lending proportion and drama. The director and camera crew, squatting like guerrillas on strategic hillocks, directed our passage through walkie-talkies. We gazed hypocritically through them into solitude. The four camels which did not officially exist coughed unseen in a dip of the sands. How did we look?

The cameraman worried about the slant of evening light. The dunes, he said, were pointing the wrong way. The director pondered and shuffled unsurely. Wherever the lens swung, there was cliché: skyline, camel-train, sunset, us. We were trapped in other people's daydreams.

I tried to imagine how we appeared. Compared to our surroundings, I felt, we must look weirdly insubstantial. Again I was reminded of ghosts, trying pathetically to integrate with the real. Perhaps the paranoia of Hollywood directors, I thought, was due to the terrifying precariousness of their control. A film seemed to belong to nobody. It was in the hands not only of financiers and the elements, but of cameramen and actors (myself now) and of the sheer recalcitrance of images, which never reproduced themselves predictably. And in the end, for all the arts of editing and commentary, the lens would give back to the viewer his own vision: he would see simply what he would have seen if he were standing where the camera stood.

By comparison, my trade as a writer seemed megalomaniac. I was the lens, even the viewer. Everything I wrote was subjective.

Then reality broke in. As the guide and I ascended too steep a slope, the camels floundered to their knees. They collapsed in sequence, like cards. Their leading-ropes broke. They struggled and roared. I tried to beat the hindmost to its feet, but the baggage was slipping over its humps. Its buried legs gained no purchase in the sand. Its slobbering face sank level with mine. I struck its flank several times before I noticed it was defecating—a piece of cruelty faithfully recorded by the cameras on the far dune. For minutes the sand writhed and slithered away under us, as if we were treading water. And even after we had painfully reassembled on the dune's crest, the reputation of camels was confirmed. The lead beast flailed out and lacerated my guide's shin.

I felt suddenly guilty. It was as if a fictional character had lunged out of our film, and kicked. All at once I imagined the film eating up everyone around it. Except me. I was its supposed hero, already incarnate in it. Yet I was accompanied by people who had traversed precisely the same land as I had, and who would appear on screen only as names at the end.

At dusk we put up a makeshift wind-break. Our camp-fire blazed and subsided, while an invisible haze, reaching far up the horizon, obliterated the stars. Since we had to rise for the dawn light, the camels were fed in darkness, and for hours I was kept awake by the crash of their teeth into piles of brittle foliage, and watched their profiles as they shambled back and forth between the fodder and a futile search for plants. Sometimes they would squeak in a peculiar, unofficial way, as if in distress; and one great beast, passing the shelter where we lay, sank its fangs into the newly cut tent-poles and brought them crashing on to our heads before it trotted contemptuously into the night.

The unfilmed moment touched us only with dazed ill temper. It belonged merely to life. There was no light by which to film it and besides, the journey was not meant to be happening to the others, only to me.

165 But next morning, the dawn shone perfect. The most docile beasts fell into line behind me with their baggage and continuity intact. The backlit dunes were pronounced correct, and rippled accommodatingly. And I stepped again into the legend of a real journey—a voyage through random light and circumstance, to an unknown horizon, alone.

Question

"Yet our film aimed to record the Chinese Silk Road through my eyes" (lines 15 and 16)

How effectively does Colin Thubron describe and reflect on his experience of the making of this film?

[Turn over

3. **Poetry** (*Page twenty-four*)

   *Read carefully the poem **Wind** (1957) by Ted Hughes and then answer the question that follows it.*

   ## Wind

   This house has been far out at sea all night,
   The woods crashing through darkness, the booming hills,
   Winds stampeding the fields under the window
   Floundering black astride and blinding wet

   5 Till day rose; then under an orange sky
   The hills had new places, and wind wielded
   Blade-like, luminous black and emerald,
   Flexing like the lens of a mad eye.

   At noon I scaled along the house-side as far as
   10 The coal-house door. I dared once to look up—
   Through the brunt wind that dented the balls of my eyes
   The tent of the hills drummed and strained its guyrope,

   The fields quivering, the skyline a grimace,
   At any second to bang and vanish with a flap:
   15 The wind flung a magpie away and a black-
   Back gull bent like an iron bar slowly. The house

   Rang like some fine green goblet in the note
   That any second would shatter it. Now deep
   In chairs, in front of the great fire, we grip
   20 Our hearts and cannot entertain book, thought,

   Or each other. We watch the fire blazing,
   And feel the roots of the house move, but sit on,
   Seeing the window tremble to come in,
   Hearing the stones cry out under the horizons.

Question

Make a critical evaluation of this poem.

Your evaluation should be based on careful analysis of key aspects of its language and form.

4. **Drama** (*Pages twenty-five to thirty-three*)

The following extract is the opening to the play **The Voysey Inheritance** *(1905) by Harley Granville Barker.*

Central to the play is Voysey and Son, a firm of family solicitors at the heart of the London legal establishment. As head of the firm, Mr Voysey is entrusted with the financial affairs of many families, including the safe investment of their money.

The characters in the extract are Mr Voysey, Peacey, *the firm's head clerk, and* Edward, Mr Voysey's *son and a partner in the firm.*

Read the extract carefully and then answer the question that follows it (Page thirty-three).

THE VOYSEY INHERITANCE

ACT I

The Office of Voysey and Son is in the best part of Lincoln's Inn. Its panelled rooms give out a sense of grandmotherly comfort and security, very grateful at first to the hesitating investor, the dubious litigant. Mr Voysey's own room, into which he walks about twenty past ten of a morning, radiates enterprise besides. There is polish on everything; on the
5 *windows, on the mahogany of the tidily packed writing-table that stands between them, on the brasswork of the fireplace in the other wall, on the glass of the firescreen which preserves only the pleasantness of a sparkling fire, even on Mr Voysey's hat as he takes it off to place it on the little red-curtained shelf behind the door. Mr Voysey is sixty or more and masterful; would obviously be master anywhere from his own home outwards, or wreck the*
10 *situation in his attempt. Indeed there is sometimes a buccaneering air in the twist of his glance, not altogether suitable to a family solicitor. On this bright October morning, Peacey, the head clerk, follows just too late to help him off with his coat, but in time to take it and hang it up with a quite unnecessary subservience. Relieved of his coat, Mr Voysey carries to his table the bunch of beautiful roses he is accustomed to bring to the*
15 *office three times a week and places them for a moment only near the bowl of water there ready to receive them while he takes up his letters. These lie ready too, opened mostly, one or two private ones left closed and discreetly separate. By this time the usual salutations have passed, Peacey's "Good morning, sir"; Mr Voysey's "Morning, Peacey." Then as he gets to his letters Mr Voysey starts his day's work.*

20 *Mr Voysey.*   Any news for me?

Peacey.   I hear bad accounts of Alguazils Preferred, sir.

Mr Voysey.   Oh... who from?

Peacey.   Merrit and James's head clerk in the train this morning.

Mr Voysey.   They looked all right on... Give me *The Times*.

25   Peacey *goes to the fireplace for* The Times; *it is warming there. Mr Voysey waves a letter, then places it on the table.*

    Here, that's for you... Gerrard's Cross business. Anything else?

Peacey.   [*as he turns* The Times *to its Finance page*] I've made the usual notes.

	Mr Voysey.	Thank'ee.
30	*Peacey.*	Young Benham isn't back yet.
	Mr Voysey.	Mr Edward must do as he thinks fit about that. Alguazils, Alg—oh, yes.
		He is running his eye down the columns. Peacey *leans over the letters.*
	Peacey.	This is from Mr Leader about the codicil . . . You'll answer that?
35	*Mr Voysey.*	Mr Leader. Yes. Alguazils. Mr Edward's here, I suppose.
	Peacey.	No, sir.
	Mr Voysey.	[*his eye twisting with some sharpness*] What!
	Peacey.	[*almost alarmed*] I beg pardon, sir.
	Mr Voysey.	Mr Edward.
40	*Peacey.*	Oh, yes, sir, been in his room some time. I thought you said Headley; he's not due back till Thursday.
		Mr Voysey *discards* The Times *and sits to his desk and his letters.*
	Mr Voysey.	Tell Mr Edward I've come.
	Peacey.	Yes, sir. Anything else?
45	*Mr Voysey.*	Not for the moment. Cold morning, isn't it?
	Peacey.	Quite surprising, sir.
	Mr Voysey.	We had a touch of frost down at Chislehurst.
	Peacey.	So early!
50	*Mr Voysey.*	I want it for the celery. All right, I'll call through about the rest of the letters.
		Peacey *goes, having secured a letter or two, and* Mr Voysey *having sorted the rest (a proportion into the waste-paper basket) takes up the forgotten roses and starts setting them into a bowl with an artistic hand. Then his son* Edward *comes in.* Mr Voysey *gives him one glance and goes on arranging the roses, but says cheerily . . .*
55		
	Mr Voysey.	Good morning, my dear boy.
60		Edward *has little of his father in him and that little is undermost. It is a refined face, but self-consciousness takes the place in it of imagination, and in suppressing traits of brutality in his character it looks as if the young man had suppressed his sense of humour too. But whether or no, that would not be much in evidence now, for* Edward *is obviously going through some experience which is scaring him (there is no better word). He looks not to have slept for a night or two, and his standing there, clutching and unclutching the bundle of papers he carries, his eyes on his father, half appealingly but half accusingly too, his whole being altogether so unstrung and desperate, makes* Mr Voysey's *uninterrupted arranging of the flowers seem very calculated indeed. At last the little tension of silence is broken.*
65		

	Edward.	Father...
70	*Mr Voysey.*	Well?
	Edward.	I'm glad to see you.
		This is a statement of fact. He doesn't know that the commonplace phrase sounds ridiculous at such a moment.
	Mr Voysey.	I see you've the papers there.
75	*Edward.*	Yes.
	Mr Voysey.	You've been through them?
	Edward.	As you wished me...
	Mr Voysey.	Well?
80		*Edward doesn't answer. Reference to the papers seems to overwhelm him with shame.* Mr Voysey *goes on with cheerful impatience.*
		Now, now, my dear boy, don't take it like this. You're puzzled and worried, of course. But why didn't you come down to me on Saturday night? I expected you... I told you to come. Your mother was wondering why you weren't with us for dinner yesterday.
85	*Edward.*	I went through everything twice. I wanted to make quite sure.
	Mr Voysey.	I told you to come to me.
	Edward.	[*he is very near crying*] Oh, Father!
	Mr Voysey.	Now look here, Edward, I'm going to ring and dispose of these letters. Please pull yourself together.
90		*He pushes the little button on his table.*
	Edward.	I didn't leave my rooms all day yesterday.
	Mr Voysey.	A pleasant Sunday! You must learn, whatever the business may be, to leave it behind you at the office. Life's not worth living else.
95		Peacey *comes in to find* Mr Voysey *before the fire ostentatiously warming and rubbing his hands.*
		Oh, there isn't much else, Peacey. Tell Simmons that if he satisfies you about the details of this lease it'll be all right. Make a note for me of Mr Granger's address at Mentone.
	Peacey.	Mr Burnett... Burnett and Marks... has just come in, Mr Edward.
100	*Edward.*	[*without turning*] It's only fresh instructions. Will you take them?
	Peacey.	All right.
		Peacey *goes, lifting his eyebrows at the queerness of* Edward's *manner. This* Mr Voysey *sees, returning to his table with a little scowl.*
105	*Mr Voysey.*	Now sit down. I've given you a bad forty-eight hours, have I? Well, I've been anxious about you. Never mind, we'll thresh the thing out now. Go through the two accounts. Mrs Murberry's first... how did you find it stands?
	Edward.	[*his feelings choking him*] I hoped you were playing some joke on me.

	Mr Voysey.	Come now.
110		Edward *separates the papers precisely and starts to detail them; his voice quite toneless. Now and then his father's sharp comments ring out in contrast.*
115	Edward.	We've got the lease of her present house, several agreements . . . and here's her will. Here's an expired power of attorney . . . over her securities and her property generally . . . it was made out for six months.
	Mr Voysey.	She was in South Africa.
120	Edward.	Here's the Sheffield mortgage and the Henry Smith mortgage with Banker's receipts . . . her Banker's to us for the interest up to date . . . four and a half and five per cent. Then . . . Fretworthy Bonds. There's a note scribbled in your writing that they are at the Bank; but you don't say what bank.
	Mr Voysey.	My own.
125	Edward.	[*just dwelling on the words*] Your own. I queried that. There's eight thousand five hundred in three and a half India stock. And there are her Banker's receipts for cheques on account of those dividends. I presume for those dividends.
	Mr Voysey.	Why not?
130	Edward.	[*gravely*] Because then, Father, there are her Banker's half-yearly receipts for other sums amounting to an average of four hundred and twenty pounds a year. But I find no record of any capital to produce this.
	Mr Voysey.	Go on. What do you find?
135	Edward.	Till about three years back there seems to have been eleven thousand in Queenslands which would produce . . . did produce exactly the same sum. But after January of that year I find no record of them.
	Mr Voysey.	In fact the Queenslands are missing, vanished?
	Edward.	[*hardly uttering the word*] Yes.
	Mr Voysey.	From which you conclude?
140	Edward.	I supposed at first that you had not handed me all the papers . . .
	Mr Voysey.	Since Mrs Murberry evidently still gets that four twenty a year somehow; lucky woman.
	Edward.	[*in agony*] Oh!
	Mr Voysey.	Well, we'll return to the good lady later. Now let's take the other.
145	Edward.	The Hatherley Trust.
	Mr Voysey.	Quite so.
	Edward.	[*with one accusing glance*] Trust.
	Mr Voysey.	Go on.

	Edward.	Father...
150		*His grief comes uppermost again and* Mr Voysey *meets it kindly.*
	Mr Voysey.	I know, my dear boy. I shall have lots to say to you. But let's get quietly through with these details first.
	Edward.	[*bitterly now*] Oh, this is simple enough. We're young Hatherley's trustees till he comes of age. The property was thirty-eight thousand invested in Consols. Certain sums were to be allowed for his education; we seem to be paying them.
155		
	Mr Voysey.	Regularly?
	Edward.	Quite. But where's the capital?
	Mr Voysey.	No record?
160	*Edward.*	Yes... a note by you on a half sheet: Refer Bletchley Land Scheme.
	Mr Voysey.	Oh... we've been out of that six years or more! He's credited with the interest on his capital?
	Edward.	With the Consol interest.
	Mr Voysey.	Quite so.
165	*Edward.*	The Bletchley scheme paid seven and a half.
	Mr Voysey.	At one time. Have you taken the trouble to calculate what will be due from us to the lad?
	Edward.	Yes... capital and interest... about forty-six thousand pounds.
	Mr Voysey.	A respectable sum. In five years' time?
170	*Edward.*	When he comes of age.
	Mr Voysey.	That gives us, say, four years and six months in which to think about it.
		Edward *waits, hopelessly, for his father to speak again; then says...*
	Edward.	Thank you for showing me these, sir. Shall I put them back in your safe now?
175		
	Mr Voysey.	Yes, you'd better. There's the key.
		Edward *reaches for the bunch, his face hidden.*
		Put them down. Your hand shakes... why, you might have been drinking. I'll put them away later. It's no use having hysterics, Edward. Look your trouble in the face.
180		
		Edward's *only answer is to go to the fire, as far from his father as the room allows. And there he leans on the mantelpiece, his shoulders heaving.*
		I'm sorry, my dear boy. I wouldn't tell you if I could help it.
185	*Edward.*	I can't believe it. And that you should be telling me... such a thing.
	Mr Voysey.	Let yourself go... have your cry out, as the women say. It isn't pleasant, I know. It isn't pleasant to inflict it on you.

	Edward.	[*able to turn to his father again; won round by the kind voice*] How long has it been going on? Why didn't you tell me before? Oh, I know you thought you'd pull through. But I'm your partner . . . I'm responsible too. Oh, I don't want to shirk that . . . don't think I mean to shirk that, Father. Perhaps I ought to have discovered . . . but those affairs were always in your hands. I trusted . . . I beg your pardon. Oh it's us . . . not you. Everyone has trusted us.
195	*Mr Voysey.*	[*calmly and kindly still*] You don't seem to notice that I'm not breaking my heart like this.
	Edward.	What's the extent of . . . ? Are there other accounts . . . ? When did it begin? Father, what made you begin it?
	Mr Voysey.	I didn't begin it.
200	*Edward.*	You didn't? Who then?
	Mr Voysey.	My father before me.
		Edward *stares.*
		That calms you a little.
	Edward.	But how terrible! Oh, my dear father . . . I'm glad. But . . .
205	*Mr Voysey.*	[*shaking his head*] My inheritance, Edward.
	Edward.	My dear father!
	Mr Voysey.	I had hoped it wasn't to be yours.
	Edward.	But you mean to tell me that this sort of thing has been going on here for years? For more than thirty years!
210	*Mr Voysey.*	Yes.
	Edward.	That's a little hard to understand . . . just at first, sir.
	Mr Voysey.	[*sententiously*] We do what we must in this world, Edward. I have done what I had to do.
215	*Edward.*	[*his emotion well cooled by now*] Perhaps I'd better just listen while you explain.
	Mr Voysey.	[*concentrating*] You know that I'm heavily into Northern Electrics.
	Edward.	Yes.
220	*Mr Voysey.*	But you don't know how heavily. When I got the tip the Municipalities were organising the purchase, I saw of course the stock must be up to a hundred and forty-five—a hundred and fifty in no time. Now Leeds has quarrelled with the rural group . . . there'll be no general settlement for ten years. I bought at ninety-five. What are they today?
	Edward.	Seventy-two.
225	*Mr Voysey.*	Seventy-one and a half. And in ten years I may be . . . ! I'm not a young man, Edward. That's mainly why you've had to be told.
	Edward.	With whose money are you so heavily into Northern Electrics?
	Mr Voysey.	The firm's money.
	Edward.	Clients' money?
230	*Mr Voysey.*	Yes.

	Edward.	[*coldly*] Well . . . I'm waiting for your explanation, sir.
	Mr Voysey.	[*with a shrug*] Children always think the worst of their parents, I suppose. I did of mine. It's a pity.
	Edward.	Go on, sir, go on. Let me know the worst.
235	*Mr Voysey.*	There's no immediate danger. I should think anyone could see that from the figures there. There's no real risk at all.
	Edward.	Is that the worst?
	Mr Voysey.	[*his anger rising*] Have you studied these two accounts or have you not?
240	*Edward.*	Yes, sir.
	Mr Voysey.	Well, where's the deficiency in Mrs Murberry's income . . . has she ever gone without a shilling? What has young Hatherley lost?
	Edward.	He stands to lose . . .
245	*Mr Voysey.*	He stands to lose nothing if I'm spared for a little, and you will only bring a little common sense to bear and try to understand the difficulties of my position.
	Edward.	Father, I'm not thinking ill of you . . . that is, I'm trying not to. But won't you explain how you're justified . . . ?
	Mr Voysey.	In putting our affairs in order?
250	*Edward.*	Are you doing that?
	Mr Voysey.	What else?
	Edward.	[*starting patiently to examine the matter*] How bad were things when you came into control?
	Mr Voysey.	Oh, I forget.
255	*Edward.*	You can't forget.
	Mr Voysey.	Well . . . pretty bad.
	Edward.	How was it my grandfather . . . ?
260	*Mr Voysey.*	Muddlement . . . timidity! Had a perfect mania for petty speculation. He'd no capital . . . no real credit . . . and he went in terror of his life. My dear Edward, if I hadn't found out in time, he'd have confessed to the first man who came and asked for a balance sheet.
	Edward.	How much was he to the bad then?
	Mr Voysey.	Oh . . . a tidy sum.
	Edward.	But it can't have taken all these years to pay off . . .
265	*Mr Voysey.*	Oh, hasn't it!
	Edward.	[*making his point*] Then how does it happen, sir, that such a recent trust as young Hatherley's has been broken into?
	Mr Voysey.	Well, what could be safer? There is no one to interfere, and we haven't to settle up for five years.
270	*Edward.*	[*utterly beaten*] Father, are you mad?

	Mr Voysey.	Mad? I wish everybody were as sane. As a trustee the law permits me to earn for a fund three and a half per cent . . . and that I do . . . punctually and safely. Now as to Mrs Murberry . . . those Fretworthy Bonds at my bank . . . I've borrowed five thousand on them. But I can release them tomorrow if need be.
275		
	Edward.	Where's the five thousand?
	Mr Voysey.	I needed it . . . temporarily . . . to complete a purchase . . . there was that and four thousand more out of the Skipworth fund.
	Edward.	But, my dear father—
280	Mr Voysey.	Well?
	Edward.	[*summing it all up very simply*] It's not right.
		Mr Voysey *considers his son for a moment with a pitying shake of the head.*
285	Mr Voysey.	That is a word, Edward, which one should learn to use very carefully. You mean that from time to time I have had to go beyond the letter of the law. But consider the position I found myself in. Was I to see my father ruined and disgraced without lifting a finger to help him? I paid back to the man who was most involved in my father's mistakes every penny of his capital . . . and he never even knew the danger he'd been in . . . never had one uneasy moment. It was I that lay awake. I have now somewhere a letter from that man written as he lay dying . . . I'll tell you who it was, old Thomson the physiologist . . . saying that only his perfect confidence in our conduct of his affairs had enabled him to do his life's work in peace. Well, Edward, I went beyond the letter of the law to do that service . . . to my father . . . to old Thomson . . . to Science . . . to Humanity. Was I right or wrong?
290		
295		
	Edward.	In the result, sir, right.
	Mr Voysey.	Judge me by the result, I took the risk of failure . . . I should have suffered. I could have kept clear of the danger if I'd liked.
300	Edward.	But that's all past. The thing that concerns me is what you are doing now.
305	Mr Voysey.	[*gently reproachful*] My boy, can't you trust me a little? It's all very well for you to come in at the end of the day and criticise. But I who have done the day's work know how that work had to be done. And here's our firm, prosperous, respected and without a stain on its honour. That's the main point, isn't it?
	Edward.	[*quite irresponsive to this pathetic appeal*] Very well, sir. Let's dismiss from our minds any prejudice about behaving as honest firms of solicitors do behave . . .
310	Mr Voysey.	We need do nothing of the sort. If a man gives me definite instructions about his property, I follow them. And more often than not he suffers.
	Edward.	But if Mrs Murberry knew . . .

	Mr Voysey.	Well, if you can make her understand her affairs . . . financial or other . . . it's more than I ever could. Go and knock it into her head, then, if you can, that four hundred and twenty pounds of her income hasn't, for the last eight years, come from the place she thinks it's come from, and see how happy you'll make her.
315		
320	Edward.	But is that four hundred and twenty a year as safe as it was before you . . . ?
	Mr Voysey.	Why not?
	Edward.	What's the security?
	Mr Voysey.	[*putting his coping stone on the argument*] My financial ability.

Question

Make a detailed study of the dramatic means by which in this opening to the play the playwright establishes key aspects of plot, character and theme.

[Turn over

Section 4—Reading the Media

You must answer **one question only** in this section.

Category A—Film

1. *"Editing is a crucial element in the making of films."*

    Drawing evidence from particular sequences, discuss the contribution of editing to the effectiveness of any **one** film you have studied.

2. Choose any **two** films by one director. Analyse the particular aspects of style and content that mark these films as the work of that director.

Category B—Television

3. Discuss the distinctive technical and cultural codes employed in any **one** television drama—soap, serial, series or single play—you have studied.

4. *"Essential to the success of documentary is the construction of effective narrative."*

    How far do you agree?

    You should support your answer with evidence drawn from **two** or **more than two** television documentary programmes you have studied.

Category C—Radio

5. *"Radio is a non-visual medium; so much depends on voice."*

    Discuss the importance of voice in **one** or **two** of the following radio genres: news and current affairs, sport, drama, comedy, documentary, magazine, music.

6. By what means has any **one** radio channel created its distinctive identity?

    In your answer, you should consider aspects such as programme content, scheduling, mode of address.

Category D—Print journalism

7. *"The best print journalism entertains at the same time as it informs, enlightens and educates."*

    Discuss.

    You should support your answer with evidence drawn from at least **two** newspapers.

    NB In your answer to Question 7, you **may** refer to the material provided for Question 8, but your answer must also include evidence from at least **one other** newspaper.

8. In January 2006, a bottle-nosed whale dominated the news for several days before its eventual demise.

   For this question, you are provided with an extract (*see Insert*) from the coverage of this event in *The Independent on Sunday* of 22 January, 2006.

   In a careful study of the extract, show how, through devices such as narrative and representation, the newspaper turns an event into a "legend".

Category E—Advertising

9. *"Advertising is an art—the art of persuasion."*

   How effectively, in your view, is the *"art of persuasion"* employed in a range of advertisements **or** in an advertising campaign you have studied?

   NB In your answer to Question 9, you may refer to the advertisements provided for Question 10, but your answer must also refer to **other** advertisements.

10. For this question, you are provided with two advertisements (*see Insert*) published in the *Radio Times* magazine for Vodafone.

    Make a detailed analysis of these two advertisements in which you consider:

    - technical, cultural and written codes
    - the stereotyping of gender and the extent to which it is confirmed or subverted
    - the narrative of each advertisement.

[END OF QUESTION PAPER]

Insert for Section 4 – Reading the Media Question 8

The legend of the London Whale

Lost and in distress, its plight touched the city and the world

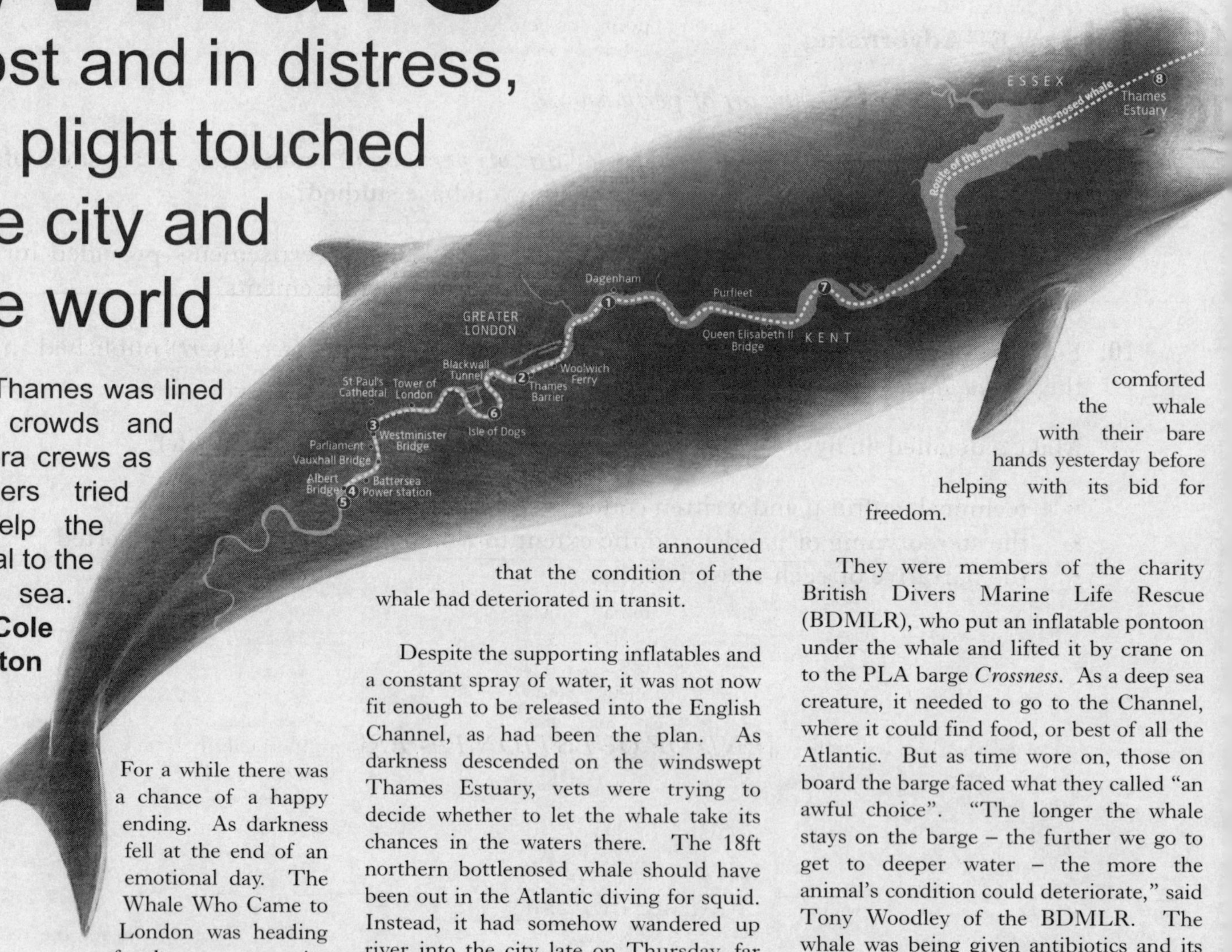

The Thames was lined with crowds and camera crews as rescuers tried to help the animal to the open sea. By **Cole Moreton**

For a while there was a chance of a happy ending. As darkness fell at the end of an emotional day. The Whale Who Came to London was heading for the open sea again, albeit in a harness and blanket on the back of a Port of London Authority (PLA) barge.

The gentle, incongruous giant spotted swimming past the House of Commons on Friday had been rescued from the shallow, polluted waters of the Thames and given the best possible odds for survival. But as television pictures of the barge heading for Tilbury were broadcast around the world, the RSPCA announced that the condition of the whale had deteriorated in transit.

Despite the supporting inflatables and a constant spray of water, it was not now fit enough to be released into the English Channel, as had been the plan. As darkness descended on the windswept Thames Estuary, vets were trying to decide whether to let the whale take its chances in the waters there. The 18ft northern bottlenosed whale should have been out in the Atlantic diving for squid. Instead, it had somehow wandered up river into the city late on Thursday, far from its mother who had been heard calling 40 miles away, off the coast of Essex.

Londoners lined the river to see it but the plight of the whale captured imaginations all round the world, not least because its story had all the elements of a modern fairytale: the child lost and lonely in an alien and dangerous place; the desperate parent calling out, and the rescuers who waded into the water and comforted the whale with their bare hands yesterday before helping with its bid for freedom.

They were members of the charity British Divers Marine Life Rescue (BDMLR), who put an inflatable pontoon under the whale and lifted it by crane on to the PLA barge *Crossness*. As a deep sea creature, it needed to go to the Channel, where it could find food, or best of all the Atlantic. But as time wore on, those on board the barge faced what they called "an awful choice". "The longer the whale stays on the barge – the further we go to get to deeper water – the more the animal's condition could deteriorate," said Tony Woodley of the BDMLR. The whale was being given antibiotics and its breathing rate monitored, but its muscles were stiffening.

"The animal has been in distress for the past couple of days," said Mr Woodley. "When it is out of the water for this length of time, the pressure on its internal organs is a problem." If the whale was released into the estuary there was still a chance it would swim back up river, or die quickly, he said. "We are pessimistic."

JOURNEY HOME	08.10 The sighting	12.30 The wrapping	13.09 The calming
Race against time to save the whale From dawn, experts fought to return the stranded mammal to open water	After the first sighting, in the Albert Bridge area, rescuers try to take control of the 15ft adolescent whale. An attempt is made to assess its health for possible transport to outside the Thames Estuary. They also weigh up the option of a mercy killing if it is too ill to travel.	At low tide, rescuers wrap the whale in a blanket and cocoon it between floating pontoons for transport. As the whale thrashes around in distress, attempts are made to assess its breathing rate. Blood and blubber samples are taken. Rescuers lubricate its eyes and blow-holes.	Medics soothe the animal before giving the go-ahead for it to be dragged gently towards a barge that will take it out of the crowded Thames. No decision has yet been made on whether it is well enough to be released, or needs to be put out of its misery.

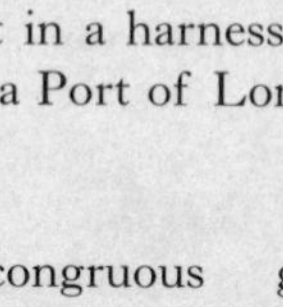

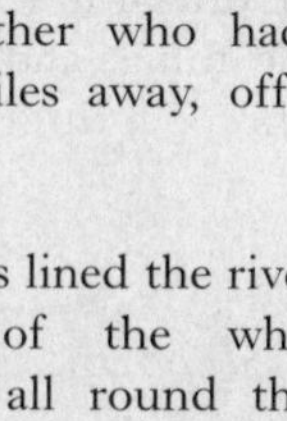

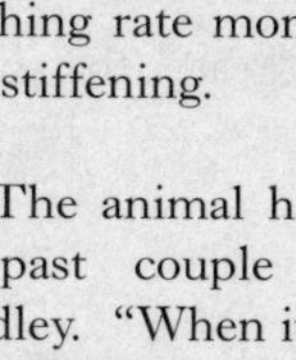

[X115/701]

THE SIGHTINGS

① **11am Thursday:** first sighting of a northern bottlenosed whale near Dagenham rouses national interest

② **3pm Thursday:** as it passes the Thames Barrier, spectators start to line riverbanks, hoping to catch a glimpse of the creature

③ **2pm Friday:** whale spotted by the Palace of Westminster. The last time that a live whale was seen in the Thames was in 1913

④ **2.30pm Friday:** the whale continues to swim upstream against a strong current, reaches Albert Bridge then appears to turn back, raising hopes that it might head downstream to the sea of its own volition. It soon becomes clear that it is disorientated

⑤ **12.30pm yesterday:** rescuers attach the beached whale to floating pontoons before towing it towards a barge, on to which it is lifted by crane

⑥ **3.45pm yesterday:** the barge carrying the whale, the "Crossness", sets off for the Thames estuary. But the whale's health deteriorates. Unable to support its own weight out of the water, it starts to suffocate

⑦ **5pm:** with regret medics cancel their appeal for an ocean-going vessel to take the whale out to sea, having decided it is now too ill to be transported to the Atlantic

⑧ **8pm:** the whale is due to be released into the Thames estuary

---

The first sighting of the whale had been on Thursday, when fishermen saw it out by the mouth of the Thames. Later that day it was spotted by staff at the Thames Barrier – which seems to have been no barrier at all. Then on Friday morning, a sharp-eyed rail commuter crossing a central London bridge looked out of the window and had the presence of mind to ring the authorities. "Unless I'm hallucinating," he said, "I've just seen a whale in the Thames."

'Unless I'm hallucinating I've seen a whale in the Thames'

This was no hallucination. Neither was it a dolphin: these visit London quite often. A dead harbour porpoise was found at Putney yesterday, by what appeared to be coincidence, although there was speculation that it might have been frightened into swimming up the Thames in the same way as the whale, possibly by naval sonar activity.

There were hopes that the whale would swim back out to sea on its own, then fears that it had died. But it was sighted again early yesterday morning by the blue and white PLA launch that then shadowed its progress up and down the river, between Battersea and Chelsea.

Noon was the deadline: that was when the vets and marine biologists expected to be able to get close to the whale, as it beached in shallow water. Trying to catch it while it swam would be too dangerous, they said. Playing whale song from closer to the mouth of the river would not work because of the level of river noise.

It was a clear, bright day, but to listen for the calls and bellows of the whale was to become aware again of the traffic, the sirens, shouts, rumbling trains and thundering jets that form the soundtrack to city life, not to mention the police and news helicopters hovering at a respectful distance overhead.

The children were mildly amused to see a huge animal surfacing to blow air in such an unlikely place. But it was the thousands of adults alongside them, lining the bridges and riverside walks, who watched for hours with childlike intensity.

Children were amused; adults watched with childlike intensity

Why are we drawn to such creatures? The size is one thing, and the grace of movement as they slip through the water, but yesterday there was something profoundly moving and attractive about the combination of power and apparent gentleness. A flick of the tail could have capsized the dinghy, but whales are curious creatures that get themselves in trouble because they like to be friendly to boats. And above all there was the curiosity value.

A whale in the Thames is not something you see every century, let alone every day. The last sighting was in 1913.

"Get back!" screamed a woman in a black rubber suit from the water as a member of the public waded in, intent on helping to rescue the whale which had become beached at low tide. "Get back you fool!" shouted her colleague and the man slowly waded away embarrassed. As the water level dropped, 18 people in rubber suits surrounded the whale, which bellowed and thrashed its tail but then became quiet and still. The hands were to calm it. Yellow bands were passed under its body, then inflated.

Mark Stevens of the BDMLR waded ashore to tell the crowds, "The whale is comfortable; it likes the pressure of the pontoons. The blood you saw in the water is because the river bed is full of dirty great boulders, and one of them cut the skin, but a whale has a lot of blood, so it is nothing to worry about."

They were waiting for the results of blood tests taken in the river, he said. But as the tide rose again it became a race against time. After a certain time the barge would not have enough room to pass under the bridges. So the *Crossness* set out without the test results, in the hope that the whale would be declared fit enough to be set free. "Go on, fella," whispered a policeman, as he helped clear spectators off the rapidly shrinking beach. "Best of luck."

14.35
The lifting
Bystanders cheer as rescuers brave cold and fast-moving currents to manouver slings under the animal's belly and lift it on to the barge. It is uncertain the exhausted whale will survive this traumatic event, but everything goes like clockwork and there is hope it may see it through.

15.50
The journey begins
Vets assess the whale's health as better than they had feared during its arduous journey on the barge towards the estuary. But they are still unsure whether they will be in a position to release it into the Channel, or have to transport it further out to open water.

Around 20.00
An uncertain end
After all the effort, spirits sink as the medics report their grim news: the whale is too ill to be transferred to another vessel for a second leg out to the Atlantic. Instead, the plan was to release it into the Channel – a worrying finale to a story that touched the nation.

Insert for Section 4 – Reading the Media Question 10

Today, Matthew,
I'm going to be a parent, a child, a grandchild, an animal handler, a man manager, an employee, a friend, a lover, an ex-friend, an ex-lover, a music lover, a bad singer, a good Samaritan, a social commentator, a philosopher, a psychologist, an interior designer, a personal shopper, a cook, a washer-upper, a player, a spectator, a film critic, a TV critic, a writer, a reader, a kids' entertainer and the beautiful princess in the bedtime story who lives happily ever after.

Make the most of now.

vodafone

It's the most

precious thing in the world. It only exists for an instant. It's here. Then it's gone. So cherish it. Love it. Use it to make someone smile. Use it to tell someone you love them. Discover great things. Laugh at daft things. Take it in your hands and stretch it. Eloooongate it. Put it through its paces. Make it earn its keep. Fill it to the brim with your favourite things. Squeeze every drop of enjoyment out of it. Whatever you do make the most of it •

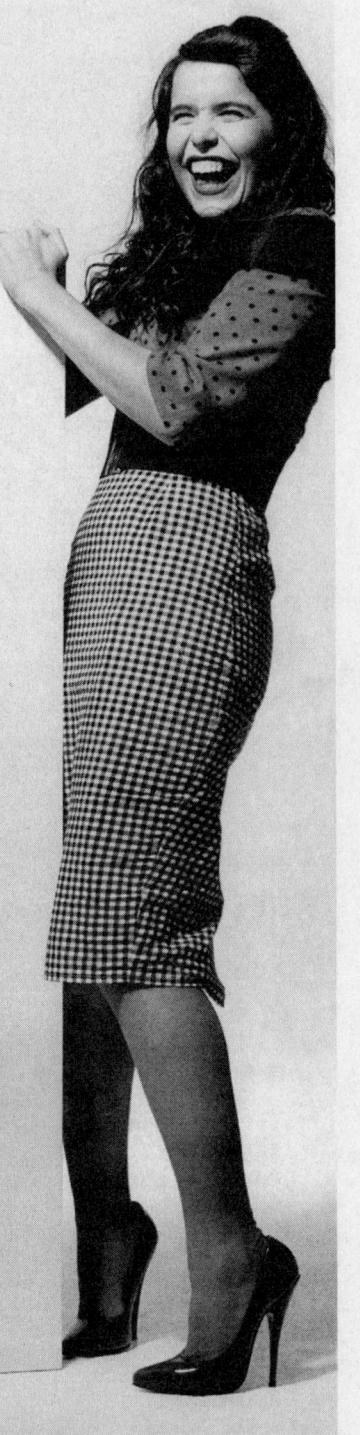

Make the most of now.

vodafone

[BLANK PAGE]

ADVANCED HIGHER
2009

[BLANK PAGE]

OFFICIAL SQA PAST PAPERS 179 ADVANCED HIGHER ENGLISH 2009

X115/701

NATIONAL
QUALIFICATIONS
2009

FRIDAY, 15 MAY
1.00 PM – 4.00 PM

ENGLISH
ADVANCED HIGHER

There are four sections in this paper.

Section 1—Literary Study	pages	2 – 9
Section 2—Language Study	pages	10 – 17
Section 3—Textual Analysis	pages	18 – 36
Section 4—Reading the Media	pages	37 – 40 (plus 2 colour inserts)

Depending on the options you have chosen, you must answer **one** or **two** questions.

If you have submitted a Creative Writing folio, you must answer only **one** question.

Otherwise, you must answer **two** questions.

If you are required to answer only **one question**

- it must be taken from **Section 1—Literary Study**
- you must leave the examination room **after 1 hour 30 minutes**.

If you are required to answer **two questions**

- your first must be taken from **Section 1—Literary Study**
- your second must be taken from **a different section**
- each answer must be written in **a separate answer booklet**
- the maximum time allowed for any question is **1 hour 30 minutes**.

You must identify each question you attempt by indicating clearly

- **the title of the section** from which the question has been taken
- **the number of the question** within that section.

You must also write inside the front cover of your Literary Study answer booklet

- **the topic** of your Specialist Study (Dissertation)
- **the texts** used in your Specialist Study (Dissertation).

SQA

LI X115/701 6/5170

Section 1—Literary Study

This section is **mandatory** for all candidates.

You must answer **one question only** in this section.

Unless otherwise indicated, your answer must take the form of a **critical essay** appropriately structured to meet the demands of your selected question.

DRAMA

1. **Beckett**

   "Although often at odds with each other, what is striking about Beckett's central characters is their need for each other, their dependence on each other."

   Discuss with reference to Vladimir and Estragon in *Waiting for Godot* **and** Hamm and Clov in *Endgame*.

2. **Byrne**

   *"Central to **The Slab Boys Trilogy** is Byrne's use of the unexpected—in terms of character, action and tone."*

   Discuss.

3. **Chekhov**

   Write an essay on the importance of time in *The Cherry Orchard*.

4. **Friel**

   Make a detailed study of the dramatic function of Owen O'Donnell in *Translations* **and** of Jack Mundy in *Dancing at Lughnasa*.

5. **Lindsay**

   Analyse and evaluate some of the principal dramatic techniques employed by Lindsay in *Ane Satyre of the Thrie Estaitis* to press for reform of Church and State and to remind those in power of their duties to the common people.

6. **Lochhead**

   Make a detailed study of the role of La Corbie in *Mary Queen of Scots Got Her Head Chopped Off* **and** of Renfield in *Dracula*.

7. **Pinter**

   Discuss Pinter's dramatic presentation of aspects of power, political or otherwise, in any **two** of the specified plays.

8. **Shakespeare**

   EITHER

   (a) ***Othello* and *Antony and Cleopatra***

   "*Excellent wretch! Perdition catch my soul
   But I do love thee; and when I love thee not,
   Chaos is come again.*"

   (Othello in Act III, Scene iii of *Othello*)

   "*Look where they come.
   Take but good note, and you shall see in him
   The triple pillar of the world transformed
   Into a strumpet's fool.*"

   (Philo in Act I, Scene i of *Antony and Cleopatra*)

   Keeping these quotations in mind, discuss Shakespeare's treatment of love in *Othello* **or** in *Antony and Cleopatra* **or** in **both** plays.

   OR

   (b) ***The Winter's Tale* and *The Tempest***

   "*The relationships between Florizel and Perdita **and** between Ferdinand and Miranda are central to the dramatic development and resolution of these plays.*"

   Discuss.

9. **Stoppard**

   "*We can't even predict the next drip from a dripping tap when it gets irregular. Each drip sets up the conditions for the next, the smallest variation blows prediction apart, and the weather is unpredictable the same way, will always be unpredictable. When you push the numbers through the computer you can see it on the screen. The future is disorder.*"

   (Valentine speaking to Hannah in Act One Scene Four of *Arcadia*)

   Discuss some of the principal dramatic means by which unpredictability and disorder are explored in *Arcadia* **and** in *Rosencrantz and Guildenstern are Dead*.

10. **Wilde**

    "*Not social analysis but social subversion by laughter through wit, style and fantasy—that was Wilde's forte.*"

    Discuss with reference to any **two** or to all **three** of the specified plays.

11. **Williams**

    "*In a Williams play, the climax of the drama comes when the central characters suffer the confrontation of past and present, when the thing they have fled from corners them . . .*"

    In the light of this assertion, make a detailed study of the climax of *A Streetcar Named Desire* **and** the climax of *Sweet Bird of Youth*.

POETRY

12. Burns

Read carefully the following extract from ***The Cotter's Saturday Night*** *and then answer questions (a) **and** (b) that follow it (Page five).*

   November chill blaws loud wi' angry sough;
    The short'ning winter-day is near a close;
   The miry beasts retreating frae the pleugh;
    The black'ning trains o' craws to their repose:
    The toil-worn Cotter frae his labour goes,
   This night his weekly moil is at an end,
    Collects his spades, his mattocks, and his hoes,
   Hoping the morn in ease and rest to spend,
And weary, o'er the moor, his course does hameward bend.

   At length his lonely cot appears in view,
    Beneath the shelter of an agèd tree;
   Th' expectant wee-things, toddlin, stacher through
    To meet their Dad, wi' flichterin' noise an' glee,
    His wee bit ingle, blinkin bonnilie,
   His clean hearth-stane, his thrifty wifie's smile,
    The lisping infant, prattling on his knee,
   Does a' his weary kiaugh and care beguile,
An' makes him quite forget his labour an' his toil.

   Belyve, the elder bairns come drapping in,
    At service out, amang the farmers roun';
   Some ca' the pleugh, some herd, some tentie rin
    A cannie errand to a neibor town:
    Their eldest hope, their Jenny, woman-grown,
   In youthfu' bloom, love sparkling in her e'e,
    Comes hame, perhaps to shew a braw new gown,
   Or deposite her sair-won penny-fee,
To help her parents dear, if they in hardship be.

   With joy unfeign'd, brothers and sisters meet,
    An' each for other's welfare kindly spiers:
   The social hours, swift-wing'd, unnoticed fleet;
    Each tells the uncos that he sees or hears;
    The parents, partial, eye their hopeful years;
   Anticipation forward points the view.
    The mother, wi' her needle an' her sheers,
   Gars auld claes look amaist as weel's the new;
The father mixes a' wi' admonition due.

> Their master's an' their mistress's command,
>   The younkers a' are warnèd to obey;
> An' mind their labours wi' an eydent hand,
>   An' ne'er, tho' out o' sight, to jauk or play:
>   "And O! be sure to fear the Lord alway,
>   An' mind your duty, duly, morn an' night!
>   Lest in temptation's path ye gang astray,
>   Implore His counsel and assisting might:
> They never sought in vain that sought the Lord aright!"
>
> But hark! a rap comes gently to the door;
>   Jenny, wha kens the meaning o' the same,
> Tells how a neebor lad cam o'er the moor,
>   To do some errands, and convoy her hame.
>   The wily mother sees the conscious flame
> Sparkle in Jenny's e'e, and flush her cheek;
>   With heart-struck anxious care, enquires his name,
> While Jenny hafflins is afraid to speak;
> Weel-pleas'd the mother hears it's nae wild, worthless rake.
>
> Wi' kindly welcome, Jenny brings him ben;
>   A strappin' youth; he takes the mother's eye;
> Blythe Jenny sees the visit's no ill ta'en;
>   The father cracks of horses, pleughs and kye.
>   The youngster's artless heart o'erflows wi' joy,
> But blate and laithfu', scarce can weel behave;
>   The mother, wi' a woman's wiles, can spy
> What makes the youth sae bashfu' an' sae grave;
> Weel-pleased to think her bairn's respected like the lave.

(a) Make a detailed analysis of Burns's treatment of Scottish rural life in this extract.

and

(b) Go on to discuss Burns's treatment of Scottish rural life elsewhere in *The Cotter's Saturday Night* **and** in **one** or **two** other poems.

13. Chaucer

Examine the poetic means by which Chaucer creates characters that extend beyond social or moral stereotypes.

In your answer you should refer to **three** or **four** characters. These characters should be drawn **both** from the General Prologue **and** from **either** or **both** of the specified Tales.

14. Donne

Discuss the uses Donne makes of aspects of Renaissance learning and discovery in *The Good Morrow, The Sun Rising, Aire and Angels* and *A Valediction: forbidding mourning*.

15. Duffy

Analyse Duffy's poetic treatment of the past in *Originally, The Captain of the 1964 "Top of the Form" Team* and *Litany*.

16. Heaney

"*Heaney explores the past to try to understand the present and to offer solutions for the future.*"

Keeping this statement in mind, discuss the principal means by which Heaney explores the past in *The Tollund Man, Funeral Rites* and *Punishment*.

17. Henryson

EITHER

(a) Read carefully the following extract from *The Testament of Cresseid* and then answer questions (i) **and** (ii) that follow it (Page seven).

> And first of all Saturne gave his sentence,
> Quhilk gave to Cupide litill reverence,
> Bot as ane busteous churle on his maneir
> Came crabitlie with auster luik and cheir.
>
> His face fronsit, his lyre was lyke the leid,
> His teeth chatterit and cheverit with the chin,
> His ene drowpit, how sonkin in his heid,
> Out of his nois the meldrop fast can rin,
> With lippis bla and cheikis leine and thin;
> The ice schoklis that fra his hair doun hang
> Was wonder greit, and as ane spear als lang:
>
> Atouir his belt his lyart lokkis lay
> Felterit unfair, ouirfret with froistis hoir
> His garmound and his gyte full gay of gray,
> His widderit weid fra him the wind out woir
> Ane busteous bow within his hand he boir,
> Under his girdill ane flasche of felloun flanis
> Fedderit with ice and heidit with hailstanis.
>
> Than Juppiter, richt fair and amiabill,
> God of the starnis in the firmament
> And nureis to all things generabill;
> Fra his father Saturne far different,
> With burelie face and browis bricht and brent,
> Upon his heid ane garland wonder gay
> Of flouris fair, as it had been in May.

> His voice was cleir, as crystal were his ene,
> As goldin wyre sa glitterand was his hair,
> His garmound and his gyte full gay of grene
> With goldin listis gilt on everie gair;
> Ane burelie brand about his middill bair,
> In his richt hand he had ane groundin speir,
> Of his father the wraith fra us to weir.

    (i) Identify and analyse in detail some of the principal poetic techniques employed in this extract to convey the character of Saturne and the character of Juppiter.

and

    (ii) Go on to examine some of the principal poetic techniques employed elsewhere in the poem to convey the character of Cresseid.

OR

(b) "In the **Morall Fabillis** the relationship between tale and moral is rarely straightforward."

Examine **two** or **three** of the *Morall Fabillis* in the light of this statement.

18. Keats

Discuss some of the principal means by which, in **two** or **three** poems, Keats explores the nature and importance of beauty.

19. MacDiarmid

EITHER

(a) Discuss some of the principal poetic means by which the search for identity, both personal and national, is explored in *A Drunk Man Looks at the Thistle*.

OR

(b) "The impact of MacDiarmid's early lyrics derives from their blend of earthly and cosmic elements."

Discuss.

20. Muir

Discuss some of the principal means by which, in *The Good Town*, *The River* and *The Refugees*, Muir explores some of the tensions he found in contemporary Europe.

21. Plath

Analyse and evaluate Plath's use of images and symbols in *The Arrival of the Bee Box*, *Daddy* and *Lady Lazarus*.

22. Yeats

Discuss in detail Yeats's poetic treatment of loss and change in *In Memory of Major Robert Gregory*, *An Irish Airman Foresees his Death* and *Easter 1916*.

PROSE FICTION

23. Atwood

Discuss some of the principal means by which Atwood presents the motivations of her characters in *Cat's Eye* **and** in *Alias Grace*.

24. Austen

"We can all **begin** freely—a slight preference is natural enough; but there are very few of us who have heart enough to be really in love without encouragement. In nine cases out of ten, a woman had better shew **more** affection than she feels."

(Charlotte Lucas to Elizabeth Bennet)

"I am no matchmaker, as you know well . . . being much too well aware of the uncertainty of all human events and calculations. I only mean that if Mr. Elliot should some time hence pay his addresses to you, and if you should be disposed to accept him, I think there would be every possibility of your being happy together. A most suitable connection everybody must consider it, but I think it might be a very happy one."

(Lady Russell to Anne Elliot)

Consider the advice offered by a range of characters to Elizabeth Bennet **and** to Anne Elliot, and discuss the effects of that advice.

25. Dickens

Discuss the contribution of humour to Dickens's characterisation in *Hard Times* **and** in *Great Expectations*.

26. Fitzgerald

"The world of a Fitzgerald novel is glamorous but essentially shallow; its characters live in an emotional and spiritual vacuum."

In the light of this statement, discuss some of the principal means by which Fitzgerald presents the worlds of *The Beautiful and Damned* **and** *Tender is the Night*.

27. Galloway

"In her novels Galloway presents to us characters that grow and develop and become stronger."

How effective, in your view, is Galloway's presentation of such characters in *The Trick is to Keep Breathing* **and** in *Foreign Parts*?

28. Gray

Discuss some of the means by which Gray explores concepts of identity in *Lanark* **and** in *Poor Things*.

29. **Hardy**

Writing of the specified texts, one critic has claimed that *"Hardy's central concerns are the social issues of his day: tradition and change in rural society, class distinctions, attitudes to marriage, the position of women . . . ."*

Discuss *The Return of the Native* **and** *Tess of the d'Urbervilles* in the light of this assertion.

30. **Hogg**

*"In **The Private Memoirs and Confessions of a Justified Sinner**, the role of the supernatural is to offer an alternative interpretation of reality."*

Discuss.

31. **Joyce**

Discuss the uses Joyce makes of "epiphanies", moments of intense revelation, in *A Portrait of the Artist as a Young Man* **and** in **one** or **two** of the stories from *Dubliners*.

32. **Stevenson**

Discuss the role of narrative voice in *The Master of Ballantrae* and in **one** or **two** of the specified short stories.

33. **Waugh**

Make a comparative study of the importance of houses both as setting and as symbol in *A Handful of Dust* **and** in *Brideshead Revisited*.

PROSE NON-FICTION

34. *"No life is really private or isolated; personal preoccupations are inevitably bound up with the larger movements of mankind."*

Discuss the treatment of "personal preoccupations" and "the larger movements of mankind" in any **one** of the specified texts.

35. It has been suggested that the writer of non-fiction *"preserves in words things that matter to him or her: people, places, events, scenes, incidents, moments"*.

Discuss some of the principal techniques employed by **one** or **two** of the specified writers in order to *"preserve in words things that matter"*.

[*Turn over*

Section 2—Language Study

You must answer **one question only** in this section.

Unless otherwise indicated, your answer must take the form of an **essay/analytical report** appropriately structured to meet the demands of your selected question.

Topic A—Varieties of English or Scots

1. Show how any **one** variety of English **or** Scots you have studied has been influenced by **one** or **more than one** of the following:

   - mass media
   - population movement
   - globalisation
   - employment patterns
   - political agendas
   - information and communication technology.

2. Describe in detail what you consider to be the distinctive features of any **one** variety of English **or** Scots you have studied.

Topic B—The historical development of English or Scots

If you choose to answer a question on this topic, you must refer to **one** of the two texts provided.

Text A is from Jonathan Swift's *A Proposal for Correcting, Improving and Ascertaining The English Tongue*, published in 1712.

Text B is from Alexander Hume's *Of the Orthographie and Congruitie of the Britan Tongue*, for which the date of publication is uncertain, but possibly 1617 or 1618.

Choose one of these texts and then answer **either** question 3 **or** question 4.

3. What linguistic features of **Text A** differ from those of present-day English **or** what linguistic features of **Text B** differ from those of present-day Scots?

   What explanations can you offer to account for the differences you have identified?

   In your answer, you may wish to consider some or all of the following:

   - spelling
   - punctuation
   - vocabulary
   - grammar.

4. Discuss some of the attitudes towards language in the text you have chosen **and** in other texts from your own reading and research.

Text A

THERE is a another Sett of Men who have contributed very much to the ſpoiling of the *Engliſh* Tongue; I mean the Poets, from the Time of the Reſtoration. Theſe Gentlemen, although they could not be inſenſible how much our Language was already overſtocked with Monoſyllables; yet, to ſave Time and Pains, introduced that barbarous Cuſtom of abbreviating Words, to fit them to the Meaſure of their Verſes; and this they have frequently done, ſo very injudiciouſly, as to form ſuch harſh unharmonious Sounds, that none but a *Northern* Ear could endure: They have joined the moſt obdurate Conſonants without one intervening Vowel, only to ſhorten a Syllable: And their Taſte in time became ſo depraved, that what was at firſt a Poetical Licence not to be juſtified, they made their Choice, alledging, that the Words pronounced at length, ſounded faint and languid. This was a Pretence to take up the ſame Cuſtom in Proſe; ſo that moſt of the Books we ſee now a-days, are full of thoſe Manglings and Abbreviations. Inſtances of this Abuſe are innumerable: What does Your LORDSHIP think of the Words, *Drudg'd, Diſturb'd, Rebuk't, Fledg'd,* and a thouſand others, every where to be met in Proſe as well as Verſe? Where, by leaving out a Vowel to ſave a Syllable, we form ſo jarring a Sound, and ſo difficult to utter, that I have often wondred how it could ever obtain.

ANOTHER Cauſe (and perhaps borrowed from the former) which hath contributed not a little to the maiming of our Language, is a fooliſh Opinion, advanced of late Years, that we ought to ſpell exactly as we ſpeak; which beſide the obvious Inconvenience of utterly deſtroying our Etymology, would be a thing we ſhould never ſee an End of. Not only the ſeveral Towns and Countries of *England*, have a different way of Pronouncing, but even here in *London*, they clip their Words after one Manner about the Court, another in the City, and a third in the Suburbs; and in a few Years, it is probable, will all differ from themſelves, as Fancy or Faſhion ſhall direct: All which reduced to Writing would entirely confound Orthography. Yet many People are ſo fond of this Conceit, that it is ſometimes a difficult matter to read modern Books and Pamphlets; where the Words are ſo curtailed and varied from their original Spelling, that whoever hath been uſed to plain *Engliſh*, will hardly know them by ſight.

Text B

To clere this point, and alsoe to reform an errour bred in the south, and now usurped be our ignorant printeres, I wil tel quhat befel my self quhen I was in the south with a special gud frende of myne. Ther rease, upon sum accident, quhither quho, quhen, quhat, etc., sould be symbolized with q or w, a hoat disputation betuene him and me. After manie conflictes (for we ofte encountered), we met be chance, in the citie of Baeth, with a Doctour of divinitie of both our acquentance. He invited us to denner. At table my antagonist, to bring the question on foot amangs his awn condisciples, began that I was becum an heretik, and the doctour spering how, ansuered that I denyed quho to be spelled with a w, but with qu. Be quhat reason? quod the Doctour. Here, I beginning to lay my grundes of labial, dental, and guttural soundes and symboles, he snapped me on this hand and he on that, that the doctour had mikle a doe to win me room for a syllogisme. Then (said I) a labial letter can not symboliz a guttural syllab. But w is a labial letter, quho a guttural sound. And therfoer w can not symboliz quho, nor noe syllab of that nature. Here the doctour staying them again (for al barked at ones), the proposition, said he, I understand; the assumption is Scottish, and the conclusion false. Quherat al laughed, as if I had bene dryven from al replye, and I fretted to see a frivolouse jest goe for a solid ansuer. My proposition is grounded on the 7 sectio of this same cap., quhilk noe man, I trow, can denye that ever suked the paepes of reason. And soe the question must rest on the assumption quhither w be a labial letter and quho a guttural syllab. As for w, let the exemples of wil, wel, wyne, juge quhilk are sounded befoer the voual with a mint of the lippes, as is said the same cap., sect. 5. As for quho, besydes that it differres from quo onelie be aspiration, and that w, being noe perfect consonant, can not be aspirated, I appele to al judiciouse eares, to quhilk Cicero attributed to mikle, quhither the aspiration in quho be not ex imo gutture, and therfoer not labial.

Topic C—Multilingualism in contemporary Scotland

5. In your own reading and research, what evidence have you found of codeswitching between languages by speakers in contemporary Scotland?

    In your answer you should consider some of the forms, contexts and purposes of such codeswitching.

6. To what extent does the Scottish Parliament encourage and support **more than** the three indigenous languages of Scotland?

Topic D—The use of Scots in contemporary literature

For both questions on this topic, you are provided with two texts written in Scots.

Text A is an extract from *The Steamie*, a play by Tony Roper.

Text B is a poem entitled *Tae makk a Martyr* by Sheena Blackhall.

Read the two texts carefully and then answer **either** question 7 **or** question 8.

7. Discuss some of the principal aesthetic effects created by each writer's use of Scots.

8. Select **one** of the texts and contrast the use of Scots in that text—vocabulary, idiom, grammar, orthography—with the use of Scots by a writer other than Tony Roper or Sheena Blackhall.

Text A

Extract from *The Steamie*

DOLLY: Wait tae ye hear this. Tell them what ye telt me Mrs Culfeathers.

MRS CULFEATHERS: Well I wis tellin' Dolly that I aye got ma mince oot o' Galloways because it is lovely mince . . . there's hardly any fat in their mince Doreen ye know.

DOREEN (slightly mystified): Aye, oh, it's good mince.

MRS CULFEATHERS: D'ye no like their mince Magrit?

MAGRIT: Aye . . . it's awright. (Looks at DOLLY.)

DOLLY: Tell them aboot whit Mr Culfeathers says aboot it.

MRS CULFEATHERS: Well . . . I wis tellin' Dolly aboot how I aye get ma mince oot o' Galloways, but sometimes I get it oot another butchers . . . ye know just for a wee change, and I was saying that when I get it oot another butchers, Mr Culfeathers can always tell, even though I havenae said whit butcher's I got it oot o'. If I pit mince doon tae him, and I havenae got it oot o' Galloways, he aye says tae me, 'where did ye get that mince fae?'

MAGRIT (slight sarcasm): Does he? ... (To DOREEN) D'ye hear that?

DOREEN: Aye ... that's ... that's ... that's eh ... very interesting.

MRS CULFEATHERS: That shows ye what good mince it is.

DOLLY: Oh it is ... aye it is good mince, isn't it Magrit?

MAGRIT: Oh ... second tae none.

DOLLY: But that's no the end o' it. There's mair.

DOREEN: Surely not.

MAGRIT: Ye mean even mair interesting than that?

DOLLY: Aye ... wait tae ye hear this.

MAGRIT: Well I don't see how you can top that but do go on.

Text B

Tae makk a Martyr

Takk ae patriot
Separate him frae kintra, kin an airmy
Croon him wi leaves like ony tattie-bogle
Makk a radge o him an his beliefs

Add nae drap o human kindness, raither
A scoosh o soor grapes, wersh as graveyaird bree
Sprinkle a jeelip o heich wirds ower the proceedins

Wheep yer warrior, bleedin ben the streets
Larded wi gobs an skaith
Beat till nearhaun fooshionless
Afore a fyauchie boorich o yer commons
Hing on the gallows till hauf-smored an thrappled

Neist, remove yer patriot,
Skewer an disembowel
While yet alive ... hate is a dish best hett

Fry his intimmers aneth his verra een
Syne chop the lave an sen tae aa the airts
Sae his puir pairts micht flegg aff similar craas
Nailin oppression's colours tae life's brig

Sit back an wyte
There's mair nur deid-flesh stewin

[Turn over

Topic E—Language and social context

9. Joan Swann has written *"the language variety you use conveys certain information about you, such as where you come from and what kind of person you are."*

To what extent does your study of language and social context support this claim?

10. What has your study of language and social context suggested about the effects of audience **and/or** topic on the linguistic choices which speakers make?

Topic F—The linguistic characteristics of informal conversation

For both questions on this topic you are provided with a transcript of a conversation between two women.

Read the transcript carefully and then answer **either** question 11 **or** question 12.

11. What linguistic features characterise this exchange as informal conversation?

12. Using the transcript provided and evidence from your own reading and research, write an essay on turn-taking in informal conversation.

The transcribers have provided the following information regarding transcription methods:

- F631 and F689 are identification numbers given to speakers
- Non-lexical sounds appear in the transcript within square brackets, eg [laugh]
- Stretches of overlapping speech are marked by the use of double slashes: // //
- Stammering, false starts and truncated words are marked by the use of hyphens: -

F631: So, you got married recently, Louise. //Tell us about your,//
F689: //[laugh]//
F631: the whole experience. [inhale]
F689: The whole experience? Oh I don't know. //I don't remember much o it now. [laugh] Sort o wiped from ma memory.//
F631: //[laugh]//
F689: Ehm, it all started, I think, it must have been September or something like that, and David just decided one day "I think we should get married soon". //An I says "Ehm,//
F631: //Mmhm// //[laugh]//
F689: //really?" [laugh]// //[laugh]//
F631: //How romantic! [laugh]//
F689: Och, it was just, I never really thought about it, cause erm, I was quite happy ploddin along, but we'd said like years ago before Rosalyn was even born that we should perhaps get married at some point, [laugh], //so it just sort o//
F631: //Mmhm//
F689: got put on hold and put on hold. And then what with the movin house and stuff. Ehm, so it originally turned out that we'd just go for a really really small do.
F631: Mmhm
F689: And [throat] of course I told Mum and she was like "Oh, we'll need to have a reception" [laugh] and things like that. //So,//
F631: //Right.//

F689: it just started out ehm tryin to keep it as simple an as sort o cheap as possible. [laugh]
F631: Mmhm
F689: Ehm, but it was quite horrendous tryin to find like a place that would accept children, //and stuff like that.//
F631: //Really?//
F689: Mmhm, it was like erm, totally, erm, "You're only allowed kids until half past eight and that's it. No exceptions." //[laugh] Uh-huh//
F631: //Up until half eight, right.//
F689: And, so we tried about four different pubs and phoned other places and it was "no no no no" //[laugh].//
F631: //Mmhm//
F689: So, and a lot of them were just really small as well, //so I was,//
F631: //Yeah.//
F689: by the time we sort o counted heads it was gonna be like fifty plus, [laugh] //[laugh]]//
F631: //Mmhm//
F689: that's what it started out like, so erm, [throat]. Pa- [tut] What else is there? Eh
F631: But it was a nice place that you had, in the end. //Mmhm//
F689: //Our hotel, uh-huh that was Mum that// sort o said, "Right, we'll go for this", even though it wisnae the cheapest //place.//
F631: //Mmhm//
F689: Ehm, so, //[laugh]//
F631: //And what about ehm// booking the registrar's? Di- when did you do that, for,
F689: Eh, it was as soon as David phoned out and found sort o the, he was like "What date shall we go for?" I was like that "Oh, any date", sort o, "preferably at the end of the month." Ehm, [tut], and, he just phoned up and they told him what dates there [laugh] were an //that was it. [laugh]//
F631: //Yeah.//
F689: oh I just sort of randomly picked that one, the Friday, and I had specifically said to him "Don't pick a Friday", [laugh] or a //a Saturday, [laugh] because you'll never find anywhere like//
F631: //Oh right. [laugh]// //Oh for a reception?//
F689: //that would uh-huh// like for a function in a pub, which was what I was wantin.
F631: Mmhm
F689: Erm so, //that//
F631: //Oops.// //[laugh]//
F689: //wis that [laugh]// that caused a wee argument, so
F631: Mmhm
F689: ehm

[Turn over

Topic G—The linguistic characteristics of political communication

13. Compare and contrast the linguistic characteristics of any **two** types of political communication.

    You may wish to consider:

    - parliamentary debates
    - parliamentary statements (including, if you wish, the statement provided in question 14)
    - political advertising
    - election leaflets
    - interviews with politicians
    - speeches by MPs, MSPs, MEPs, or any other political figures
    - any other types of political communication you have studied.

14. Identify and discuss those features of the following text that are typical of political communication.

    You should support your answer with reference to **some** or **all** of the following:

    - lexical choices
    - grammatical structures
    - rhetorical patterns
    - imagery
    - orientation to audience.

The text is an edited version of part of a statement to the Scottish Parliament made by Jack McConnell, then First Minister of Scotland, on 25 February 2004.

For ease of reference, the text has been subdivided into numbered paragraphs.

[1] Today, I wish to make a statement on our new policy to attract fresh talent to Scotland. The policy is designed to tackle the most serious long-term issue facing our country. Scotland's population is falling; it is declining at a faster rate than that of anywhere else in Europe. That decline, coupled with a significant shift in Scotland's age profile, is making a serious problem even worse. By 2009, Scotland's population will fall below the symbolic 5 million level. By 2027, there could be, on current projections, a quarter of a million fewer people of working age in Scotland. Those projections are a result of there being more deaths in Scotland than births. We know that for centuries Scots emigrated throughout the world, but net emigration is almost insignificant now. Basically, fewer people leave Scotland, but only a few come to live here.

[2] The challenge is now to counter demographic change, but before I lay out the details of our Government's plans to tackle Scotland's declining population, there is one message that I want to make very clear. The first priority of the Government in Scotland must always be to nurture and retain home-grown talent. Helping to meet the hopes and aspirations of the Scottish people should be the motivation of every one of us in this chamber. However, those hopes and aspirations will not be met if our devolved Government does not act to counter what I believe to be the greatest threat to Scotland's future prosperity.

[3] Population decline is serious. Tax revenues will fall. Falling school rolls mean that local schools will close, other local services will become less sustainable and communities will become weaker. The labour market will contract, there will be fewer consumers to underpin a domestic market and our economy will be less dynamic and more likely to contract overall. We can and must do something about that. Although future projections demonstrate demographic shifts of considerable magnitude, taken step by step the challenge looks easier to deal with.

[4] Our first target must be to avoid our population falling below 5 million. To do that, we need an additional 8,000 people living in Scotland each year between now and 2009. We want to meet that target in three ways: by retaining home-grown talent within Scotland; by encouraging Scots who have moved away to come back home; and by attracting some who are completely new to Scotland—from the rest of the United Kingdom, from the European Union and from further afield.

[5] Devolution was created for this precise purpose: to tackle a tough, long-term problem in our national interest. It is absolutely in the interest of every Scottish family that we create a country that is dynamic and growing, with opportunities for our children and our grandchildren. To do that, we need to attract and welcome new people. We need fresh talent. A more diverse, more cosmopolitan country is good for Scots. It will open minds and broaden horizons. It will stimulate ambitions and ideas—to travel, to see some of the world, to learn from others, but to come home, too. Some think that people will move only if there are job opportunities and others think that people locate only according to the quality of life. I believe that the truth is somewhere in between.

[6] Of course, Scotland needs a growing economy and Scotland's economy is growing—not as fast as it could be, but there are signs that it will grow more quickly in the medium term. More ideas are coming out of our universities, there is increased commercialisation, there are greater levels of entrepreneurial activity and more Scots are learning, training and using their skills. There are more jobs and more vacancies and, in a few sectors, there are even shortages.

[7] Scotland has a unique selling point. We are lucky that we are known to be one of the friendliest and most educated peoples in the world. We have a vibrant culture, stunning countryside, excellent schools, decent transport links and good public services. In short, it is good to live in Scotland. I believe that, in the modern world, businesses increasingly choose to locate in the places where people whom they want to employ want to live.

[8] Exactly a year ago today, I made the case that Scotland needs to attract fresh talent to our shores to secure future prosperity for Scotland. In 12 months, we have developed a national consensus that that must be a priority. I believe that the issue is too important to be party political. We cannot allow new people to be welcomed by some and not by others. We will not be able to attract fresh talent to Scotland if our country speaks with different voices. Although we in the chamber might debate the best way of attracting new people to Scotland, I hope that we can agree on one thing—Scotland's projected population decline is something that we must tackle and one important way of doing that is to welcome others to Scotland to contribute to our economy and to our country.

[Turn over

Section 3—Textual Analysis

You must answer **one question only** in this section.

Unless otherwise indicated, your answer must take the form of a **critical analysis** appropriately structured to meet the demands of your selected question.

1. **Prose fiction [*Pages eighteen to twenty-one*]**

    *The following extract is a chapter from the novel **No Great Mischief** (2000) by Alistair MacLeod.*

    The setting in this chapter is Cape Breton, Nova Scotia, Canada. The year is 1948. The narrator and his family are the descendants of emigrants who left the Scottish Highlands in 1779. They live in a community where Gaelic is still spoken.

    Read the extract carefully and then answer the question that follows it (Page twenty-one).

    My twin sister and I were the youngest children in our family, and we were three on March 28 when it was decided that we would spend the night with our grandparents.

    After he returned from naval service in the war, my father had applied for the position of lightkeeper on the island which seemed almost to float in the channel about
5 a mile and a half from the town which faced the sea. He had long been familiar with boats and the sea and, after passing the examination, was informed in a very formal letter that the job was his. He and my mother were overjoyed because it meant they would not have to go away, and the job reeked of security, which was what they wanted after the disruption of the years of war. The older generation was highly enthusiastic
10 as well. "That island will stay there for a damn long time," said Grandpa appreciatively, although he later apparently sniffed, "Any fool can look after a lighthouse. It is not like being responsible for a *whole* hospital."

    On the morning of March 28, which was the beginning of a weekend, my parents and their six children and their dog walked ashore across the ice. Their older sons, who
15 were sixteen, fifteen, and fourteen, apparently took turns carrying my sister and me upon their shoulders, stopping every so often to take off their mitts and rub our faces so that our cheeks would not become so cold as to be frozen without our realising it. Our father, accompanied by our brother Colin, who was eleven, walked ahead of us, testing the ice from time to time with a long pole, although there did not seem much
20 need to do so for he had "bushed" the ice some two months earlier, meaning he had placed spruce trees upright in the snow and ice to serve as a sort of road guide for winter travellers.

    During the coldest days of winter, the so-called "dog days", the ice became amazingly solid. It was a combination of drift ice from the region of the eastern Arctic
25 and "made" ice which resulted from the freezing of the local channel. In extremely cold winters if the ice was smooth, it was possible to move freely from the island to the mainland and back again. One could walk, or skate, or fashion an iceboat which would skim and veer with cutting dangerous speed across the stinging surface. People would venture out on the ice with cars and trucks, and on one or two weekends there would be
30 horse races to the delight of all. The sharpshod horses would pull light sleighs or even summer sulkies as they sped around yet another track staked out by temporary spruce. At the conclusion of their races, their owners would hurry to cover them with blankets as the perspiration on their coats began to turn to frost. They seemed almost, for a few brief moments, to be horses who had prematurely aged before the eyes of those
35 who watched them, their coats of black and brown turning to a fragile white. White horses frozen on a field of ice and snow.

[X115/701] *Page eighteen*

My parents welcomed the winter ice because it allowed them to do many practical things that were more difficult to accomplish in the summer. They could truck their supplies over the ice without the difficulty of first hauling everything to the wharf and then trying to load it on the boat which swayed below and then, after transporting it across to the island, having to hoist it up out of the boat to the wharf's cap and then again having to transport it up the cliff to the promontory where the lighthouse stood. They took coal and wood across in the winter, and walked and traded animals, leading them by their halters across the treacherous and temporary bridge.

Also in the winter their social life improved, as unexpected visitors crossed to see them, bringing rum and beer and fiddles and accordions. All of them staying up all night, singing songs and dancing and playing cards and telling stories, while out on the ice the seals moaned and cried and the ice itself thundered and snapped and sometimes groaned, forced by the pressures of the tides and currents, running unabated and unseen beneath the cold white surface. Sometimes the men would go outside to urinate and when they would return the others would ask, "*De chuala?*" "What did you hear?" "Nothing," they would say. "*Cha chuala sion.*" "Nothing, only the sound of the ice."

On March 28 there was a lot for my family to do. My older brothers were going to visit their cousins in the country—those who still lived in the old *Calum Ruadh* houses neighbouring the spot which my grandparents had left when they became people of the town. If they could get a ride they were going to spend the weekend there. Even if they could not get a ride, they were planning to walk, saying that ten miles on the inland sheltered roads would not be as cold as a mile and a half straight across the ice. My parents were planning to cash my father's cheque, which they hoped my grandparents had picked up at the post office, and my brother Colin was looking forward to his new parka, which my mother had shrewdly ordered from the Eaton's sale catalogue when such heavy winter garments were reduced by the coming promise of spring. He had been hoping for it since before Christmas. My sister and I were looking forward to the visit with our grandparents, who always made a great to-do about us and always told us how smart we were to make such a great journey from such a far and distant place. And the dog knew where she was going too, picking her way across the ice carefully and sometimes stopping to gnaw off the balls of snow and ice which formed between the delicate pads of her hardened paws.

Everything went well and the sun shone brightly as we journeyed forth together, walking first upon the ice so we could later walk upon the land.

In the late afternoon, the sun still shone, and there was no wind but it began to get very cold, the kind of deceptive cold that can fool those who confuse the shining of the winter sun with warmth. Relatives visiting my grandparents' house said that my brothers had arrived at their destination and would not be coming back until, perhaps, the next day.

My parents distributed their purchases into haversacks, which were always at my grandparents' house, and which they used for carrying supplies upon their backs. Because my parents' backs would be burdened and because my brothers were not there, it was decided that my sister and I would spend the night and that our brothers would take us back to the island when they returned. It was suggested that Colin also might stay, but he was insistent that he go, so that he might test the long-anticipated warmth of the new parka. When they left, the sun was still shining, although it had begun to decline, and they took two storm lanterns which might serve as lights or signs and signals for the last part of the trip. My mother carried one and Colin the other, while my father grasped the ice pole in his hand. When they set out, they first had to walk about a mile along the shore until they reached the appropriate place to get on the ice and then they started across, following the route of the spruce trees which my father had set out.

Everyone could see their three dark forms and the smaller one of the dog outlined upon the whiteness over which they travelled. By the time they were halfway across, it was dusk and out there on the ice they lit their lanterns, and that too was seen from the shore. And then they continued on their way. Then the lanterns seemed to waver and almost to dance wildly, and one described an arc in what was now the darkness and then was still. Grandpa watched for almost a minute to be sure of what he was seeing and then he shouted to my grandmother, "There is something wrong out on the ice. There is only one light and it is not moving."

My grandmother came quickly to the window. "Perhaps they stopped," she said. "Perhaps they're resting. Perhaps they had to adjust their packs. Perhaps they had to relieve themselves."

"But there is only one light," said Grandpa, "and it is not moving at all."

"Perhaps that's it," said Grandma hopefully. "The other light blew out and they're trying to get it started."

My sister and I were playing on the kitchen floor with Grandma's cutlery. We were playing "store", taking turns buying the spoons and knives and forks from each other with a supply of pennies from a jar Grandma kept in her lower cupboard for emergencies.

"The light is still not moving," said Grandpa and he began hurriedly to pull on his winter clothes and boots, even as the phone began ringing. "The light is not moving. The light is not moving," the voices said. "They're in trouble out on the ice."

And then the voices spoke in the hurriedness of exchange: "Take a rope." "Take some ice poles." "Take a blanket that we can use as a stretcher." "Take brandy." "We will meet you at the corner. Don't start across without us."

"I have just bought all his spoons and knives," said my sister proudly from the kitchen floor, "and I still have all these pennies left."

"Good for you," said Grandma. "A penny saved is a penny earned."

When they were partway to the shore, their lights picked up the dog's eyes, and she ran to Grandpa when he called to her in Gaelic, and she leaped up to his chest and his outstretched arms and licked his face even as he threw his mitts from his hands so he could bury them deep within the fur upon her back.

"She was coming to get us," he said. "They've gone under."

"Not under," someone said. "Perhaps down but not under."

"I think under," said Grandpa. "She was under, anyway. She's soaked to the spine. She's smart and she's a good swimmer and she's got a heavy, layered coat. If she just went down, she'd be down and up in a second but she's too wet for that. She must have gone down, and then the current carried her under the ice and she had to swim back to the hole to get herself back out."

They went out on the ice in single file, the string of their moving lights seeming almost like a kind of Christmas decoration; each light moving to the rhythm of the man who walked and carried it in his hand. They followed the tracks and walked towards the light which remained permanent in the ice. As they neared it, they realised it was sitting on the ice, sitting upright by itself and not held by any hand. The tracks continued until they came to the open water, and then there were no more.

Years later, my sister and I were in Grade XI and the teacher was talking to the class about Wordsworth and, as an example, was reading to us from the poem entitled "Lucy Gray". When she came to the latter lines, both my sister and I started simultaneously and looked towards each other, as if in the old, but new to us, we had stumbled upon the familiar experience:

"They followed from the snowy bank
Those footmarks, one by one,
Into the middle of the plank;
And further there were none!"

"And further there were none!" But on March 28 we were tiring of our game of store and putting the cutlery away as our grandmother prepared to ready us for bed while glancing anxiously through the window.

Out on the ice the dog began to whine when they came near the open water, and the first men in the line lay on their stomachs, each holding the feet of the man before him, so that they might form a type of human chain with their weight distributed more evenly than if they remained standing. But it was of no use, for other than the light there was nothing, and the ice seemed solid right up to the edge of the dark and sloshing void.

There was nothing for the men to do but wonder. Beyond the crater, the rows of spruce trees marched on in ordered single file in much the same way that they led up to the spot of their interruption. It was thought that perhaps only one tree had gone down and under. The section of the ice that had gone was not large, but as my grandfather said, "It was more than big enough for us."

The tide was going out when they vanished, leaving nothing but a lantern—perhaps tossed on to the ice by a sinking hand and miraculously landing upright and continuing to glow, or perhaps set down after its arc, wildly but carefully by a hand which sought to reach another. The men performed a sort of vigil out on the ice, keeping the hole broken open with their ice poles and waiting for the tide to run its course. And in the early hours of the morning when the tide was in its change, my brother Colin surfaced in one of those half-expected uncertainties known only to those who watch the sea. The white fur hood of his parka broke the surface and the half-frozen men who were crouched like patient Inuit around the hole shouted to one another, and reached for him with their poles. They thought that he had not been a great distance under, or that his clothes had snagged beneath the ice; and they thought that, perhaps, since he was not bearing a backpack, he had not been so heavily burdened and, perhaps, the new material in his parka possessed flotation qualities that had buoyed him to the top. His eyes were open and the drawstrings of his hood were still neatly tied and tucked beside his throat in the familiar manner that my mother always used.

My parents were not found that day, or the next, or in the days or months that followed.

Question

In what ways and how effectively does Alistair MacLeod present what happens on March 28?

2. **Prose non-fiction** [*Pages twenty-two to twenty-five*]

Read carefully the essay **Where Does Writing Come From?** *(1998) by Richard Ford and then answer the question that follows it (Page twenty-five).*

Where Does Writing Come From?

Where does writing come from? I've often been guilty of trying to answer this question. I've done so, I suppose, in the spirit André Breton must've had in mind when he wrote: *Our brains are dulled by the incurable mania of wanting to make the unknown known.* I've done it on public stages after readings, in panel discussions with
5 dozing colleagues, standing before rows of smirking students, at the suggestion of cruel and cynical journalists in hotel rooms at home and abroad. And I believe I can honestly say that I would never spontaneously have asked myself this question had not someone else seemed interested, or had my financial fortunes not seemed (correctly or incorrectly) tied to such speculation. I must've thought I knew the answer, or thought
10 I didn't need to know it. Yet, once the question was asked, I've over the years taken an interest in the answers I've come up with—which is to say, dreamed up—much in the way I take interest in the progress of any piece of fiction I'm writing. This, after all, is what one does, or what I do anyway when I write fiction: pick out something far-fetched or at least previously unthought of by me, something I feel a kind of
15 language-less yen for, and then see what I can dream up about it or around it that's interesting or amusing to myself in the hope that by making it make sense in words I'll make it interesting and important to someone else.

Plenty of writers for plenty of centuries have furrowed their brows over this question—where does it come from, all this stuff you write? An important part of
20 Wordsworth's answer for instance was that ". . . good poetry is the spontaneous overflow of powerful feelings". And I've seen no reason I shouldn't just as well get my two cents' worth down on the chance I might actually get to or near the bottom of the whole subject and possibly help extinguish literature once and for all—since that seems to be where the enquiry tends: let's get writing explained and turned into a neat
25 theorem, like a teasing problem in plasma physics, so we can forget about it and get back to watching *Seinfeld*. And failing that, I might at least say something witty or charming that could make a listener or a reader seek out the book I really do care about—the one I've just written and hope you'll love.

It may be that this investigation stays alive in America partly because of that
30 principally American institution, the creative writing course—of which I am a bona fide graduate, and about which Europeans like to roll their eyes. The institution has many virtues—time to write being the most precious. But it also has several faults, one of which is the unproven good of constantly having like-minded colleagues around to talk to about what one is doing, as if companionship naturally improved one's
35 important work just when one is doing it. How we do what we do and why we do it may just be a subject a certain kind of anxious person can't help tumbling to at a time in life when getting things written at all is a worry, and when one's body of work is small and not very distinguishable from one's private self, and when one comes to find that the actual thing one is writing is not a very riveting topic of conversation over
40 drinks. Among dedicated novices, the large subject of provenance may be all we have in common and all that [will pass for artily abstract speculation] of a disinterested kind.

[X115/701]   Page twenty-two

Clearly another socio-literary force which keeps the topic alive is that among many people who are not writers there's occasionally a flighty belief that writers are special people, vergers of some kind, in charge of an important interior any person would be wise to come close to as a way of sidling up to a potent life's essence. Questions about how, why, etc. become just genuflects before the medium. And writers, being generally undercharged in self-esteem and forever wanting more attention for their work, are often quite willing to become their work's exponent if not its actual avatar. I remember an anecdote about a male writer I know who, upon conducting an interested visitor to his desk overlooking the Pacific, is reported to have whispered as they tiptoed into the sacred, sun-shot room, "Well, here it is. This is where I make the magic."

Again, nothing's new here: just another instance of supposing an approach upon the writer will reveal the written thing more fully, more truly; or if not that then it's the old mistake of confusing the maker with the made thing—an object which may really have some magical pizazz about it, who knows?

Considering an actual set of mechanical connections that might have brought a piece of writing from nowhere, the "place" it resided before I'd written it, to its final condition as the book I hope you'll love, actually impresses upon me the romantic view that artistic invention is a kind of casual magic, one which can't be adequately explained the way, say, a train's arrival in Des Moines can nicely be accounted for by tracing the tracks and switches and sidings and tunnels all the way to its origin in Paducah.

You can—and scholars do—try to trace some apparent connections back from the finished work to the original blank mind and page and even to before that ("He used his father's name for the axe-murderer" . . . hmmm; "she suffered glaucoma just like the jilted sister who became a Carmelite nun, so how can you argue the whole damn story isn't about moral blindness?"). But of course such a procedure is famously unreliable and even sometimes downright impertinent, since in the first place (and there need not be a second) such investigations start at and take for granted the existence of Des Moines, whereas for the writer (and I mean soon to abandon this train business) Des Moines is not just a city but a word that has to be not merely found, but conjured from nothing. In fact the word may not even have been Des Moines to begin with—it may have been Abilene or Chagrin Falls—but became Des Moines because the writer inadvertently let Abilene slip his mind, or because Des Moines had that nice diphthong in it and looked neat and Frenchy on the page, whereas Abilene had those three clunky syllables, and there was already a dopey country song about it. Anyway, there are at least two Abilenes, one in Texas and another one in Kansas, which is confusing, and neither has rail service.

You can see what I mean: the true connections might never really be traceable because they exist only in that murky, silent but fecund interstellar night where impulse, free association, instinct and error reign. And even if I were faithfully to try explaining the etiological connections in a piece of writing I'd done, I still might lie about them, or I might just be wrong because I forgot. But in any case I'd finally have to make something up pretty much the way a scholar does—though not exactly like a writer does who, as I said before, always starts with nothing.

I remember once a complimentary reviewer of a book I'd written singling out for approval my choice of adjectives, which seemed to him surprising and expansive and of benefit to the story. One sentence he liked contained a phrase in which I'd referred to a character's eyes as "old": "He looked on her in an old-eyed way." Naturally, I was pleased to have written something that somebody liked. Only, when I was not long afterward packing away manuscripts for the attic, my eyes happened to fall upon the page and the very commended phrase, "old-eyed", and to notice that somehow in the rounds of fatigued retyping that used to precede a writer's final sign-off on a book in the days before word processors, the original and rather dully hybridised "cold-eyed" had somehow lost its "c" and become "old-eyed", only nobody'd noticed since they both made a kind of sense.

This is my larger point writ, admittedly, small, and it calls to mind the joke about the man from Alabama who couldn't understand how a thermos could keep cold things cold and hot things always hot, and expressed his wonder in a phrase akin to the title of this very essay: "How do it know?"

Anyone who's ever written a novel or a story or a poem and had the occasion later to converse about it with an agitated or merely interested reader knows the pinchy feel that comes when the reader tries to nail down the connections linking the story to some supposed "source", either as a way of illuminating the procedures that transform life to shapely art, or else of just plain diminishing an act of creation to some problem of industrial design.

In my case, this enquiry often centres on the potent subject of children, and specifically writing about children, and more prosecutorily on how it is I can write about children to such and such effect without actually having or having had any myself. (My wife and I don't have any.)

It's frequently surprising to whomever I'm speaking to that I can write persuasively about children: although the surprise is often expressed not as pure delight but in a kind of blinkingly suspicious tone whose spirit is either that I do have children (in another county, maybe) and don't want to admit it, or else that somebody in a position of authority needs to come down and take a closer look at my little minor inventions to certify that they're really as finely and truly drawn as they seem.

Myself, I try to stay in happy spirits about such questioning. Some stranger, after all, has or seems to have read at least a part of some book I've written and been moved by it, and I'm always grateful for that. He or she could also as easily have been watching *Seinfeld*. And so mostly I just try to smile and chuckle and mumble-mutter something about having been a child once myself, and if that doesn't work I say something about there being children pretty much everywhere for the watchful to study, and that my Jamesian job, after all, is to be a good observer. And finally if that isn't enough I say that if it were so hard to write about children I of all people wouldn't be able to do it, since I'm no smarter than the next guy.

But the actual truth—the one I know to be true and that sustains my stories—is that even though I was once a child, and even though there are a God's own slew of bratty kids around to be studied like lab rats, and even though I'm clearly not the smartest man in the world, I still mostly write about children by making them up. I make them up out of language bits, out of my memories, out of stories in newspapers, out of overheard remarks made by my friends and their kids, out of this and out of that, and sometimes out of nothing at all but the pleasurable will to ascribe something that might be interesting to a child instead of to an adult or to a spaceman or a horse, after which a child, a fictive child, begins to take shape on the page as a willed, moral gesture toward

135 a reader. '"All I want for Christmas is to know the difference between that and which," said little Johnny, who was just ten years old but already beginning to need some firmer discipline.' Behold: a child is born.

Occasionally if pushed or annoyed I'll come right out and say it: I make these little beggars up, that's what. So sue me. But an odd restraint almost always makes me
140 revert to my prior explanations. Some delicacy in me simply doesn't want to say, "They're invented things, these characters, you can't track them down like rabbits to their holes. They won't be hiding there." It's as though arguing for invention and its fragile wondrous efficacy was indelicate, wasn't quite nice. And even though arguing for it wouldn't harm or taint invention's marvels (we all know novels are made-up
145 things; it's part of our pleasure to keep such knowledge in our minds), still I always feel queasy doing it—not like a magician who reluctantly shows a rube how to pull a nickel out of his own ear, but more like a local parish priest who upon hearing a small but humiliating confession from a friend, lets the friend off easy just to move matters on to a higher ground.

150 Wallace Stevens wrote once that "in an age of disbelief . . . it is for the poet to supply the satisfactions of belief in his measure and his style". And that takes in how I feel about invention—invented characters, invented landscapes, invented breaks of the heart and their subsequent repairs. I believe that there are important made-up things that resist precise tracing back, and that it's a blessing there are, since our acceptance of
155 them in literature (acting as a substitute for less acceptable beliefs) suggests that for every human problem, every insoluble, every cul-de-sac, every despair, there's a chance we can conjure up an improvement—a Des Moines, where previously there was only a glum Abilene.

Frank Kermode wrote thirty years ago in his wonderful book *The Sense of an*
160 *Ending* that, "It is not that we are connoisseurs of chaos, but that we are surrounded by it, and equipped for coexistence with it only by our fictive powers". To my mind, not to believe in invention, in our fictive powers, to believe that all is traceable, that the rabbit must finally be in the hole waiting is (because it's dead wrong) a certain recipe for the squalls of disappointment, and a small but needless reproach to mankind's
165 saving capacity to imagine what could be better and, with good hope then, to seek it.

Question

"Where does writing come from?"

How effectively, in your view, does the writer explore the ideas raised by this question?

In your answer you should take account of his use of:

- personal experience and anecdote
- language and imagery
- sentence and paragraph structure
- the structure of the essay as a whole
- any other literary or rhetorical devices you consider to be important.

[Turn over

3. **Poetry (*Page twenty-six*)**

Read carefully the poem **The world is too much with us . . .** *(1807) by William Wordsworth and then answer the question that follows it.*

      The world is too much with us; late and soon,
      Getting and spending, we lay waste our powers;
      Little we see in Nature that is ours;
      We have given our hearts away, a sordid boon!
5   This Sea that bares her bosom to the moon;
      The winds that will be howling at all hours,
      And are up-gathered now like sleeping flowers;
      For this, for everything, we are out of tune;
      It moves us not.—Great God! I'd rather be
10 A Pagan suckled in a creed outworn;
      So might I, standing on this pleasant lea,
      Have glimpses that would make me less forlorn;
      Have sight of Proteus[1] rising from the sea;
      Or hear old Triton[2] blow his wreathèd horn.

[1] An ancient Greek sea god capable of taking many shapes.
[2] An ancient Greek sea god often depicted as trumpeting on a shell.

Question

Write a detailed critical analysis of this poem in which you make clear what you consider to be the significant features of its language and form.

4. **Drama** (*Pages twenty-seven to thirty-six*)

   The following extract is taken from the one-act play **Walking Through Seaweed** *(1970) by Ian Hamilton Finlay.*

   The play presents a meeting between two girls of sixteen who have previously met casually at a dance.

   The scene of the meeting is described as follows: "A city street of the 1960s, at dusk. Two teenage girls have sauntered up to look in a shop window. Three doors away is a café with a juke-box, its raucous or wistful pop songs carrying faintly into the street. Music: any wistful pop song."

   The characters are identified only as FIRST GIRL and SECOND GIRL.

   Read the extract carefully and then answer the question that follows it (Page thirty-six).

	FIRST GIRL:	I like rock-'n'-roll and jiving.
	SECOND GIRL:	I like that too – it's lovely.
	FIRST GIRL:	Everyone goes jiving.
	SECOND GIRL:	Yep. [*Pause.*] You got a boy friend?
5	FIRST GIRL:	Yep. I got lots of them.
	SECOND GIRL:	You got lots of boy friends?
	FIRST GIRL:	Yep.
	SECOND GIRL:	What d'you do with them?
	FIRST GIRL:	Not much . . . Go jiving.
10	SECOND GIRL:	That all?
	FIRST GIRL:	Go to the pictures.
	SECOND GIRL:	That all?
	FIRST GIRL:	What else?—Go jiving, go to the pictures. Play the juke-box in a café. What else?
15	SECOND GIRL:	I got a boy friend.
	FIRST GIRL:	Have you?
	SECOND GIRL:	Yep. I got a boy friend. And he's sort of special. I mean – I mean I've just the one special boy friend – and do you know what he and I do?
20	FIRST GIRL:	No.
	SECOND GIRL:	Well, guess – go on. Remember about – about the seaweed, and—. Remember he's my special boy friend . . . Now you try and guess what he and I do . . .

	FIRST GIRL:	Go to the pictures?
25	SECOND GIRL:	No.
	FIRST GIRL:	Go jiving?
	SECOND GIRL:	No.
	FIRST GIRL:	If you had enough money, you could go jiving – or something – every night.
30	SECOND GIRL:	Oh, he and I got plenty money. He and I are *loaded*.—But we don't go jiving.
	FIRST GIRL:	No? Can't he jive then?
	SECOND GIRL:	Yep. But he doesn't want to.—He ain't like an ordinary boy. He's special.
35	FIRST GIRL:	All the boys nowadays go jiving.
	SECOND GIRL:	You're supposed to be guessing what he and I do . . .
	FIRST GIRL:	No pictures . . . No jiving . . . I suppose you go in a café and play the juke-box . . .
	SECOND GIRL:	No. We never play a juke-box.
40	FIRST GIRL:	Sounds like your boy must be a square.
	SECOND GIRL:	No, he ain't a square.
	FIRST GIRL:	Well, what d'you do? You'll have to tell me.
	SECOND GIRL:	Me and my boy friend – I told you he's special – *we go walking through seaweed*.
45	FIRST GIRL:	You don't!
	SECOND GIRL:	But we do.—We go – in his car – down to where the sea is, and then – then we take off our shoes . . . and we walk through the seaweed . . . it's ever so lovely!
	FIRST GIRL:	You must be crackers – you and your boy friend.
50	SECOND GIRL:	We are not crackers. He's a very nice boy. [*Pause.*] And while we're walking along through the seaweed – he's ever such a nice boy – he takes hold of my hand . . .
	FIRST GIRL:	What does he do?
	SECOND GIRL:	When we're walking?
55	FIRST GIRL:	No, what does he *do*? What does he work at?
	SECOND GIRL:	He's – he's in advertising.
	FIRST GIRL:	What's his name?
	SECOND GIRL:	His first name's Paul.
	FIRST GIRL:	You ain't just making all of this up, are you?

60	SECOND GIRL:	How'd I be making it up? I told you his name, didn't I – Paul. His name is Paul and he's ever so handsome . . . He has nice dark hair and he's . . . kind of smooth . . .
65	FIRST GIRL:	It doesn't sound to me like a nice, smooth, handsome boy that's in advertising – a kind of a boy like this Paul – would want to go walking through a lot of seaweed . . .
	SECOND GIRL:	I beg your pardon, but he *does*. Let me tell you – he wouldn't *mind* getting bit by a crab. [*Pause*] The fact is, he's *fond* of crabs.
	FIRST GIRL:	Is he?
70	SECOND GIRL:	And we never do get bit.
	FIRST GIRL:	What kind of seaweed is that seaweed?
	SECOND GIRL:	Well, I'll tell you . . . We walk through every kind of seaweed – the liquorice stuff – and also the other poppy kind . . . And as we walk, we hold hands.
75	FIRST GIRL:	It sounds square to me.
	SECOND GIRL:	Well, it isn't.—We could take you along with us one day . . . You could come along with me and Paul, and we could all three of us go walking in the seaweed . . .
	FIRST GIRL:	I think your Paul must be bats.
80	SECOND GIRL:	He is *not* bats. He's a very sensible boy. He only sometimes gets fed-up of being in – the office . . . He gets tired of – the office – and on Saturdays – he wants a change . . . He gets sick-fed-up-to-the-teeth with that old office . . . So we go and walk through seaweed . . .
85	FIRST GIRL:	Where d'you work yourself?
	SECOND GIRL:	In a factory.
	FIRST GIRL:	How come you happened to meet this Paul fellow who's so handsome and works in advertising?
	SECOND GIRL:	You sound like you don't believe me.
90	FIRST GIRL:	I'm only asking – how come you met him?
	SECOND GIRL:	We met . . . at a dance. [*Pause*] You know – like me and you did. [*Pause*] I suppose you weren't seeing your boy friends that night?
	FIRST GIRL:	No.
95	SECOND GIRL:	Sometimes . . . you feel like being more on your own . . . Yep . . .
	FIRST GIRL:	I never met any handsome smooth fellows – out of advertising – at a dance . . .
	SECOND GIRL:	Well, maybe you will . . .
	FIRST GIRL:	I never even *saw* any fellows who looked like that . . .

100	SECOND GIRL:	Well, it's just your luck.—And then Paul and I have the same tastes . . .
	FIRST GIRL:	Yep. You both like walking through that seaweed . . .
	SECOND GIRL:	Yep. That's our favourite thing. [*Pause*.] Don't you ever get fed-up with going to the pictures? Don't you ever get sick-fed-up-to-the-teeth with just ordinary boys? And work? And all that . . . ?
105		
	FIRST GIRL:	I dunno. I don't think about it.
	SECOND GIRL:	Where d'you work?
	FIRST GIRL:	In a factory.
110	SECOND GIRL:	Same as me.
	FIRST GIRL:	Yep. Same as you. But I never met – at a dance – any handsome fellow out of advertising. I *read* of them in magazines. I read of *lots* of them in that magazine my Mum gets . . . Tall, dark and smooth . . . And come to think of it, *their* name was Paul.
115	SECOND GIRL:	Paul is a very common name in advertising.
	FIRST GIRL:	Yep. But I never met one *real* such fellow . . .
	SECOND GIRL:	Maybe you will, though . . . someday.
	FIRST GIRL:	Maybe. Yep. [*Pause*.] I only hope if I do he don't have a taste for walking through seaweed . . .
120	SECOND GIRL:	You have to walk through seaweed sometimes – if you want to get down to where the sea is . . .
	FIRST GIRL:	Who wants to get to the sea?
	SECOND GIRL:	I do sometimes. I like it. [*Pause*.] It ain't like a factory – the sea. It's big – and it's deep, and—. Well, I dunno. But I like the sea.
125		
	FIRST GIRL:	You're a queer one, you are.
	SECOND GIRL:	What's the name of *your* boy friend?
	FIRST GIRL:	I already told you – I ain't got just *one* boy friend. I got lots of boy friends. I got hundreds.
130	SECOND GIRL:	Who?
	FIRST GIRL:	I can't remember their names off-hand . . .
	SECOND GIRL:	Are they Beats?
	FIRST GIRL:	No they ain't.
	SECOND GIRL:	Do you think I'm a Beat – a Beat girl?
135	FIRST GIRL:	Yep. The things you say – you must be a Beat. Though – well, you ain't *dressed* like a Beat. But walking in seaweed – *that's* sort of a Beat thing . . .

	SECOND GIRL:	My Paul walks through seaweed. And he ain't a Beat – he's an advertising man.
140	FIRST GIRL:	What do they do in them places?
	SECOND GIRL:	Advertising places?
	FIRST GIRL:	Yep. Advertising places. What do they do there?
	SECOND GIRL:	Well, I dunno . . . I suppose . . . Well, they sort of – advertise things . . .
145	FIRST GIRL:	What does *he* do?
	SECOND GIRL:	Paul?
	FIRST GIRL:	Yep. What does Paul do in that advertising place?
150	SECOND GIRL:	He.—Well, he never talks much about it. You don't think of – of work when you're walking in the seaweed, see? You feel *romantic*.
	FIRST GIRL:	All the same you must know what he *does*.
	SECOND GIRL:	Well, as a matter of fact I do know. What he does is – is – is go to conferences.
	FIRST GIRL:	Conferences?
155	SECOND GIRL:	Yep.
	FIRST GIRL:	I read about them conferences in my Mum's magazine . . .
	SECOND GIRL:	Uh-huh.
160	FIRST GIRL:	It seems like advertising's *all* conferences. There's this boy – the one called Paul, you know – the one who's sort of smooth, and dark, and handsome – and what he does is, go to conferences.
	SECOND GIRL:	Uh-huh. Well, that's like Paul. Paul goes to conferences.
165	FIRST GIRL:	Then, after the conferences – when they've knocked off advertising – then this boy Paul – this handsome smoothy – he goes and meets his girl and they go to a rest-ur-ant. They sit and eat lobsters and maybe he's *too* smooth.
	SECOND GIRL:	My Paul isn't too smooth.
	FIRST GIRL:	Maybe. But what about the other one?
	SECOND GIRL:	I ain't *got* another one.
170	FIRST GIRL:	Oh ain't you? Come off it . . .
	SECOND GIRL:	But I *told* you – we're special.
	FIRST GIRL:	What about the one with ginger hair and a snub nose. The engineer.

[Turn over

	SECOND GIRL:	I don't *know* any engineers.
175	FIRST GIRL:	I bet *he* wouldn't walk through seaweed though. I bet the ginger one with the snub nose spends *his* Saturdays at a football match.
	SECOND GIRL:	I don't love *him*. I love Paul.
	FIRST GIRL:	You don't care about the engineer, eh?
180	SECOND GIRL:	No. If you want to know, I can't stand him.—All he *ever* wants to do is – go and jive.
	FIRST GIRL:	That's what I said. He does the same things like everyone else does.
	SECOND GIRL:	But Paul – he's different.
185	FIRST GIRL:	Yep. He's different. You're telling me he is! Any boy who spends his Saturdays just walking through seaweed is different. He's a head-case. [*Pause.*] Ain't you even *scared* of what might be in it? Ain't you scared of all them crabs and things?
	SECOND GIRL:	No. I'm more scared of every day.
190	FIRST GIRL:	What?
	SECOND GIRL:	Every day. The factory, and all that.—Just working and—. [*Pause.*] You know, when we've walked all through the seaweed– that kind like liquorice and the other poppy kind – when we've walked all the way through the seaweed, hand in hand—.
195	FIRST GIRL:	I thought *you* said you walked with your arms held up.
	SECOND GIRL:	That's right. Like a tight-rope-lady.
	FIRST GIRL:	Then how come you can hold hands?
	SECOND GIRL:	Oh, when Paul and I are walking through the seaweed – we only hold up our *outside* hands.
200	FIRST GIRL:	Then how d'you carry your shoes and socks?
	SECOND GIRL:	What?
	FIRST GIRL:	If the two of you's holding hands and you're holding up your hands like the telly-tight-rope-lady – you only got *two* hands – how d'you carry your shoes and socks? Eh?
205	SECOND GIRL:	Well — well, what d'you think? We left them up where the car is. See?
	FIRST GIRL:	Oh? [*Pause.*] One of these days you and Paul – you're going to be *sorry* for walking through seaweed.
	SECOND GIRL:	Why?
210	FIRST GIRL:	You're going to get bit. That's why.

	SECOND GIRL:	We never get bit. But we just *might* though. That's what's nice about walking through seaweed – that you might get bit . . . just a *little* . . . [*Pause.*] Them crabs don't scare *me*. I ain't scared of crabs. They're kind of on *our* side.
215	FIRST GIRL:	What? Whose side?
	SECOND GIRL:	Me and Paul's side.
	FIRST GIRL:	No one's on your side. Except you.
	SECOND GIRL:	Yes they are. The crabs are. All wee things like crabs and – and wee things like that – they *like* me and Paul. [*Pause.*] Do you tell all of them boy friends things?
220		
	FIRST GIRL:	No. They're just boy friends.
	SECOND GIRL:	I always tell my Paul *lots* of things.
	FIRST GIRL:	Do you?
	SECOND GIRL:	Yep. He's special. I tell him everything.
225	FIRST GIRL:	I can picture it.
	SECOND GIRL:	What?
	FIRST GIRL:	You and him – walking in seaweed.—The pair of you standing, walking – right up over the ankles too – in all that seaweed.—All of them crabs ready to bite you – and you and him just standing there telling things . . .
230		
	SECOND GIRL:	Well, I always feel like telling things there in the seaweed. [*Pause.*] And then – like I was saying to you – when we've walked right through it – all through the seaweed – and us holding hands too – holding our hands and telling our secret things—.
235		
	FIRST GIRL:	What sort of secret things?
	SECOND GIRL:	Like you tell yourself in bed at night . . .
	FIRST GIRL:	When I'm in bed at night I go to sleep. If we had the telly I'd sit up later though. Everyone round us has the telly. Only *we* ain't. You feel right out of it.
240		
	SECOND GIRL:	You can come round some night and see our telly.
	FIRST GIRL:	That ain't the same as if it was your *own* telly.
	SECOND GIRL:	No . . . Well, I was saying – when we've walked all through the seaweed . . .
245	FIRST GIRL:	Yep?
	SECOND GIRL:	Then me and Paul – he's a real smooth fellow – we come to where the sea is . . .
	FIRST GIRL:	Yep?
	SECOND GIRL:	Ain't you listening? We come to the sea.

[*Turn over*

250	FIRST GIRL:	I'm listening. [*Pause.*] I like those records too . . . All we got at home's an old wireless . . . My other sister – she's got a radiogram.
	SECOND GIRL:	We come to the sea and – it's ever so beautiful.
	FIRST GIRL:	Some of them's beautiful. I like the cheery ones.
255	SECOND GIRL:	I ain't talking about those records on the old juke-box – I'm telling you about Paul and me: we come to *the sea*.
260	FIRST GIRL:	Well, the sea ain't *much* – in my opinion. I don't care *that* much about the sea that I'd risk my life – and spoil my shoes maybe – just walking through a lot of seaweed, all full of crabs and things, to get to it. [*Pause.*] You could get bit like that. It just ain't nice.
	SECOND GIRL:	What ain't nice?
	FIRST GIRL:	Ain't I telling you? – Seaweed ain't nice. And the sea ain't nice. And having no telly ain't. I wouldn't put a *toe* in that seaweed . . .
265	SECOND GIRL:	But it's – beautiful – the sea.
	FIRST GIRL:	Yep. I seen it.
	SECOND GIRL:	Did you ever dream of it?
	FIRST GIRL:	I don't have dreams.—Only once I dreamed we'd a telly . . .
	SECOND GIRL:	Yep.
270	FIRST GIRL:	A great big telly with a screen as big as the screen in a picture-house. Not one of them wee old-fashioned picture-houses screens . . . . A big screen, about a hundred yards across . . .
	SECOND GIRL:	Yep?
	FIRST GIRL:	With a plastic-plated cabinet.
275	SECOND GIRL:	I ain't never dreamed of a telly set . . .
	FIRST GIRL:	Another time I had a dream of a radiogram – and once I dreamed I was married to a disc-jockey.
	SECOND GIRL:	Well, there you are. You *do* have dreams.
	FIRST GIRL:	Yep. Well . . . Maybe . . .
280	SECOND GIRL:	I dreamed – I dreamed of the sea once. . . . It was all – kind of dark – and – it was all big and dark – and—. Well, it was – beautiful!
285	FIRST GIRL:	It was a beautiful radiogram in my dream. It was kind of Hi-Fi Stereoscopic. Posh! You didn't even have to press the button. You just had to *think* and it went and switched itself on.
	SECOND GIRL:	Yep? You know what the sea was like in my dream?
	FIRST GIRL:	It was Hi-Fi Stereoscopic – with *five* extra loudspeakers.

	SECOND GIRL:	It was just kind of like *home* – it was just kind of like what a *real home* is . . .
290	FIRST GIRL:	What?
	SECOND GIRL:	I said – the sea in my dream – it was all big and dark and – just like home!
	FIRST GIRL:	You talk like a funny picture I saw.
	SECOND GIRL:	I could have stayed there by it – forever!
295	FIRST GIRL:	It made me want to giggle. *Everyone* giggled.
	SECOND GIRL:	But my Mum came and waked me up.
	FIRST GIRL:	What?
	SECOND GIRL:	I had to wake up – out of my dream.
	FIRST GIRL:	I wonder why I dreamed of a great big radiogram?
300	SECOND GIRL:	I suppose you'd like to *have* a great big radiogram.
	FIRST GIRL:	Yep.
305	SECOND GIRL:	Maybe you could come with us down to the sea. Or – well, if Paul had to work some Saturday – if he got asked to do overtime – at advertising – we could go there . . . just the two of us.
	FIRST GIRL:	And walk through that seaweed—!?
	SECOND GIRL:	I could hold your hand – like Paul holds my hand –.
	FIRST GIRL:	You ain't like a magazine fellow that would make me feel all right about that seaweed . . .
310 315 320	SECOND GIRL:	I'd hold it tight.—Ever so tight. [*Pause*.] You and I – we could hold hands – we could go walking – like dancers – like on a tight-rope – all down through all that seaweed – and we'd tell each other things – all our secret things.—Yep, you and me – we could walk through the seaweed – all the way – right to the sea! [*Pause*.] You got to walk through seaweed or – or you don't get anywhere. And seaweed – it's full of crabs and things . . . But you got to walk through it – hand in hand – with some other person – because it's lovely too – you got to walk – like a dancer – like two dancers – all through the seaweed – right to the sea . . . !
325	FIRST GIRL:	All my life I kept out of seaweed. I stayed away from seaweed. It ain't well – nice stuff. You can go and walk in all that seaweed – you can go if you want to – but not with *me*! [*Pause*.] Let's go in the café now. [*Pause*.] I like that one that's on the juke-box. Though it's kind of sad . . . Come on, let's go . . .

[Turn over

SECOND GIRL: Yep. Let's go in the café and play the juke-box.—Maybe some of all of them boy friends of yours will be in the café – perhaps.

[The music grows louder. It is a record – something like – Bobby Darin's "Beyond The Sea"]

330   Somewhere . . .
Beyond the sea . . .

[The two girls saunter off as the music grows still louder – then slowly fades]

Question

Make a detailed study of the ways in which Ian Hamilton Finlay explores the relationship that develops between the two girls.

In your answer you should pay close attention to:

- setting in time and place
- language and dialogue
- the significance of "walking through seaweed"
- the tone of the closing lines.

Section 4—Reading the Media

You must answer **one question only** in this section.

Unless otherwise indicated, your answer must take the form of a **critical essay** appropriately structured to meet the demands of your selected question.

Category A—Film

1. "*Stars are symbols: they embody the accepted values of the society of their time.*"

   How far do you agree?

   In your answer you should refer to the contribution of the "star" or "stars" to **one** or **more than one** film you have studied.

2. Show how, in **one** or **more than one** film you have studied, the conventions of a particular genre have been reworked or re-presented for a contemporary audience.

Category B—Television

3. Discuss how effectively any **one** television drama you have studied—soap, serial, series or single play—exploits the potential of its particular genre.

4. "*Television is becoming a domestic comforter, no longer watched with concentration or attended to closely.*"

   How far, in your view, does the changing relationship between television and its audience affect the ways in which serious events or issues are presented in news or current affairs programmes?

   You should support your answer with evidence drawn from **a range** of programmes you have studied.

Category C—Radio

5. "*Radio is a solitary medium to which we listen alone—but it is one of the best cures for solitude, providing a convincing illusion of company.*"

   Discuss some of the means by which radio creates a relationship of familiarity with its listeners. You may wish to consider such aspects as programme content, mode of address, channel identity.

6. How effectively does any **one** radio drama you have studied—soap, serial, series or single play—exploit the potential of sound **and** of silence?

Category D—Print journalism

7. What is it about the form, content and ideology of any **one** newspaper you have studied that makes it essential to its target audience?

8. For this question you are provided with two news stories—from *The Independent* of 16 March 2007 and *The Observer* of 18 March 2007.

   Analyse the images and written text employed by each newspaper and evaluate their effectiveness in conveying their views on global warming and climate change.

[Turn over

8. (continued)

Collapse of Arctic sea ice 'has reached tipping-point'

By Steve Connor
Science Editor

A catastrophic collapse of the Arctic sea ice could lead to radical climate changes in the northern hemisphere according to scientists who warn that the rapid melting is at a "tipping point" beyond which it may not recover.

The scientists attribute the loss of some 38,000 square miles of sea ice – an area the size of Alaska – to rising levels of carbon dioxide in the atmosphere as well as to natural variability in Arctic ice.

Ever since satellite measurements of the Arctic sea ice began in 1979, the surface area covered by summer sea ice has retreated from the long-term average. This has increased the rate of coastal erosion from Alaska to Siberia and caused problems for polar bears, which rely on sea ice for hunting seals.

However, in recent years the rate of melting has accelerated and the sea ice is showing signs of not recovering even during the cold, dark months of the Arctic winter. This has led to even less sea ice at the start of the summer melting season.

Mark Serreze, a senior glaciologist at the University of Colorado at Boulder, said the world was heading towards a situation where the Arctic will soon be almost totally ice-free during summer, which could have a dramatic impact on weather patterns across the northern hemisphere.

"When the ice thins to a vulnerable state, the bottom will drop out and we may quickly move into a new, seasonally ice-free state of the Arctic," Dr Serreze said.

"I think there is some evidence that we may have reached the tipping point, and the impacts will not be confined to the Arctic region," he said.

Some studies have linked the loss of sea ice in the Arctic to changes in atmospheric weather patterns that influence such things as rainfall in southern and western Europe and the amount of snow and heat. The summer sea ice in the Rocky Mountains of the American Midwest.

The Arctic is one of the fastest warming regions on Earth and scientists fear that temperatures could rise even faster once sea ice melts to expose dark ocean, which absorbs heat more easily without its reflective cap of ice.

"While the Arctic is losing a great deal of ice in the summer months, it now seems that it also is regenerating less ice in the winter. With this increasing vulnerability, a kick to the system just from natural climate fluctuations could send it into a tailspin," Dr Serreze said.

During the late 1980s and early 1990s, changing wind patterns flushed much of the thick sea ice out of the Arctic Ocean and into the Northern Atlantic, where it drifted south and melted away.

A thinner layer of young ice formed in its place, which more readily melts during the warmer, summer months – leading to the appearance of a greater area of open water that absorbs sunlight and heat. The summer sea ice reached an all-time minimum in September 2005, with September 2006 the second lowest.

"This ice-flushing even could be a small-scale analogue of the sort of kick that could invoke rapid collapse, or it could have been the kick itself. At this point, I don't know," again delayed, and ice extents summer by 2040.

Julienne Stroeve from the US National Snow and Ice Data Centre in Colorado said that the winter sea ice failed again this year to recover fully.

"The freeze-up this year was again delayed, and ice extents forecasts even predict an ice-free summer by 2040.

from October through to December set new record lows during the satellite era," she said. Computer models suggest that summer sea ice could disappear altogether by 2080. Some

The collapse of summer sea ice has already affected the polar bear, which relies on it for hunting seals.
JONATHAN HAYWARD/AP/CP

Ocean heat blamed for the mysterious disappearance of glaciers

By Steve Connor

A mysterious phenomenon is causing four major glaciers in the Antarctic to shrink in unison, causing a significant increase in sea levels, scientists have found.

The rise in atmospheric temperatures caused by global warming cannot account for the relatively rapid movement of the glaciers into the sea, but scientists suspect that warmer oceans may be playing a role.

"There is a possibility that heat from the ocean is somehow flowing in underneath these glaciers, but it is not related to global warming," said glaciologist Duncan Wingham of University College London. "Something has changed that is causing these glaciers to shrink.

"At this rate the glaciers will all be afloat in 150 years or so."

Satellite measurements have shown that the Antarctic glaciers are retreating in a uniform manner, suggesting a common cause. Air temperatures over Antarctica are much too cold for any significant surface melting, which suggests that the flow of glaciers into the sea is being aided by melting at their base, lubricating their movement into the ocean.

In a study in the journal Science, Dr Wingham and colleague Andrew Shepherd of Edinburgh University found that major glaciers in the Antarctic identified by Wingham and Shepherd.

"These glaciers are vulnerable to small changes in ocean temperature," he said. "A rise of less than 0.5C could have triggered the present imbalance."

However, it would take about 200 years for extra heat from the ocean to reach the underside of the glaciers, which makes it difficult to believe that the present shrinkage is due to global warming, Dr Wingham said.

While the retreat of the Greenland ice sheet can be linked to melting of the glaciers' surface, the same is not true of the four major glaciers in the Antarctic identified by Wingham and Shepherd.

"These glaciers are vulnerable over the past decade – about 12 per cent of the current global trend.

sheets have together contributed to a sea level rise of 0.35mm a year

FRIDAY 16 MARCH 2007 THE INDEPENDENT

8. (continued)

The Observer
Don't exaggerate climate dangers, scientists warn

Hollywood and the media are 'appealing to fear' and confusing the public say experts on global warming

By Juliette Jowit

LEADING CLIMATE change experts have warned of the 'Hollywoodisation' of global warning and criticised American scientists for exaggerating the message of global warming.

Professors Paul Hardaker and Chris Collier of the Royal Meteorological Society said scientists, campaign groups, politicians and the media were all guilty of making out that catastrophic events were more likely to happen when this could not be proved by scientists.

They also criticised the tendency to say individual extreme events – such as the Birmingham typhoon and the Boscastle floods – were certain evidence of climate change.

They singled out for criticism a report last month by the American Association for the Advancement of Science, which said intensification of droughts, heatwaves, floods, wildfires and storms were 'early warning signs of even more devastating damage to come'.

'It's certainly a very strong statement,' said Collier. 'To make the blanket assumption that all extreme weather events are increasing is a bit too early yet.'

Reporting of the recent report by the United Nations International Panel on Climate Change by the media was also criticised, especially the use of words not in the report such as 'catastrophic', 'shocking', 'terrifying' and 'devastating'.

'Campaigners, media and some scientists seem to be appealing to fear in order to generate a sense of urgency' said Professor Mike Hulme, director of the Tyndall Centre for Climate Change Research at the University of East Anglia and a contributor to yesterday's report. 'If they want to engage the public in responding to climate change, this is unreliable at best and counter-productive at worst.'

The report by Hardaker, Collier and other climate experts, 'Making Sense of the Weather and Climate', was launched at a conference in Oxford organised by the charity Sense About Science.

The authors said they firmly believe global warming is happening and man-made emissions of greenhouse gases are partly to blame.

Some scientists also acknowledged that dramatic warnings about climate change had helped generate public debate and support for action to reduce the threat. But Hardaker warned that exaggeration of the problems made the public confused and made it easier for sceptics to argue that the scientists were wrong.

An example of a low probability event given too much weight was the risk of the Gulf Stream, which keeps the North Atlantic relatively warm, 'switching off' and plunging the region into an ice age – the scenario dramatised by the Hollywood film *The Day after Tomorrow*, which also came in for criticism for exaggerating that problem.

As a result scientists had to be more honest about the uncertainties surrounding climate change prediction to avoid losing public trust, said Hardaker.

'Once you begin to exaggerate the science in either direction the debate gets out of control,' he said.

Their comments were backed today by other leading figures in the debate. Dr Peter Scott, manager of understanding and attributing climate change at the Hadley Centre for Climate Change, said he believes scientists have to make it clear there is a long way to go until we know how bad climate change will be.

He said: 'There is a lot more research to do to understand about exactly what effects it's going to have in the future.'

He said that while he welcomed a growing public awareness about the dangers brought about by films and deadlines, informed debate was vital.

'I think it is important that having said there is a problem, it would be unfortunate if people got the impression that there's nothing we can do about it because there is a lot we can do to change the future of climate change,' he said.

Al Gore, who has been praised for his Oscar-winning environmental film *An Inconvenient Truth* has also attracted criticism from scientists. 'I don't want to pick on Al Gore,' Don J Easterbrook, an emeritus professor of geology at Western Washington University, told hundreds of experts at the annual meeting of the Geological Society of America. 'But there are a lot of inaccuracies in the statements we are seeing, and we have to temper that with real data.'

Gore, in an email exchange about the critics, said his work made 'the most important and salient points' about climate change, if not 'some nuances and distinctions'. 'The degree of scientific consensus on global warming has never been stronger,' he said, adding. 'I am trying to communicate the essence of it in the lay language that I understand.'

Above, a tornado and the Boscastle flood. Left, disaster movie The Day After Tomorrow. Right, Oscar winner Al Gore. Getty

WEATHER WORRIES

Claim: More frequent El Ninos
Reality: El Nino is a warning of the tropical Pacific Ocean that occurs every three to seven years. The cause of El Nino is not fully understood but its frequency is not linked to global warming and it has been documented since the 16th century.

Claim: Extreme weather events like the one-in-400-years floods in Boscastle in 2004 are happening more and more frequently.
Reality: It can sound alarming to know that a major flood such as this may happen two years running, but that translates into a 0.25 per cent chance of a flood happening in any one year; the chance remains the same whatever happened in the previous 12 months.

Claim: The disappearing snows of Kilimanjaro are due to global warming.
Reality: This may not have much to do with man's activities. It appears to have begun in the 1880s and the most likely explanation seems to be the change to drier conditions in East Africa.
There is little evidence that the retreating glaciers can be blamed on rising temperatures and hence on human activity.

Source: Sense about Science charitable trust

Category E—Advertising

9. "While advertisements convey messages about particular products, services or brands, they also convey messages about society, gender, lifestyle and values."

   How far do you agree?

   In your answer to Question 9, you may refer to the advertisements provided for Question 10, but your answer **must** also include references to **other** advertisements or advertising campaigns.

10. For this question, you are provided with two advertisements—published in *The Times* and *The Sunday Times* in May 2005.

    NB These advertisements are provided separately as colour inserts.

    Make a detailed analysis of these two advertisements, examining carefully:

    - the construction of the image in each advertisement
    - the cultural codes which establish the representation of the adults and the children
    - the written codes—caption and copy
    - the gender stereotyping
    - the implied values.

[END OF QUESTION PAPER]

It's not dirt. It's breaking new ground.

When you're helping him learn how things grow for the very first time, there's nothing better than some hands-on experience. And there's nothing better than Persil non-bio to get clothes brilliantly clean, whilst caring for them and leaving them kind even next to sensitive skin. Skin can be sensitive at any age, and, reassuringly, our skin care research is supported by the British Skin Foundation.

Use Persil non-bio, and everyone's free to enjoy mucking about.

Persil non-bio – dirt is good

It's not dirt. It's breaking new ground.

It's not dirt. It's feeling safe.

It's great to be big and independent, but when you want a bit of protection, you can't beat Mum. And you can't beat Persil non-bio to clean brilliantly and leave clothes kind next to even a baby's delicate skin. It's good to know that our skin care research is supported by the British Skin Foundation. So relax. With Persil non-bio, you'll both feel happy. **Persil non-bio – dirt is good**

If you want to find out any more, call our Careline: UK 0800 776644 or visit www.persil.com

[BLANK PAGE]

Acknowledgements

Permission has been sought from all relevant copyright holders and Bright Red Publishing is grateful for the use of the following:

The poem 'Sunlight' by Seamus Heaney, taken from 'North', published by Faber & Faber Ltd, 1975 (2006 page 5);
The poem 'To Joan Eardley' by Edwin Morgan, taken from 'Collected Poems' © Carcanet Press Ltd (2006 page 6);
The Poem 'Morning Song' by Sylvia Plath, taken from 'Ariel', published by Faber & Faber Ltd, 1968 (2006 page 7);
An extract from 'Highland River' by Neil Gunn, published by Arrow. Reprinted by permission of the Random House Group Ltd (2006 page 9);
An extract from 'The Girls of Slender Means' by Muriel Spark, published by Macmillan. Reproduced with permission of David Higham Associates (2006 pages 10 & 11);
A transcript from 'Conversational Narrative: Storytelling in Everyday Talk' (2000) by Neal R Norrick, reproduced with permission of John Benjamins (2006 pages 15 & 16);
A transcript from 'Official Report of the Scottish Parliament (8th September 2004). Parliamentary material is reproduced with the permission of the Controller of HMSO on behalf of Parliament (2006 pages 16-18);
The article 'Scottish Sun is the Toast of Holyrood' by Kenny McAlpine, © The Sun/NI Syndication, September 3rd, 2004 (2006 page 19);
A transcript from 'Conversation 05: Fife couple on shared memories' Document 348 by Dr Anderson © Scots Project (2006 pages 20–22);
The poem 'Sharleen: Ah'm Shy', by Janet Paisley, from 'Cannae Win', published by Chapman © Janet Paisley (2006 page 23);
An extract from 'Almost Miss Scotland' taken from 'The Colour of Black & White' by Liz Lochhead. Reproduced with permission of Birlinn Ltd (2006 page 24);
An extract from 'Brick Lane' by Monica Ali, published by Doubleday, 2003. Reprinted by permission of The Random House Group Ltd (2006 pages 25–29);
An extract from 'Sea Burial' by James Hamilton-Paterson, taken from 'Granta 61'. Reproduced by permission of Johnson & Alcock Literary Agency (2006 page 31);
The poem 'Seen from the Train' taken from 'The Complete Poems' by C Day Lewis, published by Sinclair-Stevenson. Reprinted by permission of The Random House Group Ltd (2006 page 32);
An extract from 'The Winslow Boy' (1946) by Terence Rattigan, taken from 'Heritage of Literature' series published by Pearson Education (2006 pages 33–39);
The article 'The Last Survivors' by Cahal Milmo taken from The Independent, Thursday 5 August 2004. Reproduced by permission of The Independent (2006 pages 42–43);
An advert for Mars Delight © Mars Inc (2006 page 45);
An advert for Comfort Pure © Unilever Plc (2006 page 46);
The sonnet, 'Oh my black Soule' by John Donne, is taken from 'The Metaphysical Poets' introduced and edited by Helen Gardner. Published by Penguin (2007 page 4);
The poem, 'Blackberry Picking' by Seamus Heaney, is taken from 'New Selected Poems 1966–1987'. Published by Faber & Faber Ltd (2007 page 5);
Two poems, 'The Bonny Earl of Murray' and 'The Baron of Brackley', are taken from Scottish Ballads, published by Canongate Books Ltd, 14 High Street, Edinburgh, EH1 1TE (2007 pages 6 & 7);
A letter by Paul Coggle, taken from the T.E.S. © Paul Coggle (2007 page 11);
Transcript 'Interview 02: Glasgow woman on childhood memories' language' © Scots Project (2007 pages 12 & 13);
Extract of speech by Mr Michael Howard, MP is taken from www.conservatives.com © Crown Copyright. Reproduced under the terms of the Click-Use Licence (2007 pages 13–15);
The article 'Booze doc says start 'em young', taken from the Daily Record, Wednesday 27 April 2005 (2007 page 16);
The article 'Serve our kids drink' © The Sun/NI Syndication, Wednesday 27 April 2005 (2007 page 16);
The article 'Let children drink alcohol in the pub' by Graham Grant taken from the Scottish Daily Mail, Wednesday 27 April 2005 © Daily Mail (2007 page 17);
Transcript 'Interview 05: John Law on the Scots Language' is taken from www.scottishcorpus.ac.uk © Scots Project (2007 pages 18 & 19);
An extract from GLASGOW ZEN by Alan Spence, first published in Great Britain by Canongate Books Ltd, 14 High Street, Edinburgh, EH1 1TE (2007 page 20);
An extract from 'Da Diary o Gideon Hunter' by Peter Ratter, taken from 'The Kiste/A Chiste Anthology' Published by Nelson Thornes Ltd © Peter Ratter (2007 page 21);
An extract from The Scottish Parliament website. Parliamentary material is reproduced with the permission of the Controller of HMSO on behalf of Parliament. (2007 pages 21 & 22);
An extract from 'Poker Night' from TRUST ME by John Updike, copyright © 1987 by John Updike. Reproduced by permission of Penguin Books Ltd (2007 pages 23–27);
An extract from the Foreword by Andro Linklater of 'Eric Linklater – A Critical Biography' by Michael Parnell. Published by John Murray and reproduced with permission of Hodder Headline (2007 pages 27–30);
The poem, 'The Sunlight on the Garden' by Louis MacNeice, taken from 'The Earth Compels' published by Faber & Faber Ltd. Reproduced by permission of David Higham Associates (2007 page 31);
An extract from 'The History Boys' by Allan Bennett. Published by Faber & Faber Ltd (2007 pages 32–39);
The article, 'His second-term mission: to end tyranny on earth' by Gerard Baker © The Times/NI Syndication, Friday 21 January 2005 (2007 page 42);
A photograph © AP/Press Association Images (2007 page 42);
The article 'Smiles for the family, a fiery warning for the world' by Julian Borger, 21 January 2005. Copyright Guardian News & Media Ltd 2005 (2007 page 43);
A photograph © Alex Wong/Getty Images (2007 page 43);

Three advertisements for Pulsar watches. Reproduced with permission of Seiko UK Ltd (2007 pages 45–47);

An extract from 'Rosencrantz and Guildenstern are Dead' by Tom Stoppard (1967). Published by Faber & Faber Ltd (2008 SQP pages 3 to 5);

The poem 'In Memoriam M.K.H., 1911–1984' by Seamus Heaney, taken from 'Opened Ground: Selected Poems, 1966–1996', published by Faber & Faber Ltd (2008 SQP page 6);

The poem 'The Eemis Stane' by Hugh MacDiarmid, taken from 'Complete Poems' © Carcanet Press Ltd (2008 SQP page 7);

An extract from 'Leddy-Bird, Leddy-Bird' by Sheena Blackhall. Reproduced with permission of Sheena Blackhall (2008 SQP pages 11 & 12);

An extract from 'The Hamecomin' by Sheila Douglas. Taken from 'Scottish Short Stories' edited by Sheena Greco. Published by Harcourt Education. Reprinted by permission of Heinemann Educational Ltd (2008 SQP page 12);

Extract from 'A Wee Tatty' by Alison Kermack, taken from 'A Tongue in Yer Heid' by James Robertson, published by Black & White Publishing © Black & White Publishing (2008 SQP page 13);

A transcript from the Conservative Party Election Broadcast in 1997. Reproduced by permission of the Conservative Party Archive (2008 SQP pages 14–16);

An extract from 'Wives and Daughters' by Elizabeth Gaskell (1866). Public Domain (2008 SQP pages 17–19);

An extract from 'Moon Country' by Simon Armitage and Glyn Maxwell (1996). Published by Faber & Faber Ltd (2008 SQP pages 21–22);

The poem 'At Marsden Bay' by Peter Reading, from 'Collected Poems 1: Poems 1970–1984' (Bloodaxe Books, 1995) (2008 SQP page 23);

An extract from the play 'All My Sons' by Arthur Miller. Published by Penguin Classics (2000). Reproduced by permission of Penguin Books Ltd (2008 SQP pages 24–28);

Two adverts for the Karen Hughes diamond and the Sarah Wesson Diamond De © Beers UK Limited (2008 SQP pages 30–31);

An extract from 'Bhudda Da' by Anne Donovan, published by Canongate Books Ltd, 14 High Street, Edinburgh, EH1 1TE (2008 page 7);

The poem 'SOS SOS' taken from 'Blethertoun Braes' by Sheena Blackhall. Published by Black & White Publishing/Itchy Coo © Black & White Publishing (2008 page 8);

The poem 'A Manifesto for MSPs' taken from 'Voyage of Intent' by James Roberstson, published by Luath Press (2008 page 8);

The poem 'The Corrie Sailin' by John Law taken from Lallans. Published by Scots Language Society © John Law (2008 page 9);

A transcript taken from 'Crossing: Language and ethnicity among adolescents' by Ben Rampton © Ben Rampton (2008 page 10);

The short story 'Soldiers Home' taken from 'The Snows of Kilimanjaro and Other Stories' by Ernest Hemingway. Published by Jonathan Cape. Reprinted by permission of The Random House Group Ltd (2008 pages 13–19);

An extract from 'The Old Silk Route' taken from 'GRANTA #26' Spring 1989 by Colin Thubron © Granta (2008 pages 19–23);

The poem 'Wind' taken from 'Hawk in the Rain' by Ted Hughes. Published by Faber & Faber Ltd (2008 page 24);

An extract from 'The Voysey Inheritance' by Harley Granville Barker (1905). By permission of Oxford University Press (2008 pages 25–33);

The article 'The Legend of the London Whale' by Cahal Milmo, taken from The Independent, Sunday 22 January 2006. Reproduced by permission of The Independent (2008 pages 36–37);

Extract from 'Arcadia' by Tom Stoppard, published by Faber & Faber Ltd (2009 page 3);

An extract from 'The Cotter's Saturday Night' by Robert Burns, 1796. Published by Penguin Popular Classics 1996. Public Domain (2009 pages 4 & 5);

Extract from 'The Poetry of Scotland, Gaelic, Scots and English' by Henryson and edited by Roderick Watson. Published by Edinburgh University Press (2009 pages 6 & 7);

Extract from 'The Steamie' by Tony Roper in 'Scot-Free: New Scottish Plays' selected by Alistair Cameron copyright © 1990 Tony Roper, reproduced by permission of the publishers, Nick Hern Books Ltd: www.nickhernbooks.co.uk (2009 pages 12 & 13);

The poem 'Tae makk a Martyr' by Sheena Blackhall. Taken from 'The Wallace Muse', published by Luath Press © Sheena Blackhall (2009 page 13);

An extract taken from www.scottishcorpus.ac.uk © Scots Project (2009 pages 14 & 15);

A Scottish Parliament Official Record taken from: www.scottishparliament.uk Parliamentary material is reproduced with the permission of the Controller of HMSO on behalf of Parliament. (2009 pages 16 & 17);

An extract from 'No Great Mischief' by Alistair MacLeod © McClelland & Stewart (2009 pages 18–21);

The essay 'Where Does Writing Come From?' by Richard Ford, from 'GRANTA #62' (Spring 1998) © Granta (2009 pages 22–25);

The poem 'The world is too much with us...' by William Wordsworth, published 1807. Public Domain (2009 page 26);

An extract from 'Walking Through Seaweed' by Iain Hamilton Finlay. Taken from 'The Dancers Inherit the Party' published by Polygon in association with the Scottish Library. Reproduced with permission of Birlinn Ltd (2009 pages 27–36);

Two articles from The Independent, Friday 16th March 2007, 'Collapse of Arctic Sea Ice has reached tipping point' by Steve Connor and 'Ocean heat blamed for mysterious disappearance of glaciers' by Steve Connor. Reproduced by permission of The Independent (2009 page 38);

The article 'Don't exaggerate climate dangers, scientists warn' by Juliette Jowit, 18 March 2007. Copyright Guardian News & Media Ltd 2007 (2009 page 39);

Two adverts for Persil © Unilever Plc (2009 insert).